T0293750

Mathematical Techniques in Finance

Founded in 1807, John Wiley & Sons is the oldest independent publishing company in the United States. With offices in North America, Europe, Australia and Asia, Wiley is globally committed to developing and marketing print and electronic products and services for our customers' professional and personal knowledge and understanding.

The Wiley Finance series contains books written specifically for finance and investment professionals as well as sophisticated individual investors and their financial advisors. Book topics range from portfolio management to e-commerce, risk management, financial engineering, valuation and financial instrument analysis, as well as much more.

For a list of available titles, visit our Web site at www.WileyFinance.com.

Mathematical Techniques in Finance

An Introduction

AMIR SADR

WILEY

Library of Congress Cataloging-in-Publication Data:

Names: Sadr, Amir, author.
Title: Mathematical techniques in finance : an introduction / Amir Sadr.
Description: Hoboken, New Jersey : John Wiley & Sons, Inc., [2022] |
    Series: Wiley finance series | Includes index.
Identifiers: LCCN 2022000565 (print) | LCCN 2022000566 (ebook) | ISBN
    9781119838401 (cloth) | ISBN 9781119838425 (adobe pdf) | ISBN
    9781119838418 (epub)
Subjects: LCSH: Finance–Mathematical models.
Classification: LCC HG106 .S23 2022 (print) | LCC HG106 (ebook) | DDC
    332.01/5195–dc23/eng/20220112
LC record available at https://lccn.loc.gov/2022000565
LC ebook record available at https://lccn.loc.gov/2022000566

To my students

Contents

Preface

Finance as a distinct field from economics is generally defined as the science or study of the management of funds. The creation of credit, savings, investments, banking institutions, financial markets and products, and risk management all fall under the purview of finance. The unifying themes in finance are time, risk, and money.

Mathematical or quantitative finance is the application of mathematics to these core areas. While simple arithmetic was enough for accounting and keeping ledgers and double-entry bookkeeping, Louis Bachelier's doctoral thesis, *Théorie de la spéculation* and published in 1900, used Brownian motion to study stock prices, and is widely recognized as the beginning of quantitative finance. Since then, the use of increasingly sophisticated and specialized mathematics has created the modern field of quantitative finance encompassing investment theory, asset pricing, derivatives, financial data science, and the emerging area of crypto assets and Decentralized Finance (DeFi).

BACKGROUND

This book is the collection of my lecture notes for an elective senior level undergraduate course on mathematics of finance at NYU Courant. The mostly senior and some first year graduate students come from different majors with an even distribution of mathematics, engineering, economics, and business majors. The prerequisites for the book are the same as the ones for the course: basic calculus, probability, and linear algebra. The goal of the book is to introduce the mathematical techniques used in different areas of finance and highlight their usage by drawing from actual markets and products.

BOOK STRUCTURE

A simple definition of finance would be the study of money; quantitative finance could be thought of as the *mathematics of money*. While reductive and simplistic, this book uses this metaphor and *follows the money* across different markets to motivate and introduce concepts and mathematical techniques.

Bonds

In Chapter 2, we start with the basic building blocks of interest rates and time value of money to price and discount future cash flows for fixed income and bond markets. The concept of compound interest and its limit as continuous compounding is the first foray into mathematics of finance. Coupon bonds make regular interest payments, and we introduce the Geometric series to derive the classic bond price-yield formula.

As there is generally no closed form formula for implied calculations such as implied yield or volatility given a bond or option price, these calculations require numerical root-solving methods and we present the Newton-Raphson method and the more robust and popular bisection method.

The concept of risk is introduced by considering the bond price sensitivity to interest rates. The Taylor series expansion of a function provides the first and second order sensitivities leading to duration and convexity for bonds in Chapter 2, and delta and gamma for options in Chapter 6. Similar first and second order measures are the basis of the mean-variance theory of portfolio selection in Chapter 3.

In the United States, households hold the largest amount of net worth, followed by firms, while the U.S. government runs a negative balance and is in debt. Most of consumer finance assets and liabilities are in the form of level pay home mortgage, student, and auto loans. These products can still be tackled by the application of the Geometric series, and we can calculate various measures such as average life and time to pay a given fraction of the loan via these formulas. A large part of consumer home mortgage loans are securitized as mortgage-backed securities by companies originally set up by the U.S. government to promote home ownership and student loans. The footprint of these giants in the financial markets is large and is the main driver of structured finance. We introduce tools and techniques to quantify the negative convexity risk due to prepayments for these markets.

While the analytical price-yield formula for bonds, loans, and mortgage-backed securities can provide pricing and risk measures for single products in isolation, a variety of bonds and fixed income products trade simultaneously in markets giving rise to different yield and spread curves. We introduce the bootstrap and interpolation methods to handle yields curves and overlapping cash flows of multiple instruments in a consistent manner.

Stocks, Investments

In Chapter 3, we focus on investments and the interplay between risk-free and risky assets. We present the St. Petersburg paradox to motivate the concept of utility and to highlight the problem of investment choice, ranking, and decision-making under uncertainty. We introduce the concept of risk-preference and show the personalist nature of ranking of random payoffs. We present utility theory and its axioms, certainty-equivalent lotteries, and different measures of risk-preference (risk-taking, risk-aversion, risk-neutrality) as characterized by the utility function. Utility functions representing different classes of Arrow-Pratt measures (CARA, CRRA, HARA) are introduced and discussed.

The mean-variance theory of portfolio selection draws from the techniques of constrained and convex optimization, and we discuss and show the method of Lagrange multipliers in various calculations such as the minimum-variance portfolio, minimum-variance frontier, and tangency (market) portfolio. The seminal CAPM formula relating the excess return of an asset to that of the market portfolio is derived by using the chain rule and properties of the hyperbola of feasible portfolios.

Moving from equilibrium results, we next introduce statistical techniques such as regression, factor models, and PCA to find common drivers of asset returns and statistical measures such as the alpha and beta of portfolio performance. Trading strategies such as pairs trading and mean-reversion trades are based on these methods. We conclude by showing the use of recurrence equations and optimization techniques for risk and money management leading to the gambler's ruin formula and Kelly's ratio.

Forwards, Futures

In Chapter 4, we introduce the forward contract as the gateway product to more complicated contingent claims and options and derivatives. The basic cash-and-carry argument shows the method of static replication and arbitrage pricing. This method is used to compute forward prices in equities with discrete dividends or dividend yields, forward exchange rate via covered interest parity, and forward rates in interest rate markets.

Risk-Neutral Option Pricing

Chapter 5 presents the building blocks of the modern risk-neutral pricing framework. Starting with a simple one-step binomial model, we flesh out the full details of the replication of a contingent claim via the underlying asset and a loan and show that a contingent claim's replication price can be computed by taking expectations in a risk-neutral setting. This basic building block is extended to multiple steps through dynamic hedging of a self-financing replicating portfolio, leading to martingale relative prices and the fundamental theorems of asset pricing for complete and arbitrage-free economies.

Option Pricing

In Chapter 6, we use the risk-neutral framework to derive the Black-Scholes-Merton (BSM) option pricing formula by modeling asset returns as the continuous-time limit of a random walk, that is a Brownian motion with risk-adjusted drift. We recover and investigate the underlying replicating portfolio by considering the option Greeks: delta, gamma, theta. The interplay between these is shown by applying the Ito's lemma to the diffusion process driving an underlying asset and its derivative, leading to the BSM partial differential equation and its solution via methods from the classical boundary value heat equations.

We discuss the Cox-Ross-Rubinstein (CRR) model as a popular and practical computational method for pricing options that can also be used to compute the price of options with early exercise features via the backward induction algorithm from dynamic programming. For path-dependent options such as barrier or averaging options, we present numerical models such as the Monte Carlo simulation models and variance reduction techniques.

Interest Rate Derivatives

Chapter 7 introduces interest rate swaps and their derivatives used in structured finance. A plain vanilla swap can be priced via a static replication argument from a bootstrapped discount factor curve. In practice, simple European options on swaps and interest rate products are priced and risk-managed via the normal version of Black's formula for futures. We introduce this model under the risk-neutral pricing framework and show the pricing of the mainstream cap/floors, European swaptions, and CMS products. For complex derivatives, one needs a model for the evolution of multiple maturity zero-coupon bonds in a risk-neutral framework. We present the popular Hull-White mean-reverting model for the short rate and show the typical implementation methods and techniques, such as the forward induction method for yield curve inversion. We show the pricing of Bermudan swaptions via these lattice models. We conclude our discussion by presenting methods for calculating interest rate curve risk and VaR.

Exercises and Python Projects

The end-of-chapter exercises are based on real-world markets and products and delve deeper into some financial products and highlight the details of applying the techniques to them. All exercises can be solved by using a spreadsheet package like Excel. The Python projects are longer problems and can be done by small groups of students as a term project.

It is my hope that by the end of this book, readers have obtained a good toolkit of mathematical techniques, methods, and models used in financial markets and products, and their interest is piqued for a deeper journey into quantitative finance.

New York, New York   —Amir Sadr
December 2021

Acknowledgments

One learns by teaching and I have learned much from my students at NYU. Many thanks to all of my students over the years who have asked good questions and kept me on my toes.

Thanks to my editors at John Wiley & Sons: Bill Falloon, Purvi Patel, Samantha Enders, Julie Kerr, and Selvakumaran Rajendiran for patiently walking me through this project and correcting my many typos. All remaining errors are mine, and I welcome any corrections, suggestions, and comments sent to asadr@panalytix.com.

A.S.

About the Author

Amir Sadr received his PhD from Cornell University with his thesis work on the Foundations of Probability Theory. After working at AT&T Bell Laboratories, he started his Wall Street career at Morgan Stanley, initially as a Vice President in quantitative modeling and development of exotic interest rate models, and later as an exotics trader. He founded Panalytix, Inc., to develop financial software for pricing and risk management of interest rate derivatives. He was a Managing Director for proprietary trading at Greenwich Capital, Senior Trader in charge of CAD exotics and USD inflation trading at HSBC, the COO of Brevan Howard U.S. Asset Management in the United States, and co-founder of Yield Curve Trading, a fixed income proprietary trading firm. He is currently a partner at CorePoint Partners and is focused on crypto and DeFi.

bp	basis points, 1% of 1%, 0.0001
FV	future value
IRR	internal rate of return
PnL	profit and loss
PV	present value
YTM	yield to maturity
p.a.	per annum
$DF, D(T)$	discount factor, today's value unit payment at future date T
$D(t, T)$	dicount factor at t for unit payment at $T > t$
r	interest rate
r_m	compounding interest rate with m compoundings per year
y	yield
APR	annual percentage rate – stated interest rate without any compoundings
APY	annual pecentage yield – yield of a deposit taking compoundings into consideration: $1 + APY = (1_A PR/m)^m$ for m compoundings per year
CF	cash flow
C	coupon rate
$P, P(C, y, N, m)$	price of an N-year bond with coupon rate C, paid m times per year, with yield y
w	accrual fraction between 2 dates according to some day count basis
P_{Clean}	clean price of a bond = Price – accrued interest
$P_Z(y, N, M)$	price of an N-year zero-coupon bond with yield y, m compoundings per year
$P_A(C, y, N, m)$	price of an N-year annuity with annuity rate of C, paid m times per year, with yield y
$P_{Bill}(y, T)$	price of T-maturity Treasury Bill with discount yield y
PV01	present value change due to an "01" bp change in yield

PVBP	present value change due to a 1 bp change in coupon, present value of a 1 bp annuity
B_n	balance of a level pay loan after n periods
P_n, I_n	principal and interest payments of a level pay loan in the nth period
$P_L(C, y, N, m)$	price of N-year level pay loan with loan rate of C, paid m times per year, with yield y
AL	average life
B'_n	balance of a level pay loan after n periods with prepayments
P'_n, I'_n	principal and interest payments of a level pay loan within the nth period with prepayments
SMM	single monthly mortality rate
CPR	constant prepayment ratio
s, s_n	periodic prepayment speed
$U(x)$	utility of wealth x
$X \prec Y$	lottery Y is preferred to X
c_X	certainty-equivalent of random payoff X, $U(c_X) = E[U(X)]$
π_A, π_R	absolute risk premium, relative risk premium
V, V_P, V_i	value, value of a portfolio, value of ith asset
Q_i, P_i	quantity, price
w_i	weight of ith asset in a portfolio, $\sum_i w_i = 1$
R_A	return of an asset over a period t: $R_A = A(t)/A(0) - 1$. Can be divided by t to give rate of return
$R_A \sim (\mu_A, \sigma_A)$	asset A's return, with mean μ and standard deviation σ_A
$\mu, \sigma, \mathbf{C}$	mean vector, standard deviation vector, and covariance matrix of asset returns
R_0	return of a risk-free asset
M, R_M	market portfolio, return of the market portfolio
β_X	beta of an asset X, $Cov(R_X, R_M)/\sigma_M^2$
$\hat{x}$	empirical estimate of x
$\bar{x}$	arithmetic average of n samples of x, $1/n \sum_{i=1}^{n} x_i$
T	forward date, future date
$F_A(t, T)$	forward value of asset A at time t for forward date T
$VF_A(t, T, K)$	t-value of a forward agreement on asset A for forward date T and price K
$f(t, [T_1, T_2])$	simple (noncompounding) forward rate that can be locked at t for forward deposit period $[T_1, T_2]$. The first term may be omitted when $t = 0$.

$f_c(t, [T_1, T_2])$	continuously compounding forward rate that can be locked at t for forward deposit period $[T_1, T_2]$. The first term may be omitted when $t = 0$.
FX	foreign currency exchange rate
r_d, r_f	domestic and foreign interest rates for forward exchange rate calculations
$F_X(t, T)$	the T-forward exchange rate that can be locked at t
$A_0, A(0)$	today's value of an asset A
$C_0, C(0)$	today's value of a contingent claim C
ω	generic random sample path
$M(t), M(t, \omega)$	value of a money-market account at time t along sample path ω
$N(\mu, \sigma^2)$	normal or Gaussian random variable with mean μ and variance σ^2
$LN(\mu, \sigma^2)$	lognormal random variable whose log is $N(\mu, \sigma^2)$
CDF	cumulative ditribution function
pdf	probability density function
pmf	probability mass function
$N(x)$	cumulative distribution function of a standard ($N(0,1)$) normal random variable, $N(x) = \frac{1}{\sqrt{2\pi}} \int_{-\infty}^{x} e^{-u^2/2} du$
$N'(x)$	probability density function of a standard normal random variable, $N'(x) = \frac{1}{\sqrt{2\pi}} e^{-x^2/2}$
BM	Brownian motion
$B(t), B(t, \omega)$	Brownian motion at time t along sample path ω
σ	proportional, lognormal volatility
ATM, ATMF	at-the-money spot, at-the-money forward
$\delta(x)$	Dirac's delta function, $\int f(x)\delta(x - a)dx = f(a)$
σ_N	absolute, normalized volatility
CMS	constant maturity swap rate
AD, $AD(t_i, j)$	Arrow-Debreu price, today's price of unit payoff at state j on future date t_i
i.i.d.	independent and identically distributed

Mathematical
Techniques
in Finance

## CHAPTER 1

Finance

While economics as a social science studies the behavior of economic agents in the generation, acquisition, and expenditure of goods and services, finance is focused on the acquisition and management of capital in financial markets.

Focusing on the end user, finance can be divided into personal finance, corporate finance, and government finance. Savings, investments, and loans, such as credit card, student, automobile, and home mortgage, insurance products, and estate planning are examples of personal finance. The raising of capital by borrowing and debt or selling shares and equity by a company and the management of a company's funds are the focus of corporate finance. Monetary policy, central banking, tax systems, and the oversight of the banking sector and financial markets fall under government finance.

1.1 FOLLOW THE MONEY

Using the reductive definition of finance as the study of money, we follow the money to get our bearings. In accounting, a balance sheet is a snapshot of an entity's (person, corporation, country) net worth or equity: assets minus liabilities equals equity. Table 1.1 shows a snapshot of the net worth of the three dominant players in the U.S. economy: households, firms, and government.

As the table shows, households hold the largest amount of equity, followed by firms, while the U.S. government runs a negative balance and is in debt. Indeed, the U.S. government is the world's biggest borrower and routinely borrows money to finance its expenditures. The breakdown of households' net worth is shown in Table 1.2.

Bonds, stocks, foreign exchange, commodities, and their derivatives are the major sectors of financial markets. Tables 1.3 through 1.5 show the market size as of year end 2020.

TABLE 1.1 Balance sheet of the United States at 2020 year end.

Sector	Net Worth ($Trillions)
Households	123.35
Firms	33.9
Government	−26.8
Total	130.46

Source: U.S. Federal Reserve Z.1 Statistical Release.

TABLE 1.2 Households sector balance sheet as of 2020 year end.

Category	$Trillions	Percentage
Real estate	32.8	24%
Consumer durable goods	6.1	4%
Checking, savings, money market accounts	15.2	11%
Debt securities, bonds	5.1	4%
Equities, mutual funds, investments	79	57%
Misc	1.3	1%
Total assets	**139.6**	100%
Home mortgage loans	10.9	67%
Credit card, auto loans	4.2	26%
Other loans	1.1	7%
Total liabilities	**16.2**	100%
Net worth	**123.35**	

TABLE 1.3 Market size ($Trillions).

	U.S.	World
Bonds	50.1	123.5
Stocks	40.7	93.6
Derivatives		15.8
Foreign Exchange		6.6/day

Sources: World Bank, BIS, SIFMA.

TABLE 1.4   U.S. bond market ($Trillions).

Type	Outstanding debt	
Treasury	21.0	42%
Mortgage-related	11.2	22%
Corporate debt	9.8	8%
Municipal	4	8%
Federal agency securities	1.7	3%
Asset-backed	1.5	3%
Money markets	1	2%
Total	50.1	

Source: SIFMA.

TABLE 1.5   Global derivatives market size ($Trillions).

Market	Gross market value
Interest rate contracts	11.4
Foreign exchange contracts	3.2
Equity-linked contracts	0.8

Source: BIS.

1.2   FINANCIAL MARKETS AND PARTICIPANTS

Households typically earn wages and receive salary from firms, while firms earn income when households consume their goods and services. The government collects taxes from households and firms for its expenditures for defense, government services, infrastructure, public health, and transfer payments such as social security and Medicare. Banks and financial intermediaries facilitate the transfer of funds between these three sectors: households and firms deposit their excess funds in banks and earn interest, and banks avail these funds in the form of consumer and corporate loans. Other financial intermediaries such as investment banks, insurance companies, and investment companies provide capital and financial services to firms and individuals.

The capital markets and financial instruments facilitate the flow of funds between different sectors of the economy. Focusing on the United States, the bond market is the largest market with capitalization of $50 trillion at the end of 2020. The U.S. government routinely borrows by issuing debt in the form of coupon bonds. Similarly corporations finance their growth by issuing debt in the form of corporate coupon bonds. States

TABLE 1.6   Market participants and financial products.

Participant	Usage	Product
Households	Custody, banking, borrowing	Checking and interest bearing accounts, credit cards
	Home mortgage, auto, student loan	Level pay loans
	Investments	Cash, options brokerage accounts, financial or robo-advisor advice for asset allocation
	Insurance, estate planning	Auto, home, life insurance; annuities
Corporations	Financing	Bonds, stock issuance
	Cash flow management	Commercial paper, lines of credit, swaps
	Asset liability management, interest rate risk management	Derivatives, interest rate futures, swaps, options
Insurers, mortgage servicers	Rate risk	Swaps, caps, swaptions
Pension plans	Asset allocation and insurance	Derivatives
Hedge funds	Investment, speculation	Leveraged products, derivatives, statistical methods
Banks, financial institutions	**Financial services**	**All products**
States and local government	Financing	Bullet bonds, callable bonds
Fannie Mae, Freddie Mac	Financing, risk management	Swaps, swaptions, swapped issuance
U.S. government	Financing	Bills, notes, bonds
Federal Reserve	Monetary policy	Repo and reverse, quantitative easing

and municipalities also raise capital by issuing debt for infrastructure and other projects.

Banks and other financial institutions provide home mortgage, auto, and student loans in the form of level pay loans. These loans and receivables are in turn bought and securitized as mortgage-backed and asset-backed securities by companies originally set up by the U.S. government to promote home ownership and student loans, prominent among them are Fannie Mae (Federal National Mortgage Association), Freddie Mac (Federal Home Loan Mortgage Corporation), and Sallie Mae (Student Loan Marketing Association).

Corporations raise capital by issuing stock (equity), which is publicly traded. Households participate in the stock market directly via brokerage accounts or retirement plans primarily investing in mutual funds and ETFs (Exchange Traded Funds). The allocation of investments between different assets or funds is the subject of portfolio selection.

Firms and households use insurance and derivatives markets to mitigate and manage financial risk. Consumers buy home and auto insurance to protect against loss. Corporations raise money from the capital markets and manage their interest rate exposure through interest rate swaps and derivatives. Producers use commodity futures and derivatives to manage price risk, and pension plans and investors use equity derivatives for risk management and speculation.

1.3   QUANTITATIVE FINANCE

Households, corporations, governments, and financial firms, such as commercial and investment banks, insurance companies, asset management companies, and hedge funds, all participate in financial markets and employ a variety of products and increasingly sophisticated quantitative methods (see Table 1.6). The mathematics includes results and techniques from calculus, linear algebra, probability and statistics, numerical methods, optimization techniques, stochastic processes, differential equations, and machine learning techniques. In the following chapters, we will introduce these techniques as used in different markets and financial products.

## CHAPTER 2

Rates, Yields, Bond Math

The trade-off between delayed versus immediate consumption and the cost of waiting is a core concept in economics and finance. Discounting the future cash flows of a financial instrument such as a stock or a bond via an appropriate rate is fundamental to their pricing. The time value of money and discounting are captured by interest rates.

2.1   INTEREST RATES

Consider an investor with $100 who invests it by depositing it in an interest-bearing bank account for one year at an annual interest *rate r* = 4%. In one year's time, the investor will receive the original amount deposited, $100, and the interest *amount* of $4($100 × 4%), for a total of $104. The interest payment is in compensation for use of the money, i.e., the investor could have used the $100 for other purposes, maybe a lucrative investment, and, hence, needs to be compensated for this opportunity cost. Viewed another way, the investor is lending funds to the bank for one year and should be compensated for availing this loan.

Interest rates are generally quoted on an *annualized basis*, for example 4% per annum in the above case. For a loan of size A, the interest amount based on the annualized interest rate of r for a duration of T years is $A \times r \times T$, and the *Future Value* is the initial size plus the interest

$$FV = A + A \times r \times T = A \times (1 + rT) \tag{2.1}$$

For example, the *FV* of an initial amount $A = \$100$ in 3 months ($T = 3/12$) at the simple interest rate of 4% per annum is

$$\$100 \times \left(1 + 4\% \times \frac{3}{12}\right) = \$101$$

7

The above case is an example of a *noncompounding* interest rate. Another way of getting compensated is by compounded interest where the investor earns *compound* or interest on interest. For example, for a 2-year deposit at the same interest rate of $r = 4\%$ per annum, but compounded annually, the 1-year future value of \$100 is \$104, and the 2-year future value is $\$104 \times (1 + 4\%) = \$108.16$:

$$\$100 \times (1 + 4\%)^2 = \$108.16$$

Out of the \$8.16 in interest, \$8 is the interest for two years, \$4 for each year, and the extra \$0.16 is due to the *compounding* effect: receiving *interest on interest*.

In general, the Future Value FV of loan A at an interest rate of r per annum, *compounded m* times a year for N whole compounding periods is

$$FV = A \times \left(1 + \frac{r}{m}\right)^N \tag{2.2}$$

For example, if $m = 1$, we have annual compounding $FV = A \times (1 + r)^N$, and N is the number of years until loan maturity T. If $m = 2$, we have semi-annual compounding $FV = A \times (1 + r/2)^N$, and $N = 2 \times T$ is the number of whole semiannual periods until loan maturity T years from now (see Table 2.1). The term r/m is known as the *periodic interest rate*.

2.1.1 Fractional Periods

The compound interest Formula 2.2 can be generalized to incorporate loan durations that are not a whole number of compounding periods away. Let T be the number of years—including fractions of years—between the investment date. We can generalize Formula 2.2 to

$$FV = A \times \left(1 + \frac{r}{m}\right)^{m \times T} \tag{2.3}$$

TABLE 2.1   Future Value of \$100,000 for a 2 year ($T = 2$) loan with $r = 4\%$ per annum.

Compoundings Per Year (m)	Number of Periods ($N = T \times m$)	Periodic Interest Rate (r/m)	Future Value $FV(T)$	Interest
0=Simple			\$108,000	\$8,000
1=Annual	2	4%	\$108,160	\$8,160
2=Semiannual	4	2%	\$108,243.22	\$8,243.22
4=Quarterly	8	1%	\$108,285.67	\$8,285.67
12=Monthly	24	4%/12	\$108,314.30	\$8,314.30
365=Daily	2×365	4%/365	\$108,328.23	\$8,328.23
∞=Continuous	∞		\$108,328.71	\$8,328.71

For example, the future value of $A = \$100,000$ in 9 months $(T = 0.75)$ for a semiannual $(m = 2)$ compounded interest rate of 4% per annum is

$$FV = \$1,000,000 \times \left(1 + \frac{4\%}{2}\right)^{2 \times 0.75} = \$103,014.95$$

while the future value of $A = \$100,000$ in 3 months $(T = 0.25)$ for a semiannual compounded interest rate of 4% per annum is

$$FV = \$100,000 \times \left(1 + \frac{4\%}{2}\right)^{2 \times 0.25} = \$100,995.05$$

The first case's interest of \$3,014.95 is for 1.5 semiannual compounding periods, and exceeds the simple interest of $\$3,000 = \$100,000 \times 4\% \times 3/12$ due to compounding, while the second case is for a half (semiannual) compounding period.

Similarly, for noncompounding simple rates, we can let T be a fraction of a year. For example, the future value of $A = \$100,000$ in 2 months $(T = 2/12)$ at the simple interest rate of 4% p.a. is

$$FV = \$1,000,000 \times \left(1 + 4\% \times \frac{2}{12}\right) = \$100,666.67$$

2.1.2 Continuous Compounding

As we compound more often, in the limit we reach *continuous* compounding and Formula 2.3 becomes

$$FV = \lim_{m \to \infty} A \times \left(1 + \frac{r}{m}\right)^{m \times T} = A \times e^{rT}$$

While seldom used in real-world loans and deposits, continuously compounded interest rates provide an easy way to derive analytical formulas when interest rates are not the primary object of study, for example in investment analysis or option pricing for equities.

2.1.3 Discount Factor, PV, FV

Given an interest rate r for a time horizon T, let $FV(T)$ be the future value of unit $(A = 1)$ currency. For a simple (noncompounding) interest rate r, we have

$$FV(T) = 1 + rT \qquad (2.4)$$

and for any given initial amount A, its future value is then simply $A \times FV(T)$.

Alternatively, we can ask how much we need to invest today at the prevailing interest rates to receive unit currency at some future date T:

$$A \times (1 + rT) = 1$$

In this case, we are setting the future value to 1 and solving for A, the *Present Value*, $PV(T)$, of unit currency to be received at T. It is easy to see that

$$PV(T) = \frac{1}{1 + rT} = 1/FV(T)$$

for simple interest rates. In the above formula, we are using the interest rate to *discount* the future unit cash flow to compute its today's value, and $PV(T)$ is also known as the *Discount Factor*, $D(T) = PV(T)$.

For compounding interest rates, we have

$$D(T) = \frac{1}{(1 + r/m)^{mT}}$$

which for continuously compounded interest rates becomes

$$D(T) = e^{-rT}$$

The graph of $D(T)$ versus T is known as the *discount factor curve* and is a decreasing (non-increasing) function of T for positive (non-negative) interest rates. Given a discount factor curve, we compute today's price of a series of known cash flows $C_1, \ldots, C_N$ at futures dates $T_1, \ldots, T_n$, as

$$\sum_{i=1}^{N} C_i \times D(T_i)$$

2.1.4 Yield, Internal Rate of Return

The interest rate of a loan describes the amount and timing of the interest payments for a loan and is *fixed* at the inception of a loan, usually reflecting prevailing market interest rates at the time. For a given loan of size A and interest rate r, one can know with certainty the future interest and principal cash flows: \$100 in, \$100$(1 + rT)$ out at T if we use the simple interest rate r.

On the other hand, given the future cash flows of an investment (FV) and its today's value (PV), we can ask for the interest rate r in a cash flow *equivalent* loan that would have given us the same cash flows. The interest rate for this equivalent hypothetical loan is called *Internal Rate of Return (IRR)* or *Yield to Maturity (YTM)* or simply *yield*. Said another way, the yield is the discounting rate that will recover today's price of future cash flows.

For example, suppose there is an investment that for $100 today will pay $102 in six months ($T = 0.5$). We can ask what is the *yield* of this investment, i.e., the *implied* or equivalent interest or discounting rate that would have given us the same $FV = 102$ for $PV = 100$. The yield, just like the interest rate, can be quoted in various ways:

1. Simple (add-on, noncompounding) yield: Solve for $100(1 + y/2) = 102$.

$$y = (FV/PV - 1)/T, \quad T = 1/2$$

2. Periodically compounded yield: Solve for $100(1 + y/m)^{mT} = 102$.

$$y = m[(FV/PV)^{1/(Tm)} - 1], \quad T = 1/2$$

3. Continuously compounded yield: Solve for $100e^{y/2} = 102$.

$$y = \ln(FV/PV)/T, \quad T = 1/2$$

4. *Discount* yield: Solve for $100 = 102(1 - y/2)$.

$$y = (1 - PV/FV)/T, \quad T = 1/2$$

Note that the same cash flows, $PV = 100$, $FV = 102$, can give rise to yields quoted in different ways. When comparing the yields of different investments, one needs to use a consistent convention (semiannual, continuous, simple, ...) to ensure we are comparing apples to apples.

2.2 ARBITRAGE, LAW OF ONE PRICE

An *arbitrage* opportunity is the ability to generate profits with no risk. For example, two financial instruments with identical futures cash flows should have the same price today. Otherwise, one can sell the more expensive instrument and buy the cheaper instrument, generating a positive amount today with zero liability in the future: whatever the future cash flows of the instrument one had sold and need to be paid will be offset by the instrument one has bought and which generate the identical cash flows. Lack of arbitrage then leads to both instruments having the same price today.

The usual arbitrage pricing argument relates the future cash flows of a financial instrument to those of a risk-free investment, for example, depositing money at a bank account and receiving the simple interest rate r for a future date T. We use the relationship

$$D = D(T) = \frac{1}{1 + rT}$$

as today's value of receiving 1 at T. We assume we can invest (lend) *and* borrow for T at the same rate r.

Now consider the simplest financial instrument whose only cash flow is payment of 1 at T, and let P be today's price of this instrument. If $P < D$, then we could borrow D at the rate r and pay P for the instrument, and be left with a positive amount $D - P > 0$. At time T we will receive 1 from the instrument, while we owe $D \times (1 + rT) = 1$ to whoever lent it to us. These future cash flows exactly offset, and we have therefore made a profit today of $D - P$ with no risk.

Alternatively, let $P > D$. In this case, we sell the instrument for P and lend/invest part of it, D, at r. Again, we are left with a positive amount $P - D > 0$. At time T, we will receive $D \times (1 + rT) = 1$ from whoever we lent to, and need to pay 1 to whoever we sold the instrument to. These two cash flows exactly offset and we have made a profit of $P - D$ with no risk.

Therefore, in an arbitrage-free economy, today's price, D, of the instrument consisting of receiving 1 at T cannot be different than $D(T) = 1/(1 + rT)$.

Note that when $P < D$, the instrument's price is too low and its yield too high, and we can lend at this high yield while financing/borrowing at the lower rate r. On the other hand, when $P > D$, the price is too high and the yield too low, so we borrow at this low yield and lend/invest at the higher rate r. Lack of arbitrage can then be expressed as absence of *borrow low, lend high* opportunities. If such opportunities exist, then investors will start buying the cheap (high-yield) instrument and drive up its price, or sell the expensive (low-yield) instrument and drive down its price to the no-arbitrage price.

2.3 PRICE-YIELD FORMULA

Discount factors are the fundamental building blocks for valuing fixed income securities. Given a series of known cash flows $(C_1, \ldots, C_N)$ to be received at various times $(T_1, \ldots, T_N)$ in the future, if we know the discount factor $D(T_i)$ for each payment date T_i, then today's value of this package is

$$PV(\text{portfolio of cash flows}) = \sum_{i=1}^{N} C_i D(T_i)$$

For example, today's price P of a T-year bond paying an annualized coupon rate C m times a year (so $N = T \times m$ payments left) is

$$P = \sum_{i=1}^{N} \frac{C}{m} D(T_i) + D(T_N)$$

The standard pricing formula for bonds uses a compounded yield y with the same compounding frequency as the coupons. So, $D(T_i) = 1/(1 + y/m)^i$ results in the classical bond pricing formula

$$P(C, y, N, m) = P = \sum_{i=1}^{N} \frac{C/m}{(1 + y/m)^i} + \frac{1}{(1 + y/m)^N}$$

$$= \frac{C}{y}\left(1 - \frac{1}{(1 + y/m)^N}\right) + \frac{1}{(1 + y/m)^N} \tag{2.5}$$

where we have used the Geometric Series Formula for $\sum_{i=m}^{N} \alpha^i$. If $\alpha = 1$, the sum is simply $N - m + 1$. For $\alpha \neq 1$, we observe

$$(\alpha^m + \alpha^{m+1} + \ldots + \alpha^N)(1 - \alpha)$$

$$= (\alpha^m + \alpha^{m+1} + \ldots + \alpha^N)$$

$$- (\alpha^{m+1} + \ldots + \alpha^N + \alpha^{N+1})$$

$$= \alpha^m - \alpha^{N+1}$$

$$\sum_{i=m}^{N} \alpha^i = \frac{\alpha^m - \alpha^{N+1}}{1 - \alpha}$$

Formula 2.5 is for when there are $N = T \times m$ *whole* future coupon periods left. When valuing a bond between coupon payment dates, the discount factors are modified as $D(T_i) = 1/(1 + y/m)^{i-w}$ where w measures the *accrued* fraction (measured using some day-count convention: Act/Act, Act/365, ...) of the current coupon period

$$P(C, y, N, m) = \sum_{i=1}^{N} \frac{C/m}{(1+y/m)^{i-w}} + \frac{1}{(1+y/m)^{N-w}}$$

$$= \frac{1}{(1+y/m)^{-w}} \left[\sum_{i=1}^{N} \frac{C/m}{(1+y/m)^{i}} + \frac{1}{(1+y/m)^{N}} \right] \qquad (2.6)$$

$$= (1+y/m)^{w} \left[\frac{C}{y} \left(1 - \frac{1}{(1+y/m)^{N}} \right) + \frac{1}{(1+y/m)^{N}} \right]$$

EXAMPLE 1

Consider a 2-year bond issued on 31-Dec-2020 with maturity date of 31-Dec-2022 and semiannual coupon rate of 4% per annum. Its semiannual coupon dates are 30-Jun-2021, 31-Dec-2021, 30-Jun-2022, and 31-Dec-2022. Assume we are valuing the bond on 8-Oct-2021. In this case, there are three remaining coupons, and the fraction of time using the Actual/Actual method is

$$w = \frac{\text{Number of days between 30-Jun-2021 and 8-Oc-2021}}{\text{Number of days between 30-Jun-2021 and 31-Dec-2021}}$$

$$= \frac{100}{184} = 0.54348$$

If the yield is 3.25%, the price of the bond using Formula 2.6 is

$$P = \left(1 + \frac{0.0325}{2} \right)^{0.54348}$$

$$\left[\frac{0.04}{2} \left(1 - \frac{1}{(1+0.0325/2)^3} + \frac{1}{(1+0.325/2)^3} \right) \right]$$

$$= 1.0197889 = 101.97889\%$$

If you were to purchase $100,000 face value of this bond, you will have to pay $101,978.89 to receive the remaining cash flows: three semiannual coupons of $2,000 on 31-Dec-2021, 30-Jun-2022, and 31-Dec-2022, and $100,000 on 31-Dec-2022.

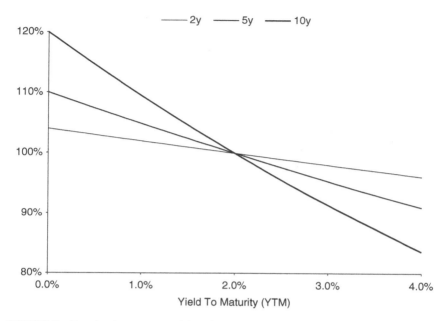

FIGURE 2.1 Bond price versus yield with coupon rate = 2% p.a.

Figure 2.1 shows the graph of the price as a function of YTM. As can be seen, when YTM equals the coupon rate, the price of the bond is *Par* (100%). When $C > y$, the price is greater than 100%, resulting in a *premium* bond. When $C < y$, the price is less than 100%, resulting in a *discount* bond. Finally, note that as yields approach zero, then the price of a bond simply becomes the sum of the remaining cash flows with no discounting.

2.3.1 Clean Price

Formula 2.6 is known as the *Dirty (Invoice/Gross/Full) Price* of a bond, that is, how much cash is needed to purchase this bond. The graph of the dirty price of a bond versus remaining time to maturity is shown in Figure 2.2. As time goes by, since one is receiving the same cash flows except earlier, the value increases. Right after any coupon payment the value drops by the periodic coupon amount since there is one less coupon remaining.

While the dirty price of a bond is discontinuous, for bond traders focused on quoted *price* of a bond, this drop in price—while real in terms of PV of *remaining* cash flows—is artificial in terms of worthiness/value of

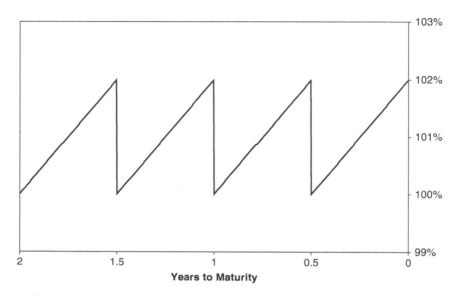

FIGURE 2.2 Price of bond versus remaining years to maturity.

a bond, and they prefer a smoother measure. By subtracting the *accrued interest*, wC/m, from the dirty price, one arrives at the *Clean/Quoted Price*

$$P_{Clean} = (1 + y/m)^w \left[\frac{C}{y} \left(1 - \frac{1}{(1 + y/m)^N} \right) + \frac{1}{(1 + y/m)^N} \right] - w\frac{C}{m} \quad (2.7)$$

In Example 1, the clean price of the bond is

$$1.0197889 - 0.54348 \times \frac{0.04}{2} = 1.0089194 = 100.89194\%$$

Even though the clean price is quoted, the amount paid for the bond uses the true economic value of the remaining cash flows, that is, the dirty price of the bond.

Figure 2.3 shows the evolution of the clean price for a 2-year, 4% semi-annual coupon bond as we get closer to maturity while holding yields constant for three yield scenarios: $y = 5\%$ leading to a discount bond $(C < y)$, $y = 3\%$ leading to a premium bond $(C > y)$, and $y = 4\%$ leading to a par $(C = y)$ bond. Notice the *Pull-to-Par Effect* for the bond regardless of the assumed yield scenario: A discount bond gets pulled *up* to par, while a premium bond gets pulled *down* to par.

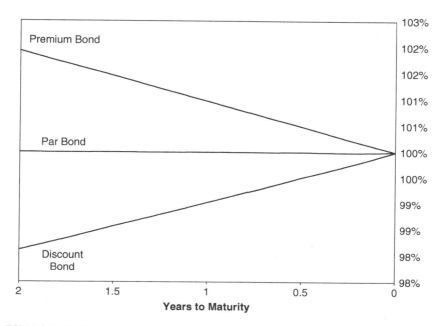

FIGURE 2.3 Pull to par effect for a 2-year, 4% semiannual coupon bond.

2.3.2 Zero-Coupon Bond

If the coupon rate is zero, $C = 0$, then the only cash flow is the principal repayment at maturity versus the amount paid for it, and the bond is aptly called a *zero-coupon bond*. Since for one unit of face value, its only future cash flow is unit payment at maturity, its price is simply the discount factor

$$P_Z(y, N, m) = D(T) = \frac{1}{(1 + y/m)^{N-w}} \qquad (2.8)$$

2.3.3 Annuity

An *annuity* is a financial product that pays a series of regular cash flows to the owner and variants of it are widely offered by insurance companies as retirement and estate planning products. For example, a $1,000,000 5-year annuity with monthly payments of 3% per annum pays

$$\$1,000,000 \times \frac{3\%}{12} = \$2,500$$

each month for the next five years (60 payments). As opposed to a coupon bond, an annuity does not have a final principal payment, and the $1,000,000 is called a *notional* principal.

Using a compounding yield with the same frequency as the payments, the price of an annuity, $P_A(C, y, N, m)$, with N periodic payments with an annuity rate of C per annum paid m times a year is

$$P_A(C, y, N, m) = \sum_{i=1}^{N} \frac{C/m}{(1 + y/m)^i} = \frac{C}{y} \left(1 - \frac{1}{(1 + y/m)^N} \right)$$

Note that a coupon bond can be considered as a combination of an annuity and a zero-coupon bond (see Figure 2.4).

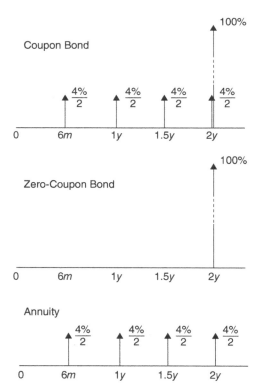

FIGURE 2.4 Cash flows of a 2-year 4% semiannual coupon bond versus a 2-year 4% semiannual annuity versus a 2-year zero-coupon bond.

2.3.4 Fractional Years, Day Counts

The calculation of fractions of years between two arbitrary dates can be thorny and nuanced, and different *day-count conventions* are used in practice. The most obvious way to calculate a fraction of a year is to compute the number of days in the relevant period and divide it by 365, giving rise to the *Actual/365* method. A variant used for U.S. *money-market instruments*—instruments with one year or less in maturity—is to divide the number of days by 360 instead of 365, *Actual/360*.

The Act/365 method, however, runs into trouble for leap years (when February has 29 days instead of 28), which happens every four years when the year is a multiple of 4, unless the year is a multiple of 100 but not a multiple of 400 (the year 2000 *was* a leap year while 1900 was *not*). One remedy could be to ignore the leap day(s) in a period, giving rise to Actual/365 No Leap (*Act/365 NL*). This method is used for Japanese government bonds.

Another method to tackle leap years is to divide the interest period into annual or fractions thereof, or subperiods, and divide the number of days in each subperiod by 365 or 366 depending on whether the subperiod is part of a leap year. Adding up the fractions for each subperiod gives the fraction of the year for the whole period. This is the method prescribed by International Swap Dealers Association (ISDA) for interest calculations in swap markets and is commonly referred to as *Actual/Actual ISDA*.

None of the above methods in general provides a whole fraction of a year for one or more whole months. For example, one would expect that the fraction of a year from the nth (say 15th) day of a month to the nth day of the next month should be 1/12. But unless the starting month has exactly 30 days (April, June, September, and November), this will not be the case. To resolve this, the 30/360 method is based on assuming each month has 30 days, and is computed as

$$360 \times (y_2 - y_1) + 30 \times (m_2 - m_1) + (d_2 - d_1)$$

divided by 360 for the calculation period $[y_1/m_1/d_1, y_2/m_2/d_2]$. While this might seem a straight-forward process, it introduces nuances when month ends are considered, and has led to different variants to tackle them. The most common variant is: if $d_2 = 31$ and $d_1 = 30,31$, change d_2 to 30. If $d_1 = 31$, change d_1 to 30. Having made these changes, apply above formula.

Finally, a common method to calculate the *accrual fraction* for accrued interest and discounting for bonds paying a periodic interest rate (m times a year) is to divide the actual number of days during the fractional period by the actual number of days in the full coupon period, resulting in a number between 0 and 1. This method is also called Actual/Actual and mainly used for bonds *Actual/Actual Bond* (see Table 2.2).

TABLE 2.2 Interest for principal of $1,000,000 and interest rate $r = 4\%$ per year for the 3-month period [2019-Dec-15 2020-Mar-15], which includes the 2020-02-29 leap day. For Act/Act ISDA, the period is broken into two subperiods: [2019-Dec-15, 2020-Jan-01] (17 days) and [2020-Jan-01, 2020-Mar-15] (74 days). For Act/Act Bond, it is assumed that semiannual coupon dates are December 15th and May 15th, hence, 183 days in current coupon period.

Day Count	N	D	N/D	Interest ($)
Act/360	91	360	0.25278	10,111.11
Act/365	91	365	0.24932	9,972.60
Act/365 NL	90	365	0.24585	9,863.01
Act/Act ISDA	17,74	365,366	0.24876	9,950.45
30/360	90	360	0.25	10,000.00
Act/Act Bond	91	183×2	0.24863	9,945.36

Note that when calculating the number of days between two dates, the number *includes* the begin date and *excludes* the end date, effectively counting the number of *nights* between two dates. For example, the number of days between Monday and Tuesday is one, i.e., one night (Monday).

2.3.5 U.S. Treasury Securities

The U.S. Treasury routinely issues short-term (4-week, 8-week, 13-week, 26-week, and 52-week) zero-coupon bonds known as Treasury Bills (T-Bills). T-Bill yields are quoted using a *discount yield*

$$P_{Bill}(y, T) = 1 - y \times T$$

where T is calculated via the Act/360 method. For example, if for settlement date 8-Oct-2021 the discount yield of a 26-week ("6 month") T-Bill maturing on 8-Apr-2022 is 2%, its price is calculated as

$$P_{Bill} = 1 - 0.02 \times \frac{\text{Number of days between 8-Oct-2021 and 8-Apr-2022}}{360}$$

$$= 1 - 0.02 \times \frac{182}{360} = 0.989889 = 98.9889\%$$

If one were to purchase $100,000 face value of this T-Bill, one would have to pay $98,988.89 on 8-Oct-2021 to receive $100,000 on 8-Apr-2022.

The U.S. Treasury also regularly borrows money by issuing semiannual coupon 2-, 3-, 5-, 7-, and 10-year *notes* and 20- 30-year *bonds*.

2.4 SOLVING FOR YIELD: ROOT SEARCH

For single cash flows, one can write a formula for the yield as a function of price. However, for products with multiple cash flows like bonds and annuities, the price-yield formula cannot be inverted easily and one has to use a *root search* method to compute the implied yield for a given price.

The *root search* problem for a function f is solving for x so that $f(x) = 0$. The related problem of finding x where $f(x) = c$ for a given constant c can be reduced to finding the root of the function g defined as $g(x) = f(x) - c$

$$g(x) = 0 \Leftrightarrow f(x) = c$$

2.4.1 Newton-Raphson Method

The Newton-Raphson method is a numerical algorithm to solve for the root of a monotonic (increasing or decreasing) function, and is based on the following intuition

$$f(x) - f(y) \approx f'(x) \times (y - x)$$

where $f'(x)$ denotes the derivative of f with respect to x

$$f'(x) = \frac{df(x)}{dx} = \lim_{h \to 0} \frac{f(x + h) - f(x)}{h}$$

The Newton-Raphson method, as shown in Figure 2.5, starts with an initial guess x_0 and using the heuristic

$$f(x_{n+1}) - f(x_n) \approx f'(x_n) \times (x_{n+1} - x_n)$$

and with the objective $f(x_{n+1}) = 0$, updates each new guess as follows

$$x_{n+1} = x_n - \frac{f(x_n)}{f'(x_n)}$$

2.4.2 Bisection Method

A root search method that does not require $f'(x)$ is the commonly used *bisection method*. The bisection method starts with two *bracketing* levels $[x_1, x_2]$ where $f(x_1) \times f(x_2) < 0$, i.e., $f(x_1)$ and $f(x_2)$ have different signs so the root x where $f(x) = 0$ is *bracketed* between x_1 and x_2. At each step, one calculates

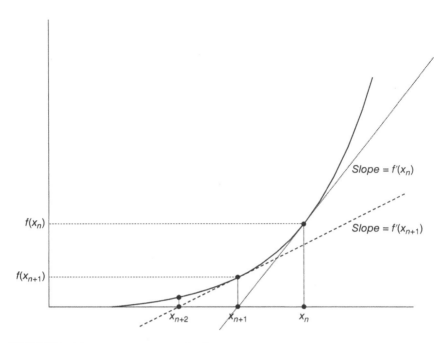

FIGURE 2.5   Newton-Raphson method.

$f(x_{Mid})$, where x_{Mid} is the halfway point $x_{Mid} = (x_1 + x_2)/2$ and updates x_1 or x_2 as follows:

- If $f(x_{Mid})$ and $f(x_1)$ have the same sign, replace x_1 by x_{Mid}.
- If $f(x_{Mid})$ and $f(x_2)$ have the same sign, replace x_2 by x_{Mid}.

After each update, the new bracket is half the width of the previous bracket, and the bracket exponentially tightens to the root.

In case the initial choices x_1, x_2 do not bracket the root, one can start with their midpoint and keep on doubling the range centered around that midpoint until the root is bracketed. This is always achievable if the function is strictly monotonic and has a root.

2.5   PRICE RISK

Asset prices and their economic drivers constantly change. When one owns a financial asset, one is not only interested in its current value, but also how this value changes due to changing market conditions. The question of how much the price changes as the yields change is known as the price sensitiv-ity or price risk, and can be answered by calculating the derivatives of the pricing formula.

2.5.1 PV01, PVBP

The main driver for bond prices is the general level of market interest rates. When market rates rise, the bond's fixed coupon rate becomes less attrac-tive relative to new market rates, and the bond value drops accordingly. Alternatively, when market yields drop, then a bond's coupon becomes more attractive and the bond value increases. The sensitivity of a bond price to changes in interest rates, known as the market risk, is the primary source of risk to a bond holder. Other risks include credit risk, liquidity risk, inflation risk, re-investment, and prepayment risk.

It is the standard to consider price changes due to 1 *basis point* (bp, $0.0001 = 1\%$ of 1%) move in yields/rates, giving rise to PV01: the change in Present Value of the bond due to 1 basis point change in implied yields:

$$PV01 = \frac{dP}{dy} \times 0.0001$$

where dP/dy is the first derivative of the bond price formula with respect to yield.

Starting with the bond price-yield formula, $P(C, y, N, m)$, we calculate

$$\frac{dP}{dy} = \frac{C}{y^2}\left(\frac{1}{(1+y/m)^N} - 1\right) + \frac{N}{m}\frac{C/y - 1}{(1+y/m)^{N+1}} \qquad (2.9)$$

The relative or percentage change in price is known as the *Modified Duration*

$$\text{Modified Duration} = \frac{1}{P}\frac{dP}{dy},$$

and has a unit of years. In bond markets, PV01 and modified duration are usually defined using $-dP/dy$ instead of dP/dy. This is to ensure that a pos-itive amount signifies a *long* position, i.e., *owning* a bond. We will ignore this market practice.

A similar but not identical concept to PV01, is $PVBP$: Present Value of 1 bp. This is the change in price due to changing the coupon rate by 1 bp

$$PVBP = \frac{dP}{dC} \times 0.0001$$

where
$$\frac{dP}{dC} = \frac{1}{y}\left(1 - \frac{1}{(1+y/m)^N}\right) \tag{2.10}$$

PVBP is equivalent to PV'ing a 1 bp per annum annuity, paid m times a year, and can be related to the *Annuity Formula*

$$PVBP = P_A(C = 0.0001, y, N, m) = \frac{0.0001}{y}\left(1 - \frac{1}{(1+y/m)^N}\right)$$

For par bonds $(C = y)$, receiving 1 bp extra in a coupon is almost equivalent to yields dropping by 1 bp, and PV01 and PVBP are sometimes used interchangeably in practice. For non-par bonds, however, the difference can become significant (see Figure 2.6) and the appropriate formula should be used depending on the application.

2.5.2 Convexity

Looking at the price-yield graph of a bond, we observe that the PV01 at a given yield is the slope of the curve at that point. We also observe that the

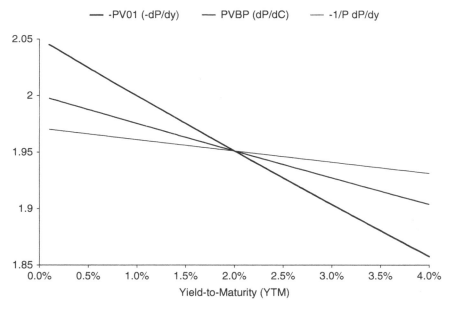

FIGURE 2.6 PV01, PVBP, and modified duration of a coupon bond.

graph is not linear and has a positive curvature, and as bond yields move, so does the slope or the PV01. We can show (see Exercises) that the price is a *convex* function of the yield.

A function f is said to be *convex* if for any $x < y$ and $0 \leq w \leq 1$, the following holds

$$f(wx + (1 - w)y) \leq wf(x) + (1 - w)f(y) \qquad (2.11)$$

A strictly convex function is when the right-hand side is strictly larger. A concave function (also called convex down) has the inequality going the other way.

The *convexity* of a bond is a measure of the curvature of the price-yield graph, and is defined as the second derivative of price with respect to yield, that is, how PV01 changes as yields move.

$$\text{Convexity} = \frac{d^2 P}{dy^2} = \frac{N(N + 1)}{m^2} \frac{1 - C/y}{(1 + y/m)^{N+2}}$$
$$- \frac{2CN/(my^2)}{(1 + y/m)^{N+1}} + \frac{2C}{y^3}\left(1 - \frac{1}{(1 + y/m)^N}\right) \qquad (2.12)$$

2.5.3 Taylor Series Expansion

PV01 and convexity can be used to estimate the price change due to a small change (Δy) in yields via the Taylor Series. For a function of one variable, $f(x)$, the Taylor Series formula is

$$f(x + \Delta x) = f(x) + f'(x)\Delta x + 1/2f''(x)(\Delta x)^2 + \ldots + \frac{f^{(n)}(x)}{n!}(\Delta x)^n + \ldots.$$

where $f'(x)$ is the first derivative, $f''(x)$ the second derivative, $f^{(n)}(x)$ the nth derivative, and so on.

In practice, we usually just use the first two derivatives, and ignore the effect of the remaining *higher-order* terms

$$f(x + \Delta x) - f(x) = f'(x)\Delta x + 1/2f''(x)(\Delta x)^2 + \text{Higher Order Terms}$$

Considering the price-yield formula for bonds, let h be the number of bps change in yields. We have

$$\text{Price change} \approx \text{PV01} \times h + 1/2 \times \text{convexity} \times (h \times 0.0001)^2.$$

In practice, however, one is primarily interested in the PV01, ignoring even the convexity effect in the above formula except for long maturity bonds, or for large yield movements.

$$\text{Price change} \approx \text{PV01} \times h$$

EXAMPLE 2

Let us consider the 10-year bond shown in Table 2.3. For a $1,000,000 face amount, its cash flows are $20,000 coupon payments every 6 months for 10 years (20 payments), plus $1,000,000 principal payment in 10 years. Since its coupon rate of 4% is below the market yield of 5%, it is trading at a *discount*: its price of 0.92205419 = 92.205419% is less than 1 = 100% (*par*), and one needs to pay $922,054.19 to buy this bond.

TABLE 2.3   Sensitivity measures for three different bonds.

T	m	N	C	y	P	dP/dy	$(dP/dy)/P$	dP/dC	d^2P/dy^2
2	2	4	4%	3%	1.019272	−1.9507	−1.9139	1.9272	4.758
5	2	10	4%	4%	1	−4.4913	−4.4913	4.4913	23.499
10	2	20	4%	5%	0.922054	−7.4264	−8.0542	7.7946	71.101

If market yields change from 5% to 5.10%, then $\Delta y = 0.0010$, and yields have moved by 10 bps. Using the first two terms of Taylor Series, we expect the new price to be approximately

$$P(y = 5.10\%) \approx P(y = 5\%) + (-7.4264) \times 0.0010 + \frac{1}{2} \times 71.101$$

$$\times (0.0010)^2$$

$$= 0.91466330$$

If we compare this to the actual price at the new yield, $P(y = 5.10\%) = 0.91466318$, we observe that the approximation error is quite small, amounting to

$$\$1,000,000 \times (0.91466330 - 0.91466318) = \$0.12$$

in market value change for the $1,000,000 face value.

For a \$1,000,000 face value, the PV01 is \$1,000,000 $\times$ $(-7.42644) \times 0.0001 = -\$742.64$. Had we just used the PV01 and ignored the convexity effect, we would have estimated the change in value to be $10 \times -\$742.64 = -\$7,426.44$, leading to a new price estimate of 0.91462775 or a market value of \$914,627.75, an error of $-\$35.43$.

2.5.4 Expansion Around *C*

Another use of the Taylor Series is to come up with an approximation for prices or yields when yields are close to the coupon rate. We know that when $C = y$, then $P(C = y, y, N, m) = 1$. If we know the dP/dy of a bond, we can approximate a new price or a new yield via the formula

$$P(y) = P(C + (y - C)) \approx P(C) + \frac{dP}{dy}(C) \times (y - C)$$

$$\Rightarrow P(y) \approx 1 + \frac{dP}{dy}(C) \times (y - C)$$

$$y \approx C + \frac{P(y) - 1}{dP/dy(C)}$$

For example, for the 5-year $C = 4\%$ bond in Table 2.3, $dP/dy = -4.49129$. We can approximate $P(4.5\%)$ as

$$P(4.5\%) \approx 1 + (-4.49129)(4.5\% - 4\%) = 97.754\%$$

Alternatively, if the bond's price is 99%, then we can approximate its yield as

$$y \approx 4\% + \frac{0.99 - 1}{-4.49129} = 4.223\%$$

2.5.5 Numerical Derivatives

For most financial instruments, a closed-form formula does not exist, and the derivatives are calculated by numerical approximation. For the first derivative, the usual method is to estimate $f'(x)$ as

$$f'(x) \approx \frac{f(x + h) - f(x)}{h}$$

for a small value of h, say $h = 10^{-8}$.

The second derivative is usually calculated by the *central difference* approximation

$$f''(x) \approx \frac{(f(x+h) - f(x))/h - (f(x) - f(x-h))/h}{h}$$

$$= \frac{f(x+h) + f(x-h) - 2f(x)}{h^2}$$

for small h, say $h = 10^{-6}$. Care needs to be taken so that the h^2 term does not become too small relative to minimum computer precision (typically 10^{-16}) resulting in arithmetic *underflow*.

2.6 LEVEL PAY LOAN

While coupon bonds are the main debt instruments for governments and corporations, most consumer finance (home, auto, student, credit card) loans are structured as *level pay* loans. A level pay loan of size B_0 with interest rate of C per annum and paid m times a year (usually monthly, $m = 12$) has the following cash flows: starting with loan balance of B_0, one makes fixed (*level*) periodic payments of size L that covers the periodic interest payment *and* pays down some of the balance, so that the loan is paid off after N periods. For example, for a 30-year home *mortgage* (backed by property) loan with monthly payments, $N = 360 = 30 \times 12$.

Starting with loan size B_0, let B_i be the remaining balance at the ith period. At each period, part of L is the interest payment, $B_i C/m$, and the remainder is the reduction in the balance:

$$B_{i+1} = B_i - (L - B_i C/m) = B_i(1 + C/m) - L$$

By inspecting the first few terms

$$B_1 = B_0(1 + C/m) - L$$

$$B_2 = B_1(1 + C/m) - L = B_0(1 + C/m)^2 - L(1 + C/m) - L$$

$$\ldots$$

we get

$$B_n = B_0(1 + C/m)^n - L \sum_{i=0}^{n-1} (1 + C/m)^i$$

$$= B_0(1 + C/m)^n - L \frac{(1 + C/m)^n - 1}{C/m}$$

If we want the loan to terminate in N periods, we set $B_N = 0$, and solve for L

$$L = B_0 \frac{(C/m)(1 + C/m)^N}{(1 + C/m)^N - 1} = B_0 \frac{C/m}{1 - 1/(1 + C/m)^N} \qquad (2.13)$$

Using Formula 2.13, we can calculate the balance B_n for any period n

$$B_n = B_0 \frac{1 - 1/(1 + C/m)^{N-n}}{1 - 1/(1 + C/m)^N}$$

To calculate how many periods it takes to pay off $0 \leq \alpha \leq 1$ of the initial loan, we need to solve

$$B_n = (1 - \alpha)B_0 \Rightarrow 1 - \alpha = \frac{1 - 1/(1 + C/m)^{N-n}}{1 - 1/(1 + C/m)^N}$$

to get

$$n(\alpha) = N - \frac{\ln(1 - (1 - \alpha)(1 - 1/(1 + C/m)^N))}{\ln(1/(1 + C/m))}$$

Note that $n(1) = N$ as expected.

EXAMPLE 3

You want to purchase a car costing \$30,000, and you are offered a 5-year auto loan at the rate of 4% per annum with monthly payments: $B_0 = \$30,000, C = 4\%, m = 12, N = 60$. Your monthly payment is

$$L = \$30,000 \times \frac{0.04/12}{1 - 1/(1 + 0.04/12)^{60}} = \$552.50$$

Your first payment at the end of the first month consists of $\$100 = \$30,000 \times 4\%/12$ interest and balance payment of \$452.50 resulting in a remaining balance of \$29,457.50 at the beginning of the second month.

2.6.1   Interest and Principal Payments

Using Formula 2.13, we can solve for the amount of interest I_n and principal P_n at each period n (see Figure 2.7). For notation ease, let $d = 1/(1 + C/m)$. We have

$$(0 \leq n \leq N) \quad B_n = B_0 \frac{1 - d^{N-n}}{1 - d^N}$$

$$(0 \leq n < N) \quad I_n = \frac{C}{m} B_n = B_0 \frac{C}{m} \frac{1 - d^{N-n}}{1 - d^N}$$

$$(0 \leq n < N) \quad P_n = L - I_n = B_0 \frac{C}{m} \frac{d^{N-n}}{1 - d^N} \qquad (2.14)$$

$$(0 \leq n < N) \quad L = I_n + P_n = B_0 \frac{C/m}{1 - d^N}$$

Using a constant yield-to-maturity (y) with the same compounding frequency as the interest payment frequency (m), we can compute the price of a unit $(B_0 = 1)$ loan as a function of yield

$$P_L(C, y, N, m) = L \sum_{n=1}^{N} \frac{1}{(1 + y/m)^n}$$

$$= \frac{C/m}{1 - 1/(1 + C/m)^N} \frac{1/(1 + y/m) - 1/(1 + y/m)^{N+1}}{1 - 1/(1 + y/m)}$$

$$= \frac{C}{y} \frac{1 - 1/(1 + y/m)^N}{1 - 1/(1 + C/m)^N}$$

$$(2.15)$$

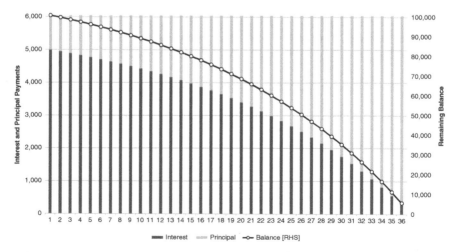

FIGURE 2.7   Interest and principal payments of a level pay loan.

2.6.2 Average Life

As opposed to a bond where the principal is only paid at maturity, a level pay loan's principal is paid throughout its lifetime, and instead of maturity, one can compute its *Average Life (AL)*. At the end of each period n, a portion of the loan payment is the repayment of principal, P_n, or equivalently P_n is the amount of principal outstanding for $n + 1$ periods. Average Life is defined as the weighted average number of periods that the loan is outstanding per unit loan $(B_0 = 1)$

$$AL = \sum_{n=0}^{N-1} (n + 1)P_n$$

Using Formula 2.14 for P_n, we have

$$AL = \sum_{n=0}^{N-1} (n + 1)P_n$$

$$= \sum_{n=0}^{N-1} (n + 1)\frac{C}{m}\frac{d^{N-n}}{1 - d^N}, \qquad d = \frac{1}{1 + C/m}$$

$$= \frac{N}{1 - 1/(1 + C/m)^N} - \frac{m}{C}$$

where we have used the identity (see Exercises)

$$S(x, m, N) = \sum_{n=m}^{N} nx^n$$

$$= \frac{mx^m - (m - 1)x^{m+1} - (N + 1)x^{N+1} + Nx^{N+2}}{(1 - x)^2} \qquad (2.16)$$

leading to

$$\sum_{n \geq 1} nx^n = \frac{x}{(1 - x)^2} \text{when } |x| < 1. \qquad (2.17)$$

If the P_n's were constant, say C is almost zero, then $P_n = 1/N$, and $AL = (N + 1)/2$. For example, the monthly payments of a 1-year monthly level pay loan with a very low interest rate are 1/12th of the principal and occur on month 1, month 2, ..., month 12, resulting in $AL = 6.5$, halfway between the sixth and seventh month.

2.6.3 Pool of Loans

Collection of similar (in maturity and coupon rate) loans are typically aggregated into a pool to form an *asset-backed* security/bond and sold to investors. For example, a *mortgage-backed security (MBS)* is formed by an entity buying a collection of individual home mortgage loans from banks, and issuing a new bond. The most common type of MBS is a *pass-through* bond: the payments of the new bond are simply the aggregate of the payments (principal and interest) of the underlying loans and are passed on to the bond investors.

2.6.4 Prepayments

A common feature of U.S. home mortgage loans is the ability of the borrower to prepay—in part or in full—the balance of the loan. For an individual loan, the prepayment simply accelerates the loan maturity: if we are at the nth period with balance B_n, paying an extra amount PP (prepayment) in addition to the scheduled level monthly payment L, the loan jumps k periods ahead to the period where the balance is $B_{n+k} = B_n - PP$.

At the pool level, the usual method to model prepayments is to assume that at each nth period, a certain amount of underlying loans *completely* prepay, so that successive *actual* balances, B'_n's, and *scheduled* balances (no prepayments), B_n's, are related as follows

$$(0 \leq n < N) \qquad \frac{B'_{n+1}}{B'_n} = (1 - s_n)\frac{B_{n+1}}{B_n}$$

Using the above relationship, we have

$$(0 \leq n \leq N) \qquad B'_n = \left[\prod_{i=0}^{n-1}(1 - s_i) \right] B_n$$

If we assume a constant periodic prepayment rate, $s_i = s$, the above expression simplifies to

$$(0 \leq n \leq N) \qquad B'_n = (1 - s)^n B_n = (1 - s)^n \frac{1 - d^{N-n}}{1 - d^N}$$

where $d = 1/(1 + C/m)$, and C/m is the periodic coupon of the bond. In the U.S. market, MBS payments are monthly, $m = 12$, and the periodic (monthly) prepayment rate s is called *single monthly mortality (SMM)* rate. The annualized version of the SMM rate is called *constant prepayment rate (CPR)*: $1 - CPR = (1 - SMM)^{12}$.

We can similarly relate actual (with prepayments) pass-through interest payments, I'_n, to the scheduled (no prepayments) version

$$(0 \le n < N) \quad I'_n = B'_n \frac{C}{m} = \left[\prod_{i=0}^{n-1}(1-s_i)\right] B_n \frac{C}{m}$$

$$= \left[\prod_{i=0}^{n-1}(1-s_i)\right] I_n$$

$$= (1-s)^n I_n \quad \text{if } s_i = s$$

$$= (1-s)^n \frac{C}{m} \frac{1-d^{N-n}}{1-d^N}$$

The total principal payment during nth period is $B'_n - B'_{n+1}$. Part of this is the scheduled principal payment based on the beginning period balance, B'_n, and the remainder is that period's prepayment. Since $I'_n = B'_n \frac{C}{m}$, we have the following for the nth cash flow of a pass-through bond with constant periodic prepayment rate s

$$(0 \le n < N) \quad CF_n = (B'_n - B'_{n+1}) + I'_n$$

$$= (1+C/m)B'_n - B'_{n+1}$$

$$= (1+C/m)(1-s)^n \frac{1-d^{N-n}}{1-d^N} - (1-s)^{n+1}\frac{1-d^{N-(n+1)}}{1-d^N}$$

$$= (1-s)^n \frac{C/m + s[1-(1+C/m)d^{N-n}]}{1-d^N}$$

Using the above formula for nth cash flow, we can compute the price of the pass-through bond as a function of a yield and periodic prepayment speed

$$P(C,y,N,m,s) = \sum_{n=0}^{N-1} \frac{CF_n}{(1+y/m)^{n+1}}$$

$$= \sum_{n=0}^{N-1} \frac{(1-s)^n}{(1+y/m)^{n+1}} \frac{C/m + s[1-(1+C/m)d^{N-n}]}{1-d^N}$$

$$= \dots$$

$$= \frac{C/m + s}{y/m + s} \frac{1 - ((1-s)/(1+y/m))^N}{1 - 1/(1+C/m)^N}$$

$$- \frac{s}{1 - 1/(1+C/m)^N} \frac{1/(1+C/m)^N - ((1-s)/(1+y/m))^N}{(1+y/m)/(1+C/m) - (1-s)}$$

$$(2.18)$$

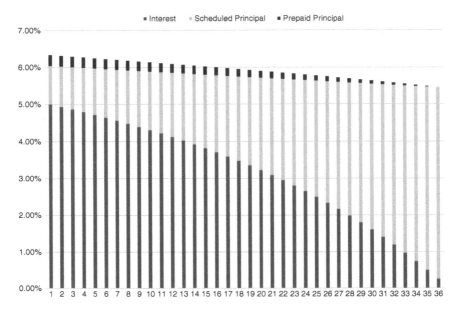

FIGURE 2.8   A pool of loans with low prepayment speed.

Note that when there are no prepayments, $s = 0$, the second term vanishes, and the first term reduces to Formula 2.15. Figures 2.8 and 2.9 show the effect of prepayments on a pool of loans.

2.6.5   Negative Convexity

Borrowers typically refinance their loans by prepaying when interest rates are low. Consider having a home mortgage loan with a 4% rate. If interest rates in general and mortgage rates drop, say to 3%, then it is beneficial for the homeowner to refinance. On the flip side, the lender will receive the balance of a loan at a high interest rate (4%) in an environment when rates are low (3%) and has to reinvest this money at low rates. The effect of faster prepayments in decreasing rate environments gives rise to the price-yield relationship for a pass-through bond shown in Figure 2.10: usually convex relationship is changed to a concave one, and is referred to as *negative convexity*.

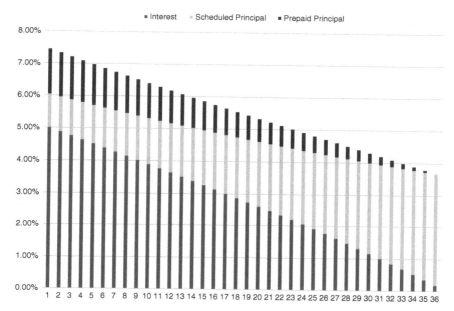

FIGURE 2.9 A pool of loans with high prepayment speed.

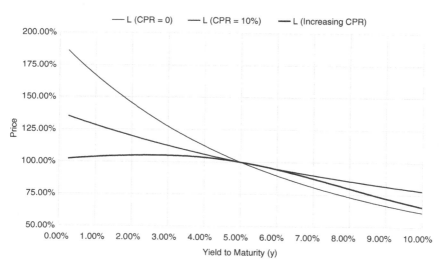

FIGURE 2.10 Negative convexity due to increased prepayments when rates are low.

2.7   YIELD CURVE

Most governments finance their infrastructure projects and any deficits by issuing bonds of various maturities at regularly scheduled auctions. For example, the U.S. government has monthly 2-year, 3-year, 5-year, and 7-year and quarterly 10-year and 30-year bond auctions. At each auction, the government borrows new money by issuing a new N-year bond ($N = 2,3,5,7,10,30$). On any day, there are a collection of outstanding (not yet matured) bonds, each with its own remaining maturity, coupon rate, price, and issue size. The graph of yield to maturity of government bonds versus their remaining maturity is known as the government/sovereign *yield curve*. Figure 2.11 shows a sample snapshot of the U.S. treasury yield curve.

Recall that the discount factor, $D(T)$, is today's value of receiving unit cash flow at a future date T. The graph of $D(T)$ versus T is the *discount factor curve*. Given a discount factor curve, the price of any financial instrument with known cash flows—for example, a coupon bond—is simply the discounted value of its remaining cash flows, with each cash flow occurring at T multiplied by $D(T)$.

In general, the market does not provide granular information about the discount factor curve. For example, a 2-year semiannual bond has cash flows at four futures dates and its price provides information about four discount factors, but not enough information about any of the individual discount factors, i.e., we have one formula and four unknowns. We have previously

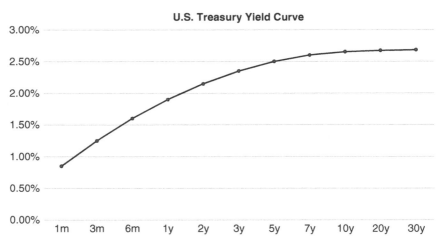

FIGURE 2.11 U.S. Treasury yield curve.

tackled this problem by assuming *flat* yields and equating the *i*th discount factor to

$$D(T_i) = 1/(1 + y/2)^i$$

While this method allows us to analyze the price-yield relationship and price sensitivities of a single bond in isolation, it is problematic when considering the collection of bonds comprising the yield curve. For example, a 2-year bond has overlapping cash flows with a 3-year bond for the first two years, and unless the 2-year and 3-year yields, y_2, y_3, are identical, we are valuing cash flows with the same payment dates differently. For example

$$D(1 \text{ year}) = \frac{1}{(1 + y_2/2)^2} = \frac{1}{(1 + y_3/2)^2}$$

which can only happen if $y_2 = y_3$.

2.7.1 Bootstrap Method

A standard method to extract the discount factor curve from a collection of bond prices is the *bootstrap* algorithm. It proceeds as follows:

1. Arrange the traded market instruments in increasing maturity $(T_1, T_2, \dots)$, and let P_i denote the market price of the *i*th instrument.
2. $D(0) = 1$. Starting with the shortest maturity instrument, generate discount factors up to T_1, $D(t), 0 \le t \le T_1$, so that the sum of its discounted cash flows equal its market price, P_1.
3. Having generated the discount factor curve up to T_n, the $n+1$th instrument might have cash flows that are on or before T_n. Generate new discount factors $D(t), T_n < t \le T_{n+1}$, so that the sum of its discounted cash flows equals its market price, $P(T_{n+1})$. In this way, we are not changing the already constructed curve, and all the previous instruments preserve their market prices $(P_1, \dots, P_n)$.

2.7.2 Interpolation Method

During each step of the bootstrap method, we are given one new constraint, market price of the $n+1$th instrument, which is a function of discount factors for many dates. Some of the dates might fall before T_n, but they don't necessarily fall on cash flow dates of previous instruments. Also there could be more than one cash flow date that falls between T_n and T_{n+1}. In short, at each bootstrap step, we have one new formula but potentially more than one unknown variable. The usual approach to resolve this is to focus only on the discount factor of the *last* date, $D(T_{n+1})$, and use interpolation for any other unknown discount factors. Two common interpolation methods are:

1. Linear in discount factors

$$(t_1 \leq t \leq t_2) \quad D(t) = D(t_1) + \frac{D(t_2) - D(t_1)}{t_2 - t_1}(t - t_1)$$

$$= D(t_1) + w(D(t_2) - D(t_1)), \quad w = \frac{t - t_1}{t_2 - t_1}$$

2. Linear in log of discount factors

$$(t_1 \leq t \leq t_2) \quad \ln D(t) = \ln D(t_1) + \frac{\ln D(t_2) - \ln D(t_1)}{t_2 - t_1}(t - t_1)$$

$$D(t) = D(t_1)\left(\frac{D(t_2)}{D(t_1)}\right)^w, \quad w = \frac{t - t_1}{t_2 - t_1}$$

EXAMPLE 4

Bootstrap with linear interpolation: Let a 2-year, 2.25% semiannual coupon bond trade at 99.50%, and let a 3-year, 2.75% semiannual coupon bond trade at 100.50%. The combined cash flow dates for the two bonds are every six months from today to three years.

Starting with $D(0) = 1$, we focus on $D(2)$, the maturity of first bond. We need to solve

$$0.995 = \frac{2.25\%}{2}[D(0.5) + D(1) + D(1.5) + D(2)] + D(2)$$

By linear interpolation, we have

$$D(0.5) = D(0) + (0.5/2)(D(2) - D(0))$$

$$D(1) = D(0) + (1/2)(D(2) - D(0))$$

$$D(1.5) = D(0) + (1.5/2)(D(2) - D(0))$$

So, all we need to solve for is $D(2)$. Algebra or trial and error gives us $D(2) = 0.951368$ as shown in Table 2.4.

TABLE 2.4 Discount factor curve construction via bootstrap method.

T	$D(T)$
0	$D(0) = 1.0$
0.5	$D(0) + .25(D(2) - D(0))$
1	$D(0) + 0.5(D(2) - D(0))$
1.5	$D(0) + 0.75(D(2) - D(0))$
2	$D(2) = ? = 0.951368$
2.5	$D(2) + 0.5(D(3) - D(2))$
3	$D(3) = ? = 0.926032$

For the 3-year, 2.75% coupon bond trading at 100.50%, we focus on $D(3)$. We need to solve

$$100.50\% = \frac{2.75\%}{2}[D(0.5) + D(1) + D(1.5) + D(2) + D(2.5) + D(3)] + D(3)$$

We already have all the discount factors except $D(2.5), D(3)$, but by linear interpolation $D(2.5) = D(2) + .5(D(3) - D(2))$, so there is only one unknown, $D(3)$. Algebra or trial and error gives us $D(3) = 0.926032$.

Note that having anchored $D(0), D(2), D(3)$, by interpolation, we can extract $D(t)$ for *any* $0 \leq t \leq 3$ by linear interpolation. For example

$$D(1.75) = D(0) + (1.75/2)(D(2) - D(0)) = 0.957447$$

which would be the *model price* of a 1.75 year zero-coupon bond.

2.7.3 Rich/Cheap Analysis

We can also come up with the *model* price or yield of a bond and compare it to the market price or yield of the bond for a rich/cheap analysis. For example, using Table 2.4, the cash flow–based model price of a 1-year, 2% semiannual bond is

$$\frac{2\%}{2}[D(0.5) + D(1)] + D(1) = 0.99532$$

which can be converted to a semiannual yield of 2.477%. If this 1-year bond's market price is lower than 99.532%, say it is trading at 99.5% (yield of 2.509%), it is flagged as too *cheap*: its yield is higher than what the model suggests. Alternatively, if its market price is higher, say 99.6% (yield of 2.407%), it is flagged as too *rich*.

2.7.4 Yield Curve Trades

Given a yield curve, there are a variety of risks and trades that can be identified. A *parallel shift* is when yields for all maturities move by the same amount, say 10 bps. Using prices and yields in Table 2.3, if there is a 10 bp parallel shift in the market, the yields of 2-year, 5-year, and 10-year bonds will be 3.10%, 4.10%, and 5.10%, respectively. For a given portfolio of bonds, if one wants to be immune to parallel shifts in the market, one can *hedge* by ensuring that the portfolio PV01 is zero. For example, the value of a portfolio of two bonds is $V = N_1 P_1 + N_2 P_2$ where N_1, N_2 are the face values of the 2-year and 10-year bonds and P_1, P_2, y_1, y_2 their respective prices and yields. The PnL is ΔV. To be hedged against parallel shift Δy means $\Delta V = 0$ when $\Delta y_1 = \Delta y_2 = \Delta y$

$$\Delta V = N_1 \Delta P_1 + N_2 \Delta P_2$$
$$\approx N_1 \frac{dP_1}{dy_1} \Delta y_1 + N_2 \frac{dP_2}{dy_2} \Delta y_2$$
$$= (N_1 \frac{dP_1}{dy_1} + N_2 \frac{dP_2}{dy_2}) \Delta y$$

For the above to be zero for a small parallel shift Δy, the following must hold

$$N_1 \frac{dP_1}{dy_1} + N_2 \frac{dP_2}{dy_2} = 0$$

Another measure of the yield curve is the slope. In Table 2.3, we observe that the 2-year to 10-year slope of the yield curve is 2% (=5%-3%), which a trader might feel is too steep compared to its historical value, and with a view that the imminent central bank tightening will cause the 2-year yield to rise by more than the increase in a 10-year yield. The trader can express this *flattening* view by selling a 2-year bond and buying a 10-year bond in dP/dy-equal amounts, that is 3.807=7.42644/1.95075 face value of the 2 year for each unit face value of the 10 year.

For example, if one sells $380.07 million face value of a 2-year bond versus buying $100 million face value of a 10-year bond, one is exposed to the slope risk of -$74,264 (=$100,000,000 × −7.42644 × 0.0001) per bp: for each 1 bp steepening/flattening of 2 year to 10 year, one loses/makes $74,264. Note that this trade is impervious to the overall level of yields: if the whole yield curve moves up or down by the same amount, there is no profit or loss except for convexity and higher order effects. Its main risk is to the slope of the yield curve.

EXERCISES

1. Use the Binomial Formula

$$(a + b)^n = \sum_{k=0}^{n} \binom{n}{k} a^k b^{n-k}$$

to show
(a)

$$e = \lim_{n \to \infty} \left(1 + \frac{1}{n}\right)^n = \sum_{k=0}^{\infty} \frac{1}{k!}$$

Hint:

$$(1 + \frac{1}{n})^n = \sum_{k=0}^{n} \frac{n!}{k!(n-k)!} \frac{1}{n^k}$$

$$\cdots$$

$$= \sum_{k=0}^{n} \frac{1}{k!} B(k, n)$$

where
$$B(k, n) = \frac{n(n-1)\ldots(n-(k-1))}{n^k} \text{ for each } k$$

(b) Use the Binomial Formula to show

$$e^x = \lim_{n \to \infty} \left(1 + \frac{x}{n}\right)^n = \sum_{k=0}^{\infty} \frac{x^k}{k!}$$

Hint: Let $n = mx$, and evaluate $(1 + x/n)^n = (1 + x/(mx))^{mx}$.
2. Using an annual interest rate $r = 4\%$, recompute Table 2.1 for $FV(T)$ for a horizon date of 6 months, $T = 0.5$. Repeat for a horizon date of 1y and 6 months, $T = 1.5$.

3. How long does it to take to double your money at a given rate r? Begin with

$$FV = PVe^{rt} = 2PV$$

and approximate $ln(2) \approx 0.72$ to come up with the Rule of 72.
   (a) At 3%, approximately how many years does it take to double your money?
   (b) How about at 8%?
4. Let r_m be the interest rate with m compoundings per year, for example, $m = 12$ means monthly compounding.
   (a) Derive the formula to convert r_m to r_n for general $m, n = 1, 2, 4, 12$.
   (b) Let r_c be the continuous compounding rate. Derive the formula to convert r_m to r_c and vice versa.
   (c) Convert a simple add-on rate, r_0, to a compounded rate r_m ($m = 1, 2, 4, 12$), and vice versa.
   (d) Convert a simple add-on rate, r_0, to a continuously compounded rate, r_c, and vice versa.
   (e) For $m < n$, what can you say qualitatively about r_m versus r_n? Explain your answer.
   (f) Convert a simple (add-on) Act/360 rate, r_1 to a simple (add-on) Act/365 rate, r_2.
   Hint: Compute the 1-year future value of unit currency invested at each rate and use the law of one price.
5. A 2-year semiannual coupon bond is issued on 1/1/2020 and matures on 1/1/2022 with a semiannual coupon rate of 4% per annum and coupon dates 7/1/2020, 1/1/2021, 7/1/2021, 1/1/2022, leading to four coupon periods consisting of 182, 184, 181, and 184 days, respectively.

Date	Remaining Coupons (N)	Accrual Fraction (w)	$P(C, y, N, m)$
1/1/2020	4	0	1
1/2/2020	4	1/182	
. . .			
6/30/2020	4	181/182	1.019889
7/1/2020	3	0	1
7/2/2020	3	1/184	1.000108
. . .			
12/31/2021	1	183/184	1.01989

(a) Keeping its semiannual yield constant at 4%, graph the daily price from 1/1/2020 to 12/31/2021, using Act/Act for fractional periods. The price ramps up from 1/1/2020 to 6/30/2020 and drops (almost 2%) from 6/30/2020 to 7/1/2020 with no change in yields. The drop is simply due to one fewer remaining coupons.

(b) Graph the clean and dirty price of the bond from 1/1/2020 to 12/31/2021 when its yield is held at 5%, resulting in a discount bond, $C < y$.

(c) Graph the clean and dirty price of the bond from 1/1/2020 to 12/31/2021 when its yield is held at 3%, resulting in a premium bond, $C > y$.

6. Geometric Series

(a) In a *Fractional Reserve* system of banking, each bank need only keep a fraction α, say 5%, of its deposits and can lend out $1 - \alpha$. The loan recipient will then deposit $1 - \alpha$ at its own bank (or it could be the same bank) and use the proceeds as/when needed. The second bank in turn can lend out $1 - \alpha$ of this amount $(1 - \alpha)^2$, and so on. Compute the *Velocity of Money*: The total amount of currency generated by each *new* unit of currency

$$1 + (1 - \alpha) + (1 - \alpha)^2 + \ldots$$

What is the velocity of money when $\alpha = 5\%$?

(b) A simple model for a company's stock value is the *Dividend Discount Model*. It is assumed that the company pays periodic dividends with growth rate g, that is each new periodic dividend $D_{n+1} = (1 + g)D_n$. Discounting each future dividend using the same periodic discount rate r, the stock value S is computed as the discounted value of future dividends

$$S = \sum_{i=1}^{\infty} D_0 (\frac{1+g}{1+r})^i$$

where D_0 is the current dividend amount. Using the above model, compute S as a function of D_0, r, g, and provide conditions to ensure the sum converges.

7. Using the bisection method, compute the semiannual yield of a 5-year bond paying a semiannual coupon of 2% per annum and trading at 98%. Start with bracketing levels of 0%, 10%, and stop when the result accuracy is better than 1.0×10^{-4}.

8. Using a semiannually compounded yield of 4% p.a., numerically or via evaluating the formula, compute the PV01 of
   (a) $1 million 5-year zero-coupon bond
   (b) $1 million 5-year 4% coupon bond with semiannual coupon payments
   (c) $1 million 5-year 4% annuity with semiannual payments
9. For a T-year zero-coupon bond with continuously compounded yield y, compute
   (a) Its modified duration, $1/P \times dP/dy$
   (b) Its convexity, d^2P/dy^2
   (c) The price, modified duration, and convexity of a 5-year zero-coupon bond with continuously compounded yield of 5%.
10. Limits at $y = 0$
    (a) Evaluate $P(C, y, N, m)$ (Formula 2.5) at $y = 0$.
    (b) Evaluate dP/dy (Formula 2.9) at $y = 0$. [Hint: L'Hôpital's Rule, or evaluate derivative of each term in the price-yield summation formula in Formula 2.5].
    (c) Evaluate dP/dC (Formula 2.10) at $y = 0$.
11. Convexity
    (a) If f'' exists, use the definition 2.11 and

$$f''(x) = \lim_{h \to 0} \frac{f(x+h) + f(x-h) - 2f(x)}{h^2}$$

    to show that $f''(x) \geq 0$ for a convex function ($f'' \leq 0$ for a concave function Formula 2.11).
    (b) For a bond with periodic coupon payments, the ith cash flow is discounted using $1/(1 + y/m)^i$. Show that $1/(1 + y/m)^i$ is a convex function of y.
    (c) Show that Formula 2.5, for the price of a coupon bond is a convex function of yield. [Hint: Use the result from part (b) of this problem.]
12. For a 30-year monthly level-pay home mortgage loan of $500,000 with a 3% interest rate
    (a) Compute the monthly level payment.
    (b) What is the total amount of interest you pay during the loan?
    (c) After how many periods have you paid off half of the principal? Find n where $B_{n-1} > \$250,000, B_n \leq \$250,000$.
    (d) After how many periods does the monthly payment start to cover more of the principal than the interest: Find n where $I_{n-1} > L/2$, $I_n \leq L/2$.

13. Derivation of $S(x, m, N)$
    (a) Derive the formula for $S(x, m, N) = \sum_{n=m}^{N} nx^n$ in Formula 2.16. *Hint:* Begin by evaluating $S(x, m, N) - xS(x, m, N)$.
    (b) Alternatively, derive the formula by noting that

$$S(x, m, N) = x \frac{d}{dx}\left(\sum_n x^n\right)$$

    and use the Geometric Series Formula.
    (c) Use the above formula and the fact that $nx^n \to 0$ as $n \to \infty$ when $|x| < 1$ to show

$$\sum_{n \geq 1} nx^n = \frac{x}{(1-x)^2} \text{ when } |x| < 1.$$

14. Let a 2-year bond with a semiannual coupon rate of 2.25% p.a. have a semiannual yield of 2% p.a., and a 10-year bond with a semiannual coupon rate of 2.5% p.a. have a semiannual yield of 3% p.a.
    (a) Calculate the PV01 of each bond.
    (b) Assume you own $N_1 = \$10M$ face value of the 2-year bond, and want to protect (hedge) yourself against parallel shifts in the yield curve by shorting the 10-year bond. How much face value of the 10-year bond do you need to sell short?
    (c) What is the Profit and Loss (PnL) of your combined (long+short) position due to a 10 bp parallel shift: the 2-year and 10-year bond yields both increase by 10 bps (10×0.0001)?
    (d) What is your PnL due to a 10 bp *steepening*: the 10-year yield change is 10 bps more than 2-year yield's change? (Assume the 2-year yield change is 0.)

15. Given instruments in the following table

Instrument	Semiannual coupon rate	Market yield	Market price
6m (182 day) T-Bill	0%	0.75%	99.62083%
2y Treasury	1.375%	1.40%	99.95086%
3y Treasury	2.125%	2.00%	100.36222%
5y Treasury	2.5%	2.50%	100%
7y Treasury	3%	2.90%	100.62942%
10y Treasury	3.25%	3.20%	100.42501%

(a) Extract the semiannual discount factors for 10 years using the bootstrap method with linear and log-linear interpolation in discount factors.
(b) On the same graph, plot the semiannual zero-coupon yields (Formula 2.8 with $w = 0$) for 6m, 1y, ..., 10y maturities for linear and log-linear interpolation methods.
(c) Using the discount factor curve from the log-linear interpolation, compute the price of a 5-year, 1% semiannual coupon bond and convert the price using Formula 2.5 to a semiannual yield. Do the same with a semiannual coupon rate of 8% to observe the *coupon effect* on yields.
Hint: See Table 2.5

TABLE 2.5   Hint for bootstrap problem.

T	Linear		Log-linear	
(years)	DF	Zero rate	DF	Zero rate
0	1		1	
0.5	0.9962083	0.761%	0.9962083	0.761%
...				
2	0.9724397	1.402%	0.9724406	1.402%
...				
7.5	0.7987633	3.018%	0.7980435	3.031%
...				
9.5	0.7373020	3.234%	0.7366574	3.243%
10	0.7219367	3.285%	0.7220633	3.283%

16. Using the price-yield Formula 2.5 for a bond with a periodic coupon of C/m with N remaining coupons, show that $P(N, m, C, y) \times (1 + y/m)^N$ equals the sum of all coupon payments reinvested to maturity at the periodic rate of y/m plus the principal payment paid at maturity.
17. U.S. Treasury Bills are quoted based on an Act/360 discount yield, $P_B = 1 - y_B N/360$, where N is the number of days from settlement date to maturity date.
    (a) Provide a formula for converting the Act/360 discount yield to an Act/360 simple (add-on) yield, $P_B \times (1 + y_s N/360) = 1$.
    (b) The semiannual coupon equivalent yield (*bond equivalent yield, BEY*) of a T-Bill is defined as follows: let $w = N/365$ (366 if there

is a leap day between settlement and maturity dates). If $w \leq 1/2$, the BEY y solves

$$P_B \times (1 + yw) = 1$$

If $w > 1/2$, y is the positive solution to the following quadratic equation

$$P_B(1 + y/2)(1 + y(w - 1/2)) = 1$$

Provide a formula for y in terms of P_B and w for each case ($w \leq 1/2$, $w > 1/2$).

(c) On Thursday, 12-Aug-2021, the U.S. Treasury issued a 52-week ("1-year") T-Bill with maturity date Monday 11-Aug-2022. If the price of this T-Bill for settlement date 8-Oct-2021 is 98%, compute its discount yield, simple (add-on) yield, and the bond-equivalent yield on the settlement date.

18. Compute price P, sensitivity dP/dy, convexity d^2P/dy^2 of 2y, 5y, 10y, 30y, 100y bonds, all with a semiannual coupon rate of 4% per annum when
  (a) $y = 4\%$
  (b) $y = 1\%$
19. Compute total interest for a level pay loan, $I = \sum_{n=0}^{N-1} I_n$, to show that $I = AL \times C/m$. Does this make sense?
20. Evaluate Formula 2.18 when $s = 1$, and explain the result.
21. For a given time series $x_1, x_2, \ldots$, the N-period arithmetic Moving Average (MA), $A(n, N)$, is defined as

$$A(n, N) = \begin{cases} (x_1 + \ldots + x_n)/n & \text{if } n < N \\ (x_n + x_{n-1} + \ldots + x_{n-(N-1)})/N & \text{if } n \geq N \end{cases}$$

Similarly, given $0 < \alpha < 1$, the Exponential Moving Average (EMA), $E(n, \alpha)$, is defined as

$$E(n, \alpha) = \begin{cases} x_1 & n = 1 \\ \alpha x_n + (1 - \alpha)E(n - 1, \alpha) & n > 1 \end{cases}$$

When computing $A(n, N), E(n, \alpha)$, the *age* of a data point x_{n-i} is i, and the *Average Age* is the weighted average age.

(a) Compute the average age of an N-period arithmetic MA.

(b) Prove the following

$$E(n, \alpha) = \sum_{i=0}^{n-2} \alpha(1 - \alpha)^i x_{n-i} + (1 - \alpha)^{n-1} x_1$$

and verify the following asymptotic approximation for large n

$$E(n, \alpha) \approx \sum_{i=0}^{\infty} \alpha(1 - \alpha)^i x_{n-i}$$

(c) Using the approximation from part (b), verify that the weights $\alpha(1 - \alpha)^i$ add up to 1, and compute the *asymptotic Average Age* of EMA

$$\sum_{i=0}^{\infty} i\alpha(1 - \alpha)^i$$

(d) An EMA with an asymptotic average age equal to an N-period arithmetic MA is called an *N-period EMA*. What is the α of an N-period EMA?

(e) A crypto exchange defines its settlement price as the 30-second EMA of the Bitcoin price. What weight is assigned to the Bitcoin price of 15 seconds ago?

PYTHON PROJECTS

1. Price-Yield Formula. To apply Formula 2.6 and 2.7 with dates, we need a series of helper functions.

(a) Write a function that for any input date *yyyymmdd* returns the last day of that month. Recall that February has 29 days in leap years, and a leap year is one that is divisible by 4, unless it is a multiple of 100 but not a multiple of 400.

```
def is_leap_year(yyyy):
    res = False
    # is yyyy a multiple of 4? change res to True
    # is yyyy a mulitple of 100? change res back to False
    # is yyyy a multiple of 400? change res back to True
    return res


def last_day_of_month(input_date):
    # input_date comes in as an int yyyymmdd, e.g,. 20000101
    # extract year, month (1 through 12)
    dict_month_days = { 1:31; 2:28; 3:31, ..., 12:31}
    res = dict_month[month]
    if is_leap_year(year) and month==2:
        res = 29

    return res
```

(b) Write a function that adds *n* months to a given date. If the start date is an end of month, then the resulting date should also be end of month: 1 month after Feb 28th is Mar 31st, not Mar 28th.

```
def add_month(input_date, num_months):
    # num_months can be 0, positive or negative integer
    # extract yyyy, mm
    months1 = 12 * yyyy + mm -1
    months2 = months1 + num_months
    # convert months2 to yyyymm
    # append appropriate dd to yyyymm

    return yyyymmdd
```

(c) Write a function that computes the number of days between two dates. This requires calculation of the *Julian day* of dates.

```
def julian_day(input_date):
    # extract y, m, d
    mm = (m + 9) // 12 - 1
    jd = (1461 * (y + 4800 + mm)) // 4 \
       + (367 * (m - 2 - 12 * mm)) // 12 \
       - (3 * ((y + 4900 + mm) // 100)) // 4 \
       + d - 32075

    return jd
def date_diff(date1, date2):
    return julian_day(date2) - julian_day(date1)
```

(d) Compute the number of remaining periodic coupons, previous coupon date, and next coupon date

```
def num_coupons(start_date, end_date, freq):
    # freq is 1 (annual), 2 (semi-annual), 4 (quarterly),
        12 (monthly)
    period_months = 12/freq
    num = 0
    while add_month(end_date, -num*period_months)
      > start_date:
        num = num + 1

    return num
def prev_coupon_date(settle_date, mat_date, freq):
    period_months = 12/freq
    num = num_coupons(settle_date, mat_date, freq)
```

```
    prev_date = add_month(mat_date, - num * period_months)

    return prev_date
def next_coupon_date(settle_date, mat_date, freq):
    period_months = 12/freq
    num = num_coupons(settle_date, mat_date, freq)
    next_date = ...

    return next_date
```

(e) Dirty and Clean price, Formulas 2.6 and 2.7

```
def price(settle_date, mat_date, coupon, yield, freq):
    N = num_coupons(settle_date, mat_date, freq)
    nxt = next_coupon_date(settle_date, mat_date, freq)
    prv = prev_coupon_date(settle_date, mat_date, freq)
    w = date_diff(prv, settle_date) / date_diff(prv, nxt)
    # Formula for dirty price

    return price
def price-clean(settle_date, mat_date, coupon, yield, freq):
    price-dirty = price(settle_date, mat_date, coupon, yield,
      freq)
    nxt = next_coupon_date(settle_date, mat_date, freq)
    prv = prev_coupon_date(settle_date, mat_date, freq)
    w = date_diff(prv, settle_date) / date_diff(prv, nxt)

    return price_dirty - w * coupon / freq
```

(f) Solve for yield given a clean price

```
def yld(settle_date, mat_date, coupon, target_price, freq):
    # find 2 yields that bracket the clean_price
    # P(y_lo) > clean_price > P(y_hi)
    prc_lo = price-clean(settle_date, mat_date, coupon, y_lo,
      freq)
    prc_hi = price-clean(settle_date, mat_date, coupon, y_hi,
      freq)
    tol = 1.0e-8
    y_mid = 0.5 * (y_lo + y_hi)
    prc_mid = price-clean(settle_date, mat_date, coupon,
      y_mid, freq)
```

```
        while abs(target_price-prc_mid) > tol:
            if prc_mid > target_price:
                y_lo = y_mid
                prc_lo = prc_mid
            else:
                y_hi = y_mid
                prc_hi = prc_mid

            y_mid = 0.5 * (y_lo + y_hi)
            prc_mid = price-clean(settle_date, mat_date, coupon,
              y_mid, freq)

        return y_mid
```

2. Bootstrap Method

Implement the bootstrap method for a given collection of N bonds using the following series of helper functions. Assume all bonds have the same coupon frequency, say $m = 2$, and let the bonds be sorted according to their maturity dates.

```
# mat_dates = [mat_date1, ..., mat_dateN]
    mat_date1<mat_date2<...
# coupons = [coupon1, ..., couponN]
# mkt_prices = [price1, ..., priceN]
#   These are Dirty/Full prices: today's value of remaining
      cashflows
```

(a) Write a function that returns the remaining cash flow dates and amounts of a bond per unit face value.

```
def cash_flows(settle_date, mat_date, coupon, freq):
    dates = [mat_date]
    amounts = [1.0]

    N = num_coupons(settle_date, mat_date, freq)
    # freq is 1 (annual), 2 (semi-annual), 4 (quarterly),
        12 (monthly)
    period_months = 12/freq

    for cf_no in range(N):
        cf_date = add_month(mat_date, -cf_no * period_months)
        dates.append(cf_date)
        amounts.append(coupon/freq)

    return dates, amounts
```

(**b**) Given a list of sorted dates (yyyymmdd) and a date strictly in between the first and last date, use bisection to write a function that returns the location of a new date: dates[location] $\leq$ date $<$ dates[location+1].

```
def locate_date(sorted_dates, new_date):
    # sorted_dates[0] <= new_date <= sorted_date[-1]
    # Use the bisection method to find the location:
    #     sorted_dates[loc_idx] <= new_date
            < sorted_dates[loc_idx+1]

    return loc_idx
```

(**c**) Represent a discount factor curve as a list of sorted dates, a list of corresponding discount factors, and an interpolation method. Write a function to return the discount factor for an arbitrary date.

```
def get_df(df_dates, df_values, interp_method, new_date):
    if new_date <= df_dates[0]:
        return df_values[0]
    if new_date >= df_dates[-1]:
        return df_value[-1]

    loc_idx = locate_date(df_dates, new_date)

    # Use the appropriate interpolation formula to
      calculate new_df
    #     based on df_values[loc_idx], df_values[loc_idx+1]

    return new_df
```

(**d**) Calculate today's value of bond given a discount factor curve.

```
def price:bond(df_dates, df_values, interp_method, \
               settle_date, mat_date, coupon, freq):
    dates, amounts = cash_flows(settle_date, mat_date,
      coupon, freq)

    sum = 0
    for cf_no in range(len(date)):
        df = get_df(df_dates, df_values, interp_method,
          dates[cf_no])
        sum = sum + amounts[cf_no] * df

    return sum
```

(e) Create a discount factor curve using the bootstrap method.

```
def df_curve(settle_date, mat_dates, coupons, mkt_prices,
interp_method):
    df_dates=[settle_date]
    df_values=[1.0]
    N = len(mat_dates)
    for bond_no in range(N):
        last_dfdate = df_dates[-1]
        new_mat = mat_dates[bond_no]
        if new_mat > last_dfdate:
            df_dates.append(new_mat)
            # Use bisection to find appropriate value to
                append to df_values
            ...

    return df_dates, df_values
```

CHAPTER **3**

Investment Theory

The future cash flows and, hence, *returns* of many investments are uncertain. Even for fixed income instruments like bonds where the cash flows are known, the future yields are not known, hence, the future price of a bond until its maturity is random: we know the current price, and we also know its final price at maturity (100%), but for any date between now and maturity, the bond price is random. Faced with this uncertainty, much of finance uses techniques and insights from probability theory and shares concepts and language of games of chance and gambling: a sound investment is a gamble with good *odds* and risk/reward profile.

One of the oldest studies of games of chance that combines elements of probability theory, decision-making under uncertainty, and behavioral finance is the following: consider a game based on successive coin flips with the payoff 2^N where N is the number of tosses to get to the first tail (see Table 3.1).

Let X be the random payoff of this game. Its expected value is infinite

$$E[X] = \sum \text{Payoff} \times \text{Probability}$$
$$= \sum_{N \geq 1} 2^N \times (1/2)^N$$
$$= \sum_{N \geq 1} 1 = \infty$$

What is the fair price of this random payoff, that is, how much should a rational person pay to play this game? One can argue that since the expected payoff is infinite, one should be willing to pay *any* finite amount. However, most people observe that the potentially large (exponential) payoffs are accompanied by very small probabilities, and will, therefore, limit their price. It has been suggested that a reasonable maximum anyone should pay is $25, a far cry from infinity.

TABLE 3.1   St. Petersburg game.

Outcome	N	Payoff	Probability
{T}	1	2	1/2
{H,T}	2	2^2	$(1/2)^2$
{H,H,T}	3	2^3	$(1/2)^3$
...			

This classic conundrum is called the *St. Petersburg Paradox*. The original and usual remedy is to posit that the *utility* of money—its value or usefulness—is not linear, but a concave function, and its incremental value decreases as wealth increases: *diminishing utility*. For example, if we model utility of wealth via a logarithm function, we can calculate the *expected utility* of the above payoff

$$E[U(X)] = E[\ln(X)] = \sum_{N \geq 1} \ln(2^N)(1/2)^N$$

$$= \ln(2) \sum_{N \geq 1} \frac{N}{2^N}$$

$$= 2\ln(2) \approx 1.4$$

using Formula 2.17.

The square root function is another concave utility function with diminishing utility as wealth increases. We have

$$\sum_{N \geq 1} \sqrt{2^N} \frac{1}{2^N} = \sum_{N \geq 1} \left(\frac{1}{\sqrt{2}} \right)^N = \frac{1}{\sqrt{2} - 1} \approx 2.5$$

3.1   UTILITY THEORY

The problem of how much to pay for a random payoff—also referred to as a *lottery*—or how to select among random payoffs starting with an initial amount of wealth are facets of decision making under uncertainty that have been studied under game theory and decision theory disciplines. In finance, the applications are in investment choice and portfolio selection.

3.1.1 Risk Appetite

Much of utility and investment theory is based on each individual's attitude toward uncertainty and risk. Let us compare a few random payoffs

$X_1 = \$100$ with probability 1, a *sure* bet with no uncertainty

$$X_2 = \begin{cases} 101 & \text{with probability } p = 1/2 \\ 99 & \text{with probability } 1 - p = 1/2 \end{cases}$$

$$X_3 = \begin{cases} 200 & \text{with probability } p = 1/2 \\ 0 & \text{with probability } 1 - p = 1/2 \end{cases}$$

$$X_4 = \begin{cases} 1,000,000 & \text{with probability } p = 1/1,000,000 \\ \dfrac{99}{1-p} \approx 99 & \text{with probability } 1 - p \end{cases}$$

$$X_5 = \begin{cases} -1,000,000 & \text{with probability } p = 1/1,000,000 \\ \dfrac{101}{1-p} \approx 101 & \text{with probability } 1 - p \end{cases}$$

and let Y_i be the profit or loss if one pays \$100 for each of the above, $Y_i = X_i - 100$: $Y_1 = 0$, $Y_2 = \pm 1$ with probability 1/2, $Y_3 = \pm 100$ with probability 1/2

$$Y_4 = \begin{cases} 999,900 & \text{with probability } p = 1/1,000,000 \\ \dfrac{-1}{1-p} \approx -1 & \text{with probability } 1 - p \end{cases}$$

$$Y_5 = \begin{cases} -1,000,100 & \text{with probability } p = 1/1,000,000 \\ \dfrac{1}{1-p} \approx 1 & \text{with probability } 1 - p \end{cases}$$

We observe that that $E[X_i] = 100$, $E[Y_i] = 0$

$$\sigma(X_1) = 0, \quad \sigma(X_2) = 1, \quad \sigma(X_3) = 100$$

$$\sigma(X_4) = \sigma(X_5) \approx 1,000$$

$\sigma(Y_i) = \sigma(X_i)$ where $\sigma(X_i)$ is the standard deviation of X_i.

Using X_1 as the base case, it should be clear that its price should be $100 as any deviation from $100 will be arbitraged away.

When comparing X_1 and X_2 either via the payoffs or the PnL (Y_1 versus Y_2), most people might consider them equivalent. This is an example of a *risk-neutral* attitude where two payoffs with different characteristics are considered equivalent when they have the same expected value.

Moving on to X_3, most people would not consider it equivalent to X_1, as it entails losing all the investment, and one might want to pay an amount less than $100 to be compensated for this risk. This is an example of *risk-aversion* where one requires a *risk premium* for taking on risk. For example, equities in general have higher risk than bonds and command a higher yield (lower price) in exchange for that risk.

X_4 is an example of a *lottery ticket*, and given the large payoff, one might be willing to pay even more than $100 for the large payoff even after consideration of the small probability of the large payoff. This is an example of *risk taking*, that is, paying up rather than receiving a premium for a risky investment.

The last case, X_5, highlights *loss aversion*. Although it has the same expected value and standard deviation as X_4, most people would be loathe to pay even $100 for it, and some might even ask to be paid to take on this risk. Examples of loss aversion are buying auto or home insurance or an extended warranty for a product. Even though the expected payoff—cost versus potential payoff—has negative expected value, most people prefer the certainty of limited maximum loss and keep insurers in business.

In the payoff space (X_is), paying less than $100 for X_5 is an example of risk-aversion, but when considered via the lens of gain and loss (Y_is), it highlights the asymmetric attitude of most people between gain and loss: a large gain with a small probability (Y_4) is desirable, while an equal size loss with the same probability (Y_5) is not. This is one of the insights of behavioral finance and can be analyzed via prospect theory.

3.1.2   Risk versus Uncertainty, Ranking

In many fields, including finance, one makes a distinction between objective versus subjective probabilities. Objective probability is associated with repeatable games of chance and is interpreted as the long-term statistical average frequencies. Games of chance such as the canonical coin flip and its associated objective probability of 1/2 is an example of decision-making under *risk*.

Making predictions or decisions for infrequent or one-off events such as Brexit or Covid are examples of using one's own subjective probabilities and decision-making under *uncertainty*.

Utility theory is a formalization and guide to rational decision-making under risk or uncertainty. It is a *normative* versus a *descriptive* approach: it shows how one *should* make decisions as opposed to describing how one actually makes them. It does not prescribe any certain attitude toward risk (risk-averse, risk-neutral, risk-seeking), but its aim is to ensure consistency and an ability to *rank* random payoffs referred to as *lotteries*, regardless of one's attitude toward risk.

In what follows, we shall use the terms lotteries and random payoffs modeled as discrete random variables interchangeably. Ranking of payoffs is denoted by " $\prec$ ": $X_1 \prec X_2$ means payoff X_2 is preferred to X_1. $X_1 \sim X_2$ means one is indifferent between X_1 and X_2, and $X_1 \preceq X_2$ means that X_2 is no worse than X_1. When choosing between a sure return X_1 versus an uncertain one X_2 with $E[X_1] = E[X_2]$, risk-averse investors would rank X_1 as better than X_2, $X_2 \prec X_1$, and are willing to pay a higher price for the sure bet X_1.

Utility theory uses simple lotteries and *compound* lotteries. Starting with two lotteries X_1, X_2, one can create a new compound lottery as follows: we first flip a loaded coin with probability of Heads equal to $0 < p < 1$, with the coin flip independent from X_1, X_2. If we get Heads, the payoff is lottery X_1, and if we get Tails, the payoff is lottery X_2 (see Figure 3.1). This new lottery X_3 has the combined payoffs of X_1 and X_2 but with probabilities $p\pi_1 + (1 - p)\pi_2$, where π_1, π_2 are the probability mass functions of each random variable

$$\pi_{1,2}(x_i) = P[X_{1,2} = x_i]$$

For example, using the two lotteries X_1, X_2

$$P[X_1 = 100] = 1, \quad P[X_2 = 80] = P[X_2 = 120] = 1/2$$

and a given $0 < p < 1$, we create the compound lottery X_3

$$P[X_3 = 100] = p, \quad P[X_3 = 80] = P[X_3 = 120] = (1 - p)/2$$

3.1.3 Utility Theory Axioms

The utility theory axioms are:

1. Completeness: Any two payoffs *can* be compared: $X \prec Y$, or $Y \prec X$ or $X \sim Y$. "*I can't/won't decide*" is not an option!
2. Transitivity: If $X \prec Y$ and $Y \prec Z$, then $X \prec Z$.
3. Continuity: Given three lotteries with $X \preceq Y \preceq Z$, one can create a new compound lottery from X, Z that is equivalent to Y: there exists a probability $0 \leq p \leq 1$, where $\pi_Y = p\pi_X + (1 - p)\pi_Z$.

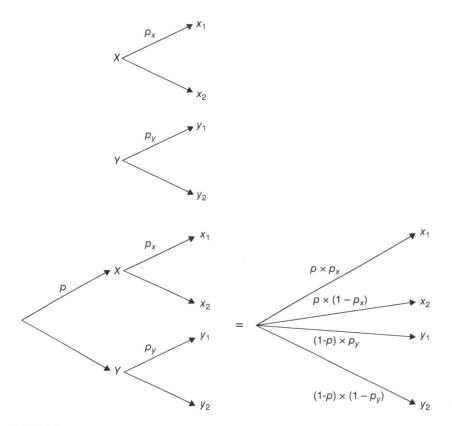

FIGURE 3.1 Compound lottery.

4. Independence/Substitution: Creating compound lotteries preserves ranking. Specifically, starting with two lotteries $X \leq Y$, and given a new lottery Z independent of X, Y, then for any probability $0 < p \leq 1$, we must have

$$p\pi_X + (1-p)\pi_Z \leq p\pi_Y + (1-p)\pi_Z$$

The axioms were posited by John von Neumann and Oskar Morgenstern (VNM), and the VNM *Expected Utility Theorem* states: a ranking $\prec$ satisfying above axioms is equivalent to the existence of a *utility function U* where $X \prec Y$ is equivalent to $E[U(X)] < E[U(Y)]$.

Armed with a utility function, the tedious pairwise comparison of simple and compound lotteries can be replaced by calculating and comparing the expected utility of their payoffs using probabilities (objective or subjective).

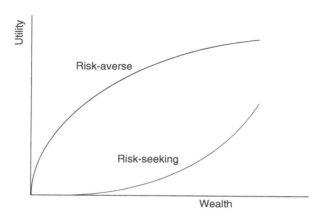

FIGURE 3.2 Risk attitude and utility function.

VNM Utility Theorem is an *existence* theorem. It does not impose any shape on the utility function. VNM utility of each person can be different than another person's, (see Figure 3.2) allowing for:

- Risk-aversion: concave utility function, $U''(x) < 0$
- Risk-seeking: convex utility function, $U''(x) > 0$
- Risk-neutrality: linear utility function, $U'(x) = c$ for a constant c, $U'' = 0$

Moreover, utility is unique up to a linear transformation: let $U_1(x)$ be the utility function of a person and $U_2(x)$ the utility function of another person with *identical* ranking of *all* lotteries. One might expect that $U_2(x) = U_1(x)$, but utility theory's axioms only show that $U_2(x) = aU_1(x) + b$ for any constant $a > 0$, b provide the same ranking of lotteries as U_1.

3.1.4 Certainty-Equivalent

Given a utility function, for any random payoff X with expected utility $E[U(X)]$, we can consider a guaranteed payoff Y with only one outcome c_X, $P[Y = c_X] = 1$, with the same expected utility as X, $E[U(Y)] = E[U(X)]$. We have

$$E[U(Y)] = U(c_X) \times P[Y = c_X]$$

$$= U(c_X) \times 1$$

$$= U(c_X)$$

The constant c_X is called the *certainty-equivalent* of X and satisfies

$$E[U(c_X)] = U(c_X) = E[U(X)]$$

It can be interpreted as the *certain* amount, c_X, that one would pay to receive an uncertain amount X to receive the same utility.

The utility function of a risk-averse investor is concave, and by Jensen's inequality

$$f(E[X]) \geq f[U(X)]$$

for any concave function f. Therefore, $U(E[X]) \geq U(c_X)$, and if we make the reasonable assumption that utility is an increasing function of wealth, we observe that $E[X] \geq c_X$ for a risk-averse investor.

The difference between $E[X]$ and c_X is defined as the *absolute risk premium* as a measure of the concavity the utility function and risk-aversion, Figure 3.3

$$\pi_A(X) = E[X] - c_X$$

while the proportional amount

$$\pi_R(X) = \frac{E[X] - c_X}{E[X]} = \frac{\pi_A(X)}{E[X]}$$

is defined as the *relative risk premium*.

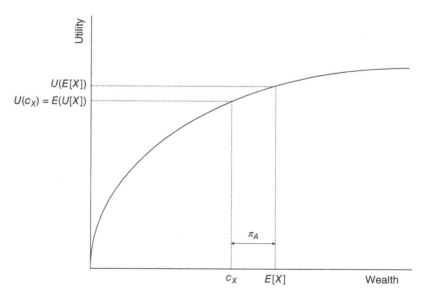

FIGURE 3.3   Risk premium for a risk-averse investor.

3.1.5 X-ARRA

Utility functions exhibiting risk aversion are concave, $U''(x) < 0$, and different functional forms of concave functions have been proposed and studied for risk-averse investors. The term $-U''(x)$ is a measure of concavity and a higher concavity and risk aversion results in a higher $-U''(x)$. Since utility of two persons with identical preference is only unique up to a linear transformation, $-U''$ is divided by U' to remove this and $-U''(x)/U'(x)$, known as *Arrow-Pratt absolute risk aversion (ARA)*, is used to classify utility functions. Note that if $U_2(x) = aU_1(x) + b$

$$
\begin{aligned}
-\frac{U_2''(x)}{U_2'(x)} &= -\frac{(aU_1(x) + b)''}{(aU_1(x) + b)'} \\
&= -\frac{aU_1''(x)}{aU_1'(x)} \\
&= -\frac{U_1''(x)}{U_1'(x)}
\end{aligned}
$$

Therefore, two persons with identical ranking of lotteries will have identical ARA.

A similar measure is the *relative risk aversion (RRA)*, which is defined as ARA multiplied by x. Note

$$
\begin{aligned}
-x\frac{U''(x)}{U'(x)} &= -\frac{d/dx\,U'(x)}{U'(x)/x} \\
&= -\frac{dU'(x)/U'(x)}{dx/x} \\
&= -\frac{\text{Relative Change in } U'(x)}{\text{Relative Change in } x}
\end{aligned}
$$

ARA and absolute risk premium can be related via the following heuristic argument. For a given random payoff X, let $\mu = E[X], \sigma^2 = Var(X)$. If we Taylor-expand $U(\cdot)$ around μ up to the first order term, we can evaluate

$$
U(c_X) \approx U(\mu) + U'(\mu)(c_X - \mu) \tag{3.1}
$$

Similarly, if we Taylor-expand $U(\cdot)$ around μ up to the second order term, we get

$$
U(X) \approx U(\mu) + U'(\mu)(X - \mu) + 1/2U''(\mu)(X - \mu)^2 \tag{3.2}
$$

Taking expected value of both sides of Formula 3.2, since $E[X] = \mu$, we get

$$E[U(X)] \approx U(\mu) + U'(\mu)E[(X - \mu)] + 1/2U''(\mu)E[(\mu)(X - \mu)^2]$$

$$= U(\mu) + 1/2U''(\mu)\sigma^2 \tag{3.3}$$

Since $U(c_X) = E[U(X)]$, combining Formulas 3.1 and 3.3, we get

$$\pi_A = \mu - c_X$$

$$= -\frac{1}{2}\frac{U''(\mu)}{U'(\mu)}\sigma^2$$

$$= \frac{1}{2}ARA(\mu)\sigma^2$$

Similarly, we can show

$$\pi_R = \frac{1}{2}RRA(\mu)s^2, \quad s^2 = Var\left(\frac{X}{E[X]}\right)$$

The two most commonly used classes of ARA and RRA are constant absolute risk aversion (CARA) with parametric form $-e^{-cx}$ for a constant c, and constant relative risk aversion (CRRA) with parametric form $x^{1-\alpha}/(1-\alpha)$ for $\alpha \neq 1$ and $\ln(x)$ when $\alpha = 1$.

Both of these parametric family of functions are special cases of the general *hyperbolic absolute risk aversion (HARA)* with parametric form

$$H(x) = \frac{\gamma}{1-\gamma}\left(\frac{x}{\gamma} + \eta\right)^{1-\gamma}$$

$H(x) = CRRA$ when $\eta = 0$ and it can be shown that $H(x) \to CARA(1/\eta)$ as $\gamma \to \infty$.

3.2 PORTFOLIO SELECTION

Utility theory in general and the parametric families expressing the utility function provide a framework to evaluate and rank investments. The ranking is based on the expected utility of the investment's future values requiring full specification of the distribution of the future value or returns of the underlying investment. The ranking of investments can aid in investment choice and portfolio construction.

3.2.1 Asset Allocation

Consider a portfolio P composed of N assets. The value of the portfolio at any time, $V_P(t)$, depends on the quantity of each asset, Q_i, and the asset's price, P_i

$$V_P = \sum_{i=1}^{N} Q_i P_i = \sum_{i=1}^{N} V_i, \quad V_i = Q_i P_i$$

The portfolio *allocation* of the ith asset is the relative value of that asset's value $V_i = Q_i P_i$ to the portfolio value

$$w_i = \frac{V_i}{V_P} = \frac{V_i}{\sum_i V_i} = \frac{Q_i P_i}{\sum_i Q_i P_i}$$

where the w_is are the portfolio *weights* of the assets. The weights add up to 1

$$\sum_i w_i = 1$$

Note that an asset's weight is its relative *value contribution*, $Q_i \times P_i$, to portfolio value, $\sum_i Q_i P_i$, *not* its relative price or its relative quantity.

Given an initial investment amount $V_P(0)$, the goal of *asset allocation* is to find w_i to maximize the future wealth $V_P(t)$.

3.2.2 Markowitz Mean-Variance Portfolio Theory

The pioneering work of Harry Markowitz (Markowitz, 1952) casts the portfolio selection problem as a trade-off between risk and reward of returns. The 1-period *rate of return*, or simply *return* of an asset, is the relative change in the value

$$R(t) = \frac{V(t) - V(0)}{V(0)} = \frac{V(t)}{V(0)} - 1$$

over the 1-period investment horizon $(0, t)$. One can annualize the return by dividing above with length of the period t measured in years.

The 1-period rate of return of a portfolio can be related to the rate of return of each asset in the portfolio. Let R_i be the ith asset's 1-period rate of return

$$R_i = \frac{V_i(t)}{V_i(0)} - 1 = \frac{Q_i P_i(t)}{Q_i P_i(0)} - 1 = \frac{P_i(t)}{P_i(0)} - 1$$

We have

$$R_P = \frac{V_P(t)}{V_P(0)} - 1 = \frac{\sum_i V_i(t)}{V_P(0)} - 1$$

$$= \frac{\sum_i V_i(0)(1 + R_i)}{V_P(0)} - 1$$

$$= \left[\frac{\sum_i V_i(0)}{V_P(0)} + \sum_i \left(\frac{V_i(0)}{V_P(0)} \right) R_i \right] - 1$$

$$= \sum_i w_i R_i$$

since $V_P(0) = \sum_i V_i(0)$.

3.2.3 Risky Assets

In general, asset returns are random. For a given 1-period investment horizon, we let R_A denote the return of an asset A over that horizon. R_A is a random variable, and we let $\mu_R = E[R]$, $\sigma_R = \sqrt{Var(R)}$, and use the following shorthand notation

$$R_A \sim (\mu_A, \sigma_A)$$

In this notation, μ_A is the expected return of asset A, while σ_A is the standard deviation of its return, commonly referred to as the risk of the asset. A risky asset is one where there is uncertainty about its return: $\sigma_R > 0$. A risk-free asset is one where there is no uncertainty about its return: $\sigma_A = 0$, and its return R_A is a constant number. The canonical example of risky assets are stocks, while bonds or interest-bearing bank deposits are considered risk-free assets.

3.2.4 Portfolio Risk

Consider a portfolio, P, of two assets, A_1, A_2, with returns $R_i = R_{A_i} \sim (\mu_i, \sigma_i)$, and let w_1, w_2 be the *weights* of the assets for a 1-period investment horizon. We have already shown

$$R_P = w_1 R_1 + w_2 R_2$$

Since expectation, E, is linear, we have

$$\mu_P = E[R_P] = E[w_1 R_1 + w_2 R_2] = w_1 E[R_1] + w_2 E[R_2]$$

$$= w_1 \mu_1 + w_2 \mu_2$$

The portfolio risk, σ_P, is related to the covariance matrix, **C**, of the two assets' returns

$$\mathbf{C} = \begin{bmatrix} \sigma_1^2 & \rho\sigma_1\sigma_2 \\ \rho\sigma_1\sigma_2 & \sigma_2^2 \end{bmatrix}$$

where ρ is the *correlation* between R_1 and R_2. We have

$$\sigma_P^2 = w_1^2\sigma_1^2 + w_2^2\sigma_2^2 + 2w_1w_2\rho\sigma_1\sigma_2$$

$$= \begin{bmatrix} w_1 & w_2 \end{bmatrix} \begin{bmatrix} \sigma_1^2 & \rho\sigma_1\sigma_2 \\ \rho\sigma_1\sigma_2 & \sigma_2^2 \end{bmatrix} \begin{bmatrix} w_1 \\ w_2 \end{bmatrix}$$

$$= \mathbf{w}^T\mathbf{C}\mathbf{w}$$

In general, for a portfolio consisting of N assets with weights $\{w_1, \ldots, w_N\}$, where each asset's return $R_i = R_{A_i} \sim (\mu_i, \sigma_i)$, we have

$$R_P = \sum_i w_i R_i$$

$$\mu_P = E[R_P] = \sum_i w_i\mu_i = \mathbf{w}^T\boldsymbol{\mu}$$

where

$$\mathbf{w} = \begin{bmatrix} w_1 \\ \ldots \\ w_N \end{bmatrix}, \qquad \boldsymbol{\mu} = \begin{bmatrix} \mu_1 \\ \ldots \\ \mu_N \end{bmatrix}$$

The portfolio variance can be expressed as

$$\sigma_P^2 = \mathbf{w}^T\mathbf{C}\mathbf{w}$$

where **C** is the $N \times N$ covariance matrix of the returns

$$[\mathbf{C}]_{ij} = Cov(R_i, R_j) = E[(R_i - \mu_i)(R_j - \mu_j)] = \rho_{ij}\sigma_i\sigma_j = \sigma_{ij}$$

with ρ_{ij} denoting the correlation between R_i and R_j.

Recall that the weights must add up to 1, $\sum_i w_i = 1$, or in matrix notation

$$\mathbf{u}^T\mathbf{w} = 1$$

where **u** is the unit column vector with N rows:

$$\mathbf{u} = \begin{bmatrix} 1 \\ \ldots \\ 1 \end{bmatrix}$$

3.2.5 Minimum Variance Portfolio

Focusing on the two-asset portfolio, let $R_1 \sim (\mu_1, \sigma_1), R_2 \sim (\mu_2, \sigma_2)$ with **C** as the 2×2 covariance matrix of the assets' returns. Since $w_2 = 1 - w_1$, both $\mu = \mu_P$ and $\sigma = \sigma_P$ become a function of w_1, and each choice of w_1 gives rise to a *feasible portfolio*, that is, a portfolio that can be constructed from the two assets.

Moreover, since $w_2 = 1 - w_1$, $\mu = w_1\mu_1 + (1 - w_1)\mu_2$, and, hence, w_1 is a linear function of μ

$$w_1 = \frac{1}{\mu_1 - \mu_2}\mu - \frac{\mu_2}{\mu_1 - \mu_2}$$

and the portfolio variance σ^2 and its mean are related as

$$\sigma^2/c_\sigma^2 - (\mu - \mu_0)^2/c_\mu^2 = 1$$

for constants μ_0, c_μ, c_σ. This is the canonical equation of a hyperbola in the risk-reward (σ, μ). Recall that a hyperbola is a conic section with canonical form in the (x, y) plane as $x^2/a^2 - y^2/b^2 = 1$ for constants a, b with asymptotes: $y = \pm(b/a)x$ (see Figure 3.4).

The hyperbola consisting of the points (μ_P, σ_P) of each feasible portfolio as we vary w_1 is referred to as the *Markowitz bullet* after the pioneering work on portfolio selection by Harry Markowitz (see Figure 3.5).

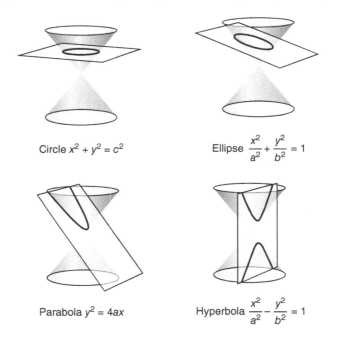

Circle $x^2 + y^2 = c^2$

Ellipse $\dfrac{x^2}{a^2} + \dfrac{y^2}{b^2} = 1$

Parabola $y^2 = 4ax$

Hyperbola $\dfrac{x^2}{a^2} - \dfrac{y^2}{b^2} = 1$

FIGURE 3.4 Conic sections.

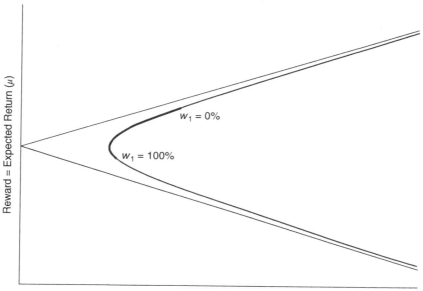

FIGURE 3.5   Feasible region for two risky assets.

The vertex of the Markowitz bullet is the portfolio with the lowest variance or equivalently lowest standard deviation (risk) among all feasible portfolios, and is referred to as the *minimum variance portfolio (MVP)*. The MVP can be found by using the fact that $w_2 = 1 - w_1$ and expressing σ_P^2 solely as a function of w_1, and then solving

$$\frac{d\sigma_P^2}{dw_1} = 0 \tag{3.4}$$

which is the necessary condition for finding the minimum. This leads to the following for the minimizing weights, (w_1^*, w_2^*), and the resulting MVP (μ_P^*, σ_P^*) when the denominator term is not zero

$$w_1^* = \frac{\sigma_2^2 - \rho\sigma_1\sigma_2}{\sigma_1^2 + \sigma_2^2 - 2\rho\sigma_1\sigma_2}, \quad w_2^* = \frac{\sigma_1^2 - \rho\sigma_1\sigma_2}{\sigma_1^2 + \sigma_2^2 - 2\rho\sigma_1\sigma_2} \tag{3.5}$$

$$\mu_P^* = \frac{\mu_1\sigma_2^2 + \mu_2\sigma_1^2 - (\mu_1 + \mu_2)\rho\sigma_1\sigma_2}{\sigma_1^2 + \sigma_2^2 - 2\rho\sigma_1\sigma_2}$$

$$\sigma_P^* = \sqrt{\frac{\sigma_1^2\sigma_2^2(1 - \rho^2)}{\sigma_1^2 + \sigma_2^2 - 2\rho\sigma_1\sigma_2}}$$

EXAMPLE 1

Let $R_1 \sim (5\%, 10\%)$ and $R_2 \sim (10\%, 20\%)$ denote the return of two risky assets. The MVP and its weights as a function of correlation ρ is shown in Table 3.2 and Figure 3.6.

TABLE 3.2 MVP portfolio for two risky assets.

ρ	(w_1^*, w_2^*)	(μ_P^*, σ_P^*)
100%	$(2, -1)$	$(0, 0)$
95%	$(1.75, -0.75)$	$(1.25\%, 5.70\%)$
50%	$(1, 0)$	$(5\%, 10\%)$
0	$(0.8, 0.2)$	$(6\%, 8.94\%)$
-75%	$(0.6875, 0.3125)$	$(6.56\%, 4.68\%)$
-100%	$(2/3, 1/3)$	$(6.67\%, 0)$

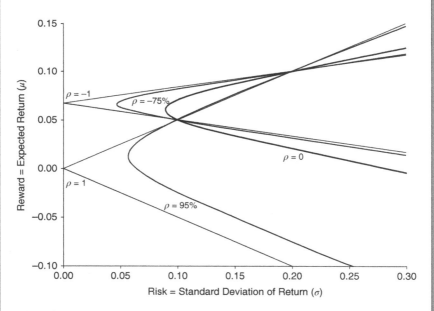

FIGURE 3.6 Feasible regions for different correlations.

3.2.6 Leverage, Short Sales

As can be seen in Table 3.2, the optimal quantities of an asset in a portfolio may turn out to be negative. The financial interpretation of negative quantities is via understanding *short sales*.

When you own an asset, you are said to be *long* the asset. To *go long* an asset means to buy an asset. If you own an asset, your position in that asset is *long*. You can buy or go long an asset either by spending money that you have, *real money*, or by borrowing money, *leverage*. When you buy an asset through leverage and eventually sell it, your position becomes zero or *flat*, and you need to pay back the lender the original amount borrowed plus interest. The difference between sales and purchase price minus the interest determines your profit and loss (PnL). Note that in this case, you are borrowing money to spend it (buying the asset).

In the opposite direction, if you own an asset and sell it, you are selling it out of inventory and your position after the sale is flat (zero). If you do not own the asset, you can borrow it and sell it. This is called *going short* or *shorting* an asset, and your position is not flat, but *short*, a negative quantity. When you eventually buy the asset back, you are *covering your short*, and you must return the asset to the asset lender. After covering your short, your position becomes flat and your profit or loss is due to the difference between purchase price versus short sale price plus any interest you might have earned on the funds received upon the sale. In this case, you are borrowing an asset to spend it (buying/receiving money).

Short sales as described above are generally only available to large institutions. For retail investors, the brokerage firm will charge a fee (via a high interest rate on the sale proceeds) for borrowing the security for your account, greatly diminishing the PnL. The fee can be quite large for difficult-to-borrow securities.

3.2.7 Multiple Risky Assets

For portfolios consisting of more than two risky assets, $N > 2$, the shape of the feasible region changes to points on *and* inside a hyperbola in the (σ, μ) plane (see Figure 3.7). The equations for μ_P and σ_P become longer as we have to consider all pair-wise terms, and the more general way to find the MVP is to solve the following *constrained optimization* problem

$$\text{Minimize } \mathbf{w}^T \mathbf{C} \mathbf{w} \text{ with } \mathbf{u}^T \mathbf{w} = 1$$

The standard technique to solve constrained optimization problems is via the method of *Lagrange Multipliers* with one multiplier λ for each constraint. This method is based on the observation that if a solution to an

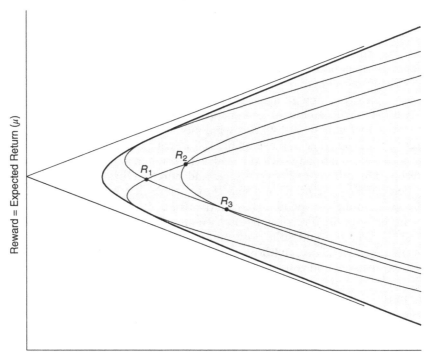

Risk = Standard Deviation of Return (σ)

FIGURE 3.7   Feasible region for three or more risky assets.

optimization $f(\cdot)$ subject to constraint $g(\cdot) = c$ exists, then the gradient of the constraint and the contour of f that just touches the constraint should be co-linear

$$\nabla f = \lambda \nabla g$$

for some λ where

$$\nabla f = \begin{bmatrix} \dfrac{\partial f}{\partial x_1} \\ \cdots \\ \dfrac{\partial f}{\partial x_N} \end{bmatrix}$$

for a function $f(x_1, \ldots, x_n)$ (see Figure 3.8).

To use this method, we first form the *Lagrangian function*

$$\mathcal{L}(\mathbf{w}, \lambda) = \mathbf{w}^T \mathbf{C} \mathbf{w} - \lambda(\mathbf{u}^T \mathbf{w} - 1)$$

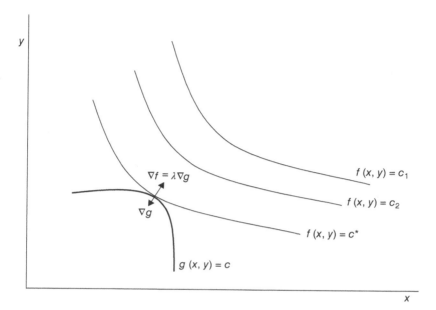

FIGURE 3.8 Method of Lagrange multipliers.

and then set its derivatives with respect to each w_i *and* each multiplier λ to zero

$$\begin{bmatrix} \dfrac{\partial \mathcal{L}}{w_1} \\ \cdots \\ \dfrac{\partial \mathcal{L}}{w_N} \\ \dfrac{\partial \mathcal{L}}{\lambda} \end{bmatrix} = \begin{bmatrix} 0 \\ \cdots \\ 0 \\ 0 \end{bmatrix}$$

The above system of equations provide the necessary conditions for the optimal $\mathbf{w}^*$.

Let us rederive the weights of the MVP for two assets via Lagrange multipliers. We first form the Lagrangian function

$$\mathcal{L}(w_1, w_2, \lambda) = \mathbf{w}^T \mathbf{C} \mathbf{w} - \lambda(\mathbf{u}^T \mathbf{w} - 1)$$

$$= \begin{bmatrix} w_1 & w_2 \end{bmatrix} \begin{bmatrix} \sigma_1^2 & \rho \sigma_1 \sigma_2 \\ \rho \sigma_1 \sigma_2 & \sigma_2^2 \end{bmatrix} \begin{bmatrix} w_1 \\ w_2 \end{bmatrix} - \lambda \left(\begin{bmatrix} 1 & 1 \end{bmatrix} \begin{bmatrix} w_1 \\ w_2 \end{bmatrix} - 1 \right)$$

$$= w_1^2 \sigma_1^2 + w_2^2 \sigma_2^2 + 2 w_1 w_2 \rho \sigma_1 \sigma_2 - \lambda(w_1 + w_2 - 1)$$

and set all its partial derivatives to 0

$$\begin{bmatrix} \partial \mathcal{L}/\partial w_1 \\ \partial \mathcal{L}/\partial w_2 \\ \partial \mathcal{L}/\partial \lambda \end{bmatrix} = \begin{bmatrix} 2\sigma_1^2 w_1 + 2\rho\sigma_1\sigma_2 w_2 - \lambda \\ 2\sigma_2^2 w_2 + 2\rho\sigma_1\sigma_2 w_1 - \lambda \\ 1 - w_1 - w_2 \end{bmatrix} = \begin{bmatrix} 0 \\ 0 \\ 0 \end{bmatrix}$$

The first two rows give us

$$2 \begin{bmatrix} \sigma_1^2 & \rho\sigma_1\sigma_2 \\ \rho\sigma_1\sigma_2 & \sigma_2^2 \end{bmatrix} \begin{bmatrix} w_1 \\ w_2 \end{bmatrix} - \lambda \begin{bmatrix} 1 \\ 1 \end{bmatrix} = \begin{bmatrix} 0 \\ 0 \end{bmatrix}$$

or in matrix format

$$2\mathbf{C}\mathbf{w} - \lambda\mathbf{u} = \mathbf{0}$$

Taking the λ term to the right-hand side of the equation, and premultiplying both sides with the matrix inverse of $\mathbf{C}$, $\mathbf{C}^{-1}$ (if it exists), provides the weights in terms of λ:

$$\begin{bmatrix} w_1 \\ w_2 \end{bmatrix} = \frac{1}{2}\lambda \begin{bmatrix} \sigma_1^2 & \rho\sigma_1\sigma_2 \\ \rho\sigma_1\sigma_2 & \sigma_2^2 \end{bmatrix}^{-1} \begin{bmatrix} 1 \\ 1 \end{bmatrix} \tag{3.6}$$

or in matrix format

$$\mathbf{w} = \frac{1}{2}\lambda\mathbf{C}^{-1}\mathbf{u}$$

Since $\mathbf{u}^T\mathbf{w} = 1$, we have

$$\frac{1}{2}\lambda \begin{bmatrix} 1 & 1 \end{bmatrix} \begin{bmatrix} \sigma_1^2 & \rho\sigma_1\sigma_2 \\ \rho\sigma_1\sigma_2 & \sigma_2^2 \end{bmatrix}^{-1} \begin{bmatrix} 1 \\ 1 \end{bmatrix} = 1$$

which allows us to calculate λ

$$\lambda = \frac{2}{\begin{bmatrix} 1 & 1 \end{bmatrix} \begin{bmatrix} \sigma_1^2 & \rho\sigma_1\sigma_2 \\ \rho\sigma_1\sigma_2 & \sigma_2^2 \end{bmatrix}^{-1} \begin{bmatrix} 1 \\ 1 \end{bmatrix}} \tag{3.7}$$

or in matrix format

$$\lambda = \frac{2}{\mathbf{u}^T\mathbf{C}^{-1}\mathbf{u}}$$

Note that the term in the denominator is a 1×1 matrix, i.e., a *scalar* or a single number.

We can now plug in Formula 3.7 for λ in Formula 3.6 to solve for w_1, w_2

$$\begin{bmatrix} w_1 \\ w_2 \end{bmatrix} = \frac{\begin{bmatrix} \sigma_1^2 & \rho\sigma_1\sigma_2 \\ \rho\sigma_1\sigma_2 & \sigma_2^2 \end{bmatrix}^{-1} \begin{bmatrix} 1 \\ 1 \end{bmatrix}}{\begin{bmatrix} 1 & 1 \end{bmatrix} \begin{bmatrix} \sigma_1^2 & \rho\sigma_1\sigma_2 \\ \rho\sigma_1\sigma_2 & \sigma_2^2 \end{bmatrix}^{-1} \begin{bmatrix} 1 \\ 1 \end{bmatrix}}$$

or in matrix format

$$\mathbf{w} = \frac{\mathbf{C}^{-1}\mathbf{u}}{\mathbf{u}^T\mathbf{C}^{-1}\mathbf{u}}$$

All that remains is to calculate $\mathbf{C}^{-1}$

$$\mathbf{C}^{-1} = \begin{bmatrix} \sigma_1^2 & \rho\sigma_1\sigma_2 \\ \rho\sigma_1\sigma_2 & \sigma_2^2 \end{bmatrix}^{-1} = \frac{1}{\sigma_1^2\sigma_2^2 - \rho^2\sigma_1^2\sigma_2^2} \begin{bmatrix} \sigma_2^2 & -\rho\sigma_1\sigma_2 \\ -\rho\sigma_1\sigma_2 & \sigma_1^2 \end{bmatrix}$$

to get

$$\begin{bmatrix} w_1 \\ w_2 \end{bmatrix} = \frac{\begin{bmatrix} \sigma_2^2 & -\rho\sigma_1\sigma_2 \\ -\rho\sigma_1\sigma_2 & \sigma_1^2 \end{bmatrix} \begin{bmatrix} 1 \\ 1 \end{bmatrix}}{\begin{bmatrix} 1 & 1 \end{bmatrix} \begin{bmatrix} \sigma_2^2 & -\rho\sigma_1\sigma_2 \\ -\rho\sigma_1\sigma_2 & \sigma_1^2 \end{bmatrix} \begin{bmatrix} 1 \\ 1 \end{bmatrix}}$$

$$= \frac{1}{\sigma_1^2 + \sigma_2^2 - 2\rho\sigma_1\sigma_2} \begin{bmatrix} \sigma_2^2 - \rho\sigma_1\sigma_2 \\ \sigma_1^2 - \rho\sigma_1\sigma_2 \end{bmatrix}$$

which is the same result as in Formula 3.5.

3.2.8 Efficient Frontier

So far, we have focused on the MVP, the portfolio that has minimum variance, σ^2, or equivalently minimum risk, σ. We can expand our search and be willing to accept different risks. As mentioned before, there can be three attitudes toward increased risk:

1. *Risk-seeker*: Given the potential higher upside, one might prefer the riskier asset, even with same expected return.
2. *Risk-averse*: Higher risk should be compensated by higher returns.
3. *Risk-neutral*: As long as expected returns are the same, one is indifferent on the risk of investments.

Risk-averse investors expect a risk premium, i.e., extra expected return to enter into a risky investment. Specifically, given two investments with respective returns $R_1 \sim (\mu_1, \sigma_1)$ and $R_2 \sim (\mu_2, \sigma_2)$, they would avoid the latter if it has higher risk for less expected return: $\mu_1 \geq \mu_2$ and $\sigma_1 \leq \sigma_2$. In this case, the first investment is said to *dominate* the second.

Given all feasible portfolios, the set of undominated ones is called the *efficient frontier*. In our graph, it is the upper half of the Markowitz bullet. Each portfolio on the efficient frontier is called the *frontier portfolio*.

3.2.9 Minimum Variance Frontier

A frontier portfolio is the highest returning portfolio for a given level of risk σ. One can ask a similar question based on returns: What is the *least risky* portfolio for a given level of return μ? The optimal weight vector, $\mathbf{w}^*(\mu)$, must satisfy the following

$$\text{Minimize } \sigma_P^2 = \mathbf{w}^T \mathbf{C} \mathbf{w}$$

$$\text{Subject to } \boldsymbol{\mu}^T \mathbf{w} = \mu, \quad \mathbf{u}^T \mathbf{w} = 1$$

This constrained optimization problem can be solved via the method of Lagrange multipliers. We form the Lagrangian, but now with two multipliers λ_1, λ_2, one for each constraint

$$\mathcal{L}(\mathbf{w}, \lambda_1, \lambda_2) = \mathbf{w}^T \mathbf{C} \mathbf{w} - \lambda_1(\boldsymbol{\mu}^T \mathbf{w} - \mu) - \lambda_2(\mathbf{u}^T \mathbf{w} - 1)$$

and form the derivative of the Lagrangian relative to weight vector, $\mathbf{w}$, and set it to zero

$$2\mathbf{C}\mathbf{w} - \lambda_1 \boldsymbol{\mu} - \lambda_2 \mathbf{u} = \mathbf{0}$$

$$\Rightarrow \quad \mathbf{w} = \frac{\lambda_1}{2}\mathbf{C}^{-1}\boldsymbol{\mu} + \frac{\lambda_2}{2}\mathbf{C}^{-1}\mathbf{u} \qquad (3.8)$$

Since $\boldsymbol{\mu}^T \mathbf{w} = \mu$ and $\mathbf{u}^T \mathbf{w} = 1$, we can multiply this formula for $\mathbf{w}$ by $\boldsymbol{\mu}^T, \mathbf{u}^T$ to get the following two formulas

$$\frac{\lambda_1}{2}\boldsymbol{\mu}^T\mathbf{C}^{-1}\boldsymbol{\mu} + \frac{\lambda_2}{2}\boldsymbol{\mu}^T\mathbf{C}^{-1}\mathbf{u} = \mu$$

$$\frac{\lambda_1}{2}\mathbf{u}^T\mathbf{C}^{-1}\boldsymbol{\mu} + \frac{\lambda_2}{2}\mathbf{u}^T\mathbf{C}^{-1}\mathbf{u} = 1$$

which can be expressed as

$$\frac{1}{2} \begin{bmatrix} \mu^T C^{-1} \mu & \mu^T C^{-1} u \\ u^T C^{-1} \mu & u^T C^{-1} u \end{bmatrix} \begin{bmatrix} \lambda_1 \\ \lambda_2 \end{bmatrix} = \begin{bmatrix} \mu \\ 1 \end{bmatrix}$$

Let D be the inverse (if it exists) of the 2×2 matrix multiplying λ

$$D = \begin{bmatrix} d_{11} & d_{12} \\ d_{21} & d_{22} \end{bmatrix} = \begin{bmatrix} \mu^T C^{-1} \mu & \mu^T C^{-1} u \\ u^T C^{-1} \mu & u^T C^{-1} u \end{bmatrix}^{-1}$$

We have

$$\begin{bmatrix} \lambda_1 \\ \lambda_2 \end{bmatrix} = 2 \begin{bmatrix} d_{11} & d_{12} \\ d_{21} & d_{22} \end{bmatrix} \begin{bmatrix} \mu \\ 1 \end{bmatrix}$$

Plugging back (λ_1, λ_2) into the expression for w in Formula 3.8, we have

$$w^*(\mu) = a\mu + b \qquad (3.9)$$

where

$$\begin{aligned} a &= d_{11} C^{-1} \mu + d_{21} C^{-1} u \\ b &= d_{12} C^{-1} \mu + d_{22} C^{-1} u \end{aligned} \qquad (3.10)$$

Note that the 2×2 matrix D and, hence, the vectors a, b *only* depend on μ and C, and have *no* dependence on the particular μ under consideration.

The optimal weights $w^*(\mu)$ characterize the least risky portfolio for a given return μ and can be used to calculate the minimum feasible variance or risk $\sigma^*(\mu)$. The collection of minimum variance portfolios as a function of μ maps out the *minimum variance frontier (MVF)*.

EXAMPLE 2

For three risky assets, let $R_1 \sim (4\%, 6\%)$, $R_2 \sim (6\%, 8\%)$, $R_3 \sim (5\%, 4\%)$ with correlation matrix

$$\begin{bmatrix} 100\% & 60\% & -10\% \\ 60\% & 100\% & 40\% \\ -10\% & 40\% & 100\% \end{bmatrix}$$

(Continued)

Then

$$D = \begin{bmatrix} 10.592 & -0.455 \\ -0.455 & 0.020 \end{bmatrix}^{-1} = \begin{bmatrix} 2.356 & 52.651 \\ 52.651 & 1225.563 \end{bmatrix}$$

$$a = \begin{bmatrix} -49.333 \\ 50.667 \\ -1.333 \end{bmatrix} \quad b = \begin{bmatrix} 2.587 \\ -2.413 \\ 0.827 \end{bmatrix}$$

3.2.10 Separation: Two-Fund Theorem

Formula 3.9 for the weights on MVF leads to a *separation* result commonly referred to as the *two-fund theorem*: given two portfolios *on* the MVF, $P_1 \sim (\mu_1, \sigma_1)$, $P_2 \sim (\mu_2, \sigma_2)$, $\mu_1 < \mu_2$, each portfolio's weight vector satisfies

$$\mathbf{w}^*(\mu_i) = \mathbf{a}\mu_i + \mathbf{b}$$

For any portfolio on the MVF with expected return μ, define

$$w = \frac{\mu - \mu_1}{\mu_2 - \mu_1} \quad \Rightarrow \quad \mu = w\mu_1 + (1 - w)\mu_2$$

we have

$$\mathbf{w}^*(\mu) = \mathbf{a}\mu + \mathbf{b}$$
$$= \mathbf{a}[w\mu_1 + (1 - w)\mu_2] + [w + (1 - w)]\mathbf{b}$$
$$= w\mathbf{w}^*(\mu_1) + (1 - w)\mathbf{w}^*(\mu_2)$$

which equals the weights of a portfolio made up of P_1, P_2 with respective allocations $(w, 1 - w)$. Since μ was arbitrary, this shows that *all* portfolios on the MVF can be composed of the two portfolios P_1, P_2.

Since the set of feasible portfolios consisting of two assets or portfolios is a hyperbola, the two-fund theorem shows that MVF of the feasible set of *any* number of risky assets is still a hyperbola (see Exercises). While for two assets, the hyperbola *is* the feasible set, for three or more risky assets, there can be portfolios inside the hyperbola, and the feasible set for three or more risky assets consists of points on *and* inside the hyperbola.

3.2.11   Risk-Free Asset

We have so far considered portfolios of risky assets, that is, $\sigma_i > 0$, for all assets A_i. We can include a risk-free asset, A_0, say a T-Bill or a CD, whose 1-period rate of return, R_0, is known with no uncertainty, $\sigma_0 = 0$. In this case, the random variable R_0 becomes a simple constant number: $R_0 \sim (\mu_0 = R_0, \sigma_0 = 0)$.

If we construct a portfolio P from a risk-free asset with return R_0 and a risky asset/portfolio A with $R_A \sim (\mu_A, \sigma_A)$ with weights $(w, w_1 = 1 - w)$, we have

$$R_P \sim (wR_0 + (1 - w)\mu_A, |1 - w|\sigma_A)$$

which shows that the feasible set of a risk-free asset and risky one is a straight line starting from $(0, R_0)$ corresponding to $w = 1$, and going through (σ_A, μ_A) corresponding to $w = 0$ in the (σ, μ) (risk-reward) plane. If we allow borrowing money at the risk-free rate of R_0, the line extends past (σ_A, μ_A) corresponding to $w < 0$.

3.2.12   Capital Market Line

We previously showed that the Markowitz bullet is the feasible region of two or more risky assets. The addition of a new asset—risk-free in this case—can only expand our portfolio choices and enlarge the feasible set, since one can always decide to invest zero in the new asset and, hence, recover the original feasible set.

If we go through every risky portfolio P in the Markowitz bullet, and consider portfolios constructed from P and the risk-free asset, we arrive at the new feasible region: a triangular region with the vertex at $(0, R_0)$ and at least one of the boundary lines just touching/kissing the Markowitz bullet, see Figure 3.9. The new triangular region *includes* the all-risky Markowitz bullet as expected.

The addition of the risk-free asset dramatically changes the shape of the feasible set from a hyperbola to a triangular region. The new efficient frontier, referred to as the *capital market line (CML)*, is simply a straight line that starts at the risk-free rate, $(0, R_0)$. If R_0 is less than the mean of the minimum variance portfolio, the line touches the top half of the Markowitz bullet at only one point, (σ_M, μ_M). The tangency portfolio M with return $R_M \sim (\mu_M, \sigma_M)$ is called the *market portfolio (MP)*.

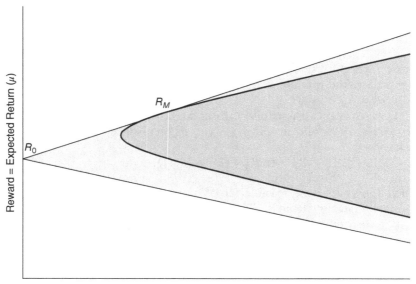

FIGURE 3.9   Relationship between CML and the feasible region of risky assets.

Since CML is a straight line connecting the risk-free asset and MP, the return $R \sim (\mu, \sigma)$ of any portfolio on CML must satisfy

$$\mu = R_0 + \frac{\mu_M - R_0}{\sigma_M} \sigma$$

The slope of CML, $(\mu_M - R_0)/\sigma_M$, is the measure of excess return required by rational investors per unit of risk, and $(\mu_M - R_0)/\sigma_M \times \sigma$ is the excess return over the risk-free rate for a given level of risk and is called the *risk premium*.

3.2.13   Market Portfolio

Let there be N investors where ith investor has V_i to invest, M risky assets, and the weights of the tangency portfolio be given as $(w_1, \ldots, w_M)$ where $\sum_{j=1}^{M} w_j = 1$. Each investor with pick their spot on the CML by investing $(1 - \alpha_i)$ of their capital V_i in the risk-free asset, and $\alpha_i V_i$ in the tangency portfolio. Each ith investor will then invest $\alpha_i V_i w_j$ in the jth risky asset.

Summing over all investors, each jth risky asset has a market capitalization of $\sum_{i=1}^{N} \alpha_i V_i w_j$. Moreover, the total risky market size is $\sum_{i=1}^{N} \alpha_i V_i$. Hence

$$\frac{\text{Market capitalization of } j\text{th asset}}{\text{Total market size}} = \frac{\sum_{i=1}^{N} \alpha_i V_i w_j}{\sum_{i=1}^{N} \alpha_i V_i} = w_j$$

justifying the term *market* portfolio.

Since the line connecting R_0 to M has the highest slope, we can solve for the weights of the market portfolio by solving the following constrained optimization problem: maximize the slope $(\mathbf{w}^T \boldsymbol{\mu} - R_0)/\sqrt{\mathbf{w}^T \mathbf{C} \mathbf{w}}$ subject to $\mathbf{w}^T \mathbf{u} = 1$, resulting in the following weights

$$\mathbf{w}_M = \frac{\mathbf{C}^{-1}(\boldsymbol{\mu} - R_0 \mathbf{u})}{\mathbf{u}^T \mathbf{C}^{-1}(\boldsymbol{\mu} - R_0 \mathbf{u})} \tag{3.11}$$

The proof is left as an exercise.

Example 3

Continuing with the previous 3-asset case in Example 2, let the risk-free rate be $R_0 = 3\%$. The weights of the market portfolio are

$$\mathbf{w}_M = \begin{bmatrix} 17.405\% \\ 6.449\% \\ 76.146\% \end{bmatrix}$$

with $R_M \sim (3.45\%, 4.89\%)$, resulting in 0.548 as the slope of the CML.

3.3 CAPITAL ASSET PRICING MODEL

What is the relationship between the market portfolio with return $R_M \sim (\mu_M, \sigma_M)$, and a given risky asset or portfolio X with return $R_X \sim (\mu_X, \sigma_X)$? The feasible set of portfolios constructed from just (M, X) is a hyperbola, and is a subset of the feasible region when *all* risky assets were considered. This sub-hyperbola is a continuous function and includes (σ_M, μ_M). If its tangent at (σ_M, μ_M) is not the CML, then there must be feasible portfolios either to the left or right of (σ_M, μ_M) and *a bove* CML, which cannot be since CML is the efficient frontier (highest reward for any risk) of risk-free and *all* risky assets. Therefore CML is the tangent of the sub-hyperbola at (σ_M, μ_M) as shown in Figure 3.10.

All that remains is to calculate the slope of the tangent (σ_M, μ_M), i.e., the derivative of the sub-hyperbola evaluated at (σ_M, μ_M). The return, $R_P \sim (\mu_P, \sigma_P)$, for any portfolio P on the (M, X) feasible set satisfies

$$R_P = wR_X + (1 - w)R_M$$

$$\mu_P = w\mu_X + (1 - w)\mu_M$$

$$\sigma_P = \sqrt{w^2\sigma_X^2 + (1 - w)^2\sigma_M^2 + 2w(1 - w)Cov(R_X, R_M)}$$

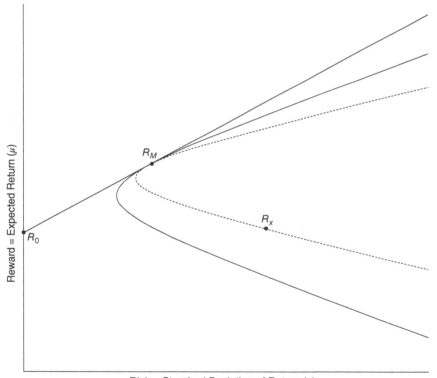

FIGURE 3.10   Proof of the CAPM formula.

for some w. By the chain rule

$$\frac{d\mu_P}{d\sigma_P} = \frac{d\mu_P}{dw}\frac{dw}{d\sigma_P} = \frac{d\mu_P/dw}{d\sigma_P/dw}$$

By observing that $P = M$ when $w = 0$, we can compute the desired slope

$$\text{Slope} = \frac{d\mu_P}{d\sigma_P}\bigg|_{w=0} = \frac{d\mu_P/dw}{d\sigma_P/dw}\bigg|_{w=0}$$

$$= \frac{\mu_X - \mu_M}{[w\sigma_X^2 - (1-w)\sigma_M^2 + (1-2w)Cov(R_X, R_M)]/\sigma_P}\bigg|_{w=0}$$

$$= \frac{\mu_X - \mu_M}{(Cov(R_X, R_M) - \sigma_M^2)/\sigma_M}$$

Setting the above to equal the slope of CML, $(\mu_M - R_0)/\sigma_M$, we can solve for μ_X to arrive at the *Capital Asset Pricing Model (CAPM) formula*, [Sharpe, 1964]

$$\frac{\mu_X - \mu_M}{(Cov(R_X, R_M) - \sigma_M^2)/\sigma_M} = \frac{\mu_M - R_0}{\sigma_M}$$

$$\Rightarrow \frac{\mu_X - \mu_M}{(Cov(R_X, R_M) - \sigma_M^2)/\sigma_M^2} = \mu_M - R_0$$

$$\Rightarrow \frac{\mu_X - \mu_M}{\beta_X - 1} = \mu_M - R_0$$

$$\Rightarrow \mu_X - R_0 = \beta_X(\mu_M - R_0) \tag{3.12}$$

where the term

$$\beta_X = \frac{Cov(R_X, R_M)}{\sigma_M^2} = \rho_{X,M}\frac{\sigma_X}{\sigma_M}$$

is called the *beta* of the asset with respect to the market portfolio and can be interpreted as a measure of systematic risk.

Writing the CAPM formula in terms of the correlation, we have

$$\frac{\mu_X - R_0}{\sigma_X} = \rho_{X,M}\frac{\mu_M - R_0}{\sigma_M}$$

which shows that the ratio of the slope of $R_0 \to \mu_X$ line to the slope of $R_0 \to \mu_M$ line equals $\rho_{X,M}$.

3.3.1 CAPM Pricing

The CAPM formula can be used to provide today's fair price of risky assets. For a given asset X with 1-period return of R_X over $(0, t)$

$$R_X = X(t)/X(0) - 1$$

$$\Rightarrow \mu_X = E[R_X] = E[X(t)]/X(0) - 1$$

$$\Rightarrow X(0) = \frac{E[X(t)]}{1 + \mu_X} = \frac{E[X(t)]}{1 + R_0 + \beta_X(\mu_M - R_0)} \tag{3.13}$$

which shows that today's value of a risky asset is equal to its expected future value discounted by the risk-free rate *plus* its risk premium

$$\mu_X - R_0 = \beta_X(\mu_M - R_0)$$

3.3.2 Systematic and Diversifiable Risk

We can use the CAPM formula (3.12) to form a simple model for any asset or portfolio's random return and relate it to its beta. Specifically, let R_X be the random return of a portfolio $X \sim (\mu_X, \sigma_X)$. The CAPM formula based on $E[R_M] - R_0, E[R_X] - R_0$ *suggests* a linear relationship between $R_X - R_0$ and $R_M - R_0$, leading us to posit the following simple linear regression

$$R_X - R_0 = \alpha + \beta(R_M - R_0) + \epsilon_X \tag{3.14}$$

where the residual error ϵ_X has zero mean and is uncorrelated to the market's (excess) return. We shall call Formula 3.14 as the *econometric CAPM* to distinguish it from the CAPM formula (see Formula 3.12). Taking the expected value of above regression formula, we get

$$\mu_X - R_0 = \alpha + \beta(\mu_M - R_0)$$

which, when compared to CAPM, shows that α should equal 0, and β should equal β_X. Taking variances of both sides of regression Formula 3.14, we have

$$\sigma_X^2 = \beta_X^2 \sigma_M^2 + Var(\epsilon_X) \tag{3.15}$$

We now have a decomposition of the portfolio risk: the term $\beta_X^2 \sigma_M^2$ is called the *systematic* risk and is driven by the correlation of the portfolio's return to the market's return. The second component, $Var(\epsilon_X)$, is called the *specific, diversifiable* risk which would be zero if the portfolio was on the efficient frontier of risk-free and risky assets (CML).

Since $\beta_X = Cov(R_X, R_M)/\sigma_M^2 = \rho_{X,M}\sigma_X/\sigma_M$, Formula 3.15 shows the following decomposition of variance

$$\sigma_X^2 = \rho_{X,M}^2 \sigma_X^2 + Var(\epsilon_X) \qquad (3.16)$$

3.4 FACTORS

CAPM as the culmination of mean-variance portfolio theory produces the major insight that excess returns (over risk-free rate) on any investment can be related to the excess return of *one* investment (market portfolio) via its beta. The econometric linear model naturally suggested by CAPM allows one to decompose the portfolio risk into two components: the risk due to the market portfolio multiplied by the strength of its linkage (beta), and portfolio-specific risk, $\sqrt{Var(\epsilon_X)}$. As there are many securities (about 3,500 listed stocks in United States) and myriad potential portfolios composed of them, this decomposition of the risk into one common systematic risk and many specific risks is a major aid in reducing the dimension of the problem, especially when the specific risk of an asset is small relative to its systematic risk.

The idea that returns on investments are driven by a few common drivers gives rise to linear *factor models* where the excess returns on assets is modeled as a linear decomposition due to a few common factors plus the asset's specific risk. Specifically, in a linear K-factor model, the return of each ith asset is modeled as

$$R_i = \alpha_i + [\beta_{i,1}F_1 + \ldots + \beta_{i,K}F_K] + \epsilon_i \qquad (3.17)$$

Note that once we find $\beta_{i,.}$, the *factor loading* for each ith asset to each factor, the systematic part of return is fully expressed via the (few) common factors.

3.4.1 Arbitrage Pricing Theory

At first look, Formula 3.17 is very similar to econometric CAPM, Formula 3.14, and econometric CAPM can be considered to be a 1-factor linear model with market portfolio's excess return, $R_M - R_0$, as its sole factor. However, while econometric CAPM ends with Formula 3.17, arbitrage pricing theory (APT) (Ross, 1976) *starts* with Formula 3.17 with general unspecified factors and is further analyzed by imposing the following structure

$$E[\epsilon_i] = 0, \quad Cov(\epsilon_i, \epsilon_j) = 0, \quad \max(Var(\epsilon_i)) \text{ is bounded}$$

$$E[F_j] = 0, \quad Cov(F_i, F_j) = 0, \quad Var[F_j] = 1$$

$$Cov(\epsilon_i, F_j) = 0$$

To understand the key insight of APT, we consider the 1-factor version of the above with diversified portfolios and with the residuals $\epsilon_{1,2}$ set to zero, which can be justified asymptotically for large diversified portfolios via the law of large numbers. In this simplified case, we have for any two arbitrary pairs of portfolios P_1, P_2,

$$R_1 = \alpha_1 + \beta_{11}F_1$$
$$R_2 = \alpha_2 + \beta_{21}F_1 \tag{3.18}$$

For a portfolio P with allocation w to the first portfolio, we have

$$R_P = wR_1 + (1-w)R_2$$
$$= [w(\alpha_1 - \alpha_2) + \alpha_2] + [w(\beta_{11} - \beta_{21}) + \beta_{21}]F_1$$

For the choice

$$w = -\beta_{21}/(\beta_{11} - \beta_{21})$$

the term multiplying the random factor F_1 becomes zero, resulting in a riskless portfolio with return

$$R_P = \alpha_2 + \frac{-\beta_{21}}{\beta_{11} - \beta_{21}}(\alpha_1 - \alpha_2)$$

APT's main insight is that to avoid arbitrage, this riskless investment should earn the risk-free rate, $R_P = R_0$

$$\alpha_2 + \frac{-\beta_{21}}{\beta_{11} - \beta_{21}}(\alpha_1 - \alpha_2) = R_0$$
$$\Rightarrow \quad \frac{\alpha_1 - R_0}{\beta_{11}} = \frac{\alpha_2 - R_0}{\beta_{21}} \tag{3.19}$$

Since the two portfolios were arbitrary, we have

$$\frac{\alpha_i - R_0}{\beta_{i1}} = \lambda_1$$

for some λ_1 for *any* ith asset, and the common ratio λ_1 is only due to the factor F_1. It can be shown (Ingersoll, 1987) to equal

$$\lambda_1 = E[R_{Z_1}] - R_0 \tag{3.20}$$

where Z_1 is a portfolio whose F_1 beta is 1, $\beta_{.1} = 1$. The 1-factor APT model leads to

$$E[R_i] - R_0 = \beta_{i,1}(E[R_{Z_1}] - R_0)$$

which can be generalized to multiple factors as

$$E[R_i] - R_0 = \sum_{j=1}^{K} \beta_{i,j}(E[R_{Z_i}] - R_0) \tag{3.21}$$

where Z_j is the "$\beta_{.j} = 1$" portfolio for jth factor.

Comparing APT Formula 3.21 with CAPM Formula 3.12, APT can be considered a generalization of CAPM, albeit starting with completely different assumptions (asymptotically arbitrage-free) rather than mean-variance optimality in an equilibrium setting.

3.4.2 Fama-French Factors

The APT conditions for a factor model are applicable to any common driver of excess returns, be they economic or derived from data. A commonly used set of economic factors proposed by Fama and French [Fama and French, 1993] are:

- Small Minus Big (SMB): It is observed that investments in stocks of companies with small market capitalization have historically outperformed investments in large capitalization companies. The SMB factor is based on the return of a representative portfolio of small-cap stocks versus the return of a representative portfolio of large-cap stocks.
- High Minus Low (HML): The *book value* of a company is the value of its assets minus its liabilities, referred to as shareholder's *equity* in a company's balance sheet. The book value of a company is often different than its market value (price times outstanding shares). *Growth* stocks tend to have high market value versus their book value, while *value* stocks have high book value compared to their market value. Value stocks have historically outperformed growth stocks and the HML factor is based on the return of a representative portfolio of value stocks versus the return of a portfolio of growth stocks.

The addition of these factors to the market's excess return gives rise to the Fama-French three-factor econometric model for the excess return of an asset

$$R - R_0 = \alpha + \beta_M(R_M - R_0) + \beta_s F_{SMB} + \beta_v F_{HML} + \epsilon \tag{3.22}$$

Additional economic factors, such as operating profitability (robust versus weak, RMW), investments and asset growth (conservative versus aggressive, CMA), and momentum (MOM), have been added to the original factors.

3.4.3 Factor Investing

The Fama-French factors are based on the fundamentals attributes of firms such as size, book value, and investments and are plausible explanations of excess returns. Factor models also allow macroeconomic drivers such as GDP growth rate, interest rates, and also purely statistical factors as drivers and explanations of excess returns. When working with historical data to determine factors and investment strategies, one needs to be keenly aware of the usual dangers of overfitting, data mining, p-hacking, etc. This has become more critical due to the advent of financial data science and the ability to explore large amounts of historical data, which has given rise to identification and quantification of more factors, and investment strategies marketed as alternative or *smart beta* index products in the format of low-cost, tax-efficient ETFs.

The identification and understanding of the factor exposure of a portfolio allows an asset manager to selectively fine-tune the exposure by adding or reducing the exposures. For example, a portfolio manager might perform a regression analysis of their portfolio relative to the Fama-French factors and decide that their portfolio is highly exposed to SMB factor (high β_s). In this case, they might decide to reduce that exposure by shorting assets with high β_s.

Another application of factor models is to use the factor loadings obtained from a regression analysis to isolate the nonsystematic driver of an asset's return. For example, using the three Fama-French factors in Formula 3.22, if for a given asset or portfolio we estimate its factor loadings $\beta_M, \beta_s, \beta_v$ via a regression analysis, we can form a new portfolio from the original by shorting $\beta_M, \beta_s, \beta_v$ of the factor portfolios, with the resulting return of α as the excess return

$$R_{New} - R_0 = \alpha$$

Having stripped away the factor exposures, the new portfolio can be used to get exposure to *only* the α of the original asset, and we have created a *portable alpha* portfolio.

3.4.4 PCA

Rather than positing and testing economic drivers as factors, a statistical method to reduce the dimensionality of the drivers of asset returns is the *principal component analysis (PCA)* method [Tsay, 2010]. In this method, starting with a matrix of K observations of the returns of N assets' (excess) returns, we subtract $1/K \sum_{i=1}^{K} R_{ij}$ from the jth column to arrive at the $K \times N$ matrix of mean-adjusted returns

$$(1 \leq i \leq K)(1 \leq j \leq N) \quad \mathbf{R} = [R_{ij}]$$

and compute the $N \times N$ sample covariance matrix $\mathbf{C}$

$$\mathbf{C} = \frac{1}{K-1} \mathbf{R}^T \mathbf{R}$$

The goal of PCA is to project the N-dimensional data onto the orthonormal (perpendicular and of length 1) eigenvectors (see Figure 3.11).

Let $(\lambda_i, \mathbf{e}_i)$ be the ith eigenvalue-eigenvector pair for $\mathbf{C}$, that is

$$\mathbf{C}\mathbf{e}_i = \lambda_i \mathbf{e}_i, \qquad \mathbf{e}_i^T \mathbf{e}_i = 1$$

with the eigenvalues sorted in decreasing size $\lambda_1 > \lambda_2 > \ldots > \lambda_N$. Since C is non-negative-definite—$\mathbf{w}^T \mathbf{C} \mathbf{w} \geq 0$ for any weight vector $\mathbf{w}$—it can be decomposed as

$$\mathbf{C} = \mathbf{E} \Lambda \mathbf{E}^T$$

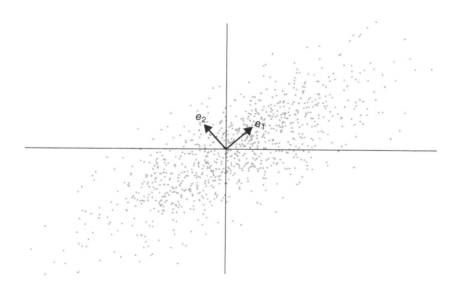

FIGURE 3.11 PCA identification of eigenvectors.

where Λ is the diagonal matrix with the eigenvalues appearing on the diagonal in decreasing size, and E consists of the corresponding eigenvectors appearing as the columns. It can be shown that the fraction of the variance (sum of the diagonals of C) explained by the ith eigenvector e_i is

$$\frac{\lambda_i}{\sum_{i=1}^{N} \lambda_i}$$

Assume that the first $M \ll N$ eigenvectors explain a large fraction, say $1 - \alpha$ for small α, of the variance

$$\frac{\sum_{i=1}^{M} \lambda_i}{\sum_{i=1}^{N} \lambda_i} = 1 - \alpha \approx 1$$

and let E_M be the truncated $N \times M$ eigenvector matrix consisting of the first M eigenvector columns. For a given $1 \times N$ mean-adjusted sample return vector R_t, the predicted value is its projection onto the first M statistically significant factors

$$\hat{R}_t = R_t E_M E_M^T$$

with the difference as the residual

$$\epsilon_t = R_t - R_t E_M E_M^T$$

3.5 MEAN-VARIANCE EFFICIENCY AND UTILITY

Mean variance portfolio theory is based on the preference of undominated portfolios: for a given level of risk, select the highest returning portfolios, and for a given level of return, select the least risky portfolios. Can the mean-variance efficiency be consistent with expected utility theory? Recall that in the expected utility framework, optimal portfolio selection is equivalent to maximizing the expected utility of future wealth. Since utility functions are unique only up to linear transformations, for a 1-period investment horizon, maximizing the expected utility of future wealth becomes equivalent to maximizing the expected utility of return.

The following conditions are sufficient in making a utility function consistent with mean-variance efficiency:

1. The utility function applied to returns depends only on the mean and standard deviation.
2. The *indifference curves*—combinations of mean and variances that provide the same expected utility level—are strictly convex and increasing functions of σ.

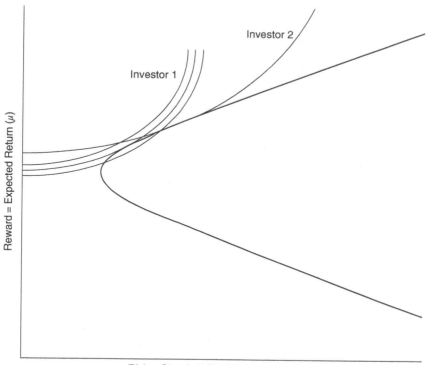

FIGURE 3.12 Utility indifference curves.

3. As one increases the expected utility level, the indifference curves shift up in the (σ, μ) plane.

A utility function satisfying the above condition will achieve its maximum only on the efficient frontier and will reject any dominated portfolio, hence, mean-variance efficient portfolios are optimal (see Figure 3.12).

3.5.1 Parabolic Utility

The *parabolic* utility function defined as $U(x) = -(x - x_0)^2$ for a constant $x_0 > 0$ satisfies the above conditions. To maximize $E[U(R)]$, we observe

$$
\begin{aligned}
E[U(R)] &= -E[(R - x_0)^2] \\
&= -E[((R - \mu) + (\mu - x_0))^2] \\
&= -(E[(R - \mu)^2] + (\mu - x_0)^2 + (\mu - x_0)E[R - \mu]) \\
&= -(\sigma^2 + (\mu - x_0)^2)
\end{aligned}
$$

The indifference curves for a given level of expected utility $c < 0$ satisfy

$$\sigma^2 + (\mu - x_0)^2 = -c$$

which is the equation of a circle centered at $(0, x_0)$ with radius $\sqrt{|c|}$ in the (σ, μ) plane. Since the sign is negative, the larger the circle, the lower the expected utility, and, hence, the maximum expected utility is achieved by shrinking the radius until it just touches the efficient frontier. Different investors can have different x_0's leading to different touch points.

While the parabolic utility satisfies these conditions, it is only concave for $x \leq x_0$ and after achieving its maximum at x_0 starts to decrease, and, hence, is an unrealistic utility function.

3.5.2 Jointly Normal Returns

A more realistic case arises if the returns of risky assets are assumed to be jointly normal, and the utility function a strictly increasing and concave (risk-averse) function. Since the returns of the assets are jointly normal, the return of any portfolio is the weighted average of these returns and is also normal and fully characterized by its mean and variance. Hence, its expected utility is a function of its mean and variance, satisfying condition 1 above. The other two conditions can be shown to hold since the utility function is strictly increasing and strictly concave.

For a specific example, we can consider the *exponential* utility defined as $U(x) = 1 - e^{-cx}$ for some constant $c > 0$. Let the return of a portfolio follow a normal distribution $R \sim N(\mu, \sigma^2)$. We have

$$E[U(R)] = \int (1 - e^{-cx}) \frac{1}{\sqrt{2\pi\sigma^2}} e^{-(x-\mu)^2/2\sigma^2} dx$$

$$= 1 - \frac{1}{\sqrt{2\pi\sigma^2}} \int e^{-cx} e^{-(x-\mu)^2/2\sigma^2} dx$$

$$= 1 - e^{-c(\mu - c\sigma^2/2)} \frac{1}{\sqrt{2\pi\sigma^2}} \int e^{-(x-(\mu-c\sigma^2))^2/2\sigma^2} dx \qquad (3.23)$$

$$= 1 - e^{-c(\mu - c\sigma^2/2)} \qquad (3.24)$$

where Formula 3.23 was obtained by completing the square in the exponent, and noticing that the integral is the total area under the pdf of an $N(\mu - c\sigma^2, \sigma^2)$ random variable, which should be 1.

Maximizing Formula 3.24 is equivalent to minimizing the term in the exponent, which in turn is equivalent to maximizing $\mu - c\sigma^2/2$ since $c > 0$. The indifference curves of $\mu - c\sigma^2/2$ for a given level of utility u satisfy

$\mu = u + c\sigma^2/2$, which are parabolas with vertex $(0, u)$, and satisfy conditions 2 and 3 above. Different investors could have different cs resulting in different touch points on the efficient frontier.

3.6 INVESTMENTS IN PRACTICE

CAPM and its econometric interpretation provide a guide and benchmark to calculate the performance of an asset, portfolio, or asset manager. CAPM by itself is a formula relating the *expected* return of a portfolio to the expected return of the market portfolio via its beta in an equilibrium setting. The empirical version of expected values derived from a historical time series of actual returns can show deviations from their equilibrium counterparts. Two of the common criticisms of mean-variance theory and CAPM are:

1. Mean-variance theory's equilibrium results are based on the assumption that all investors know and agree on an unchanging covariance matrix of all asset returns (3,500 or so stocks in the United States, so a 3500×3500 matrix) and their means. This is a tall order and in practice empirical estimates of the covariance matrix and returns are used. However, studies have shown that the tangency portfolio and slope of the CML are quite sensitive to these covariances and slight estimation variations can introduce large changes in efficient portfolios. Despite this, most investment managers still use the mean-variance theory and CAPM as a guide and starting point to portfolio selection.
2. The market portfolio's weights are each asset's market capitalization in equilibrium. For constantly moving markets, when an asset becomes overpriced, its market capitalization and weight rises, and funds newly invested or rebalanced reinforce the overvaluation by allocating more to an already overpriced asset. Similarly, undervalued assets are further punished and their valuation pushed lower.

3.6.1 Rebalancing

Since rational investors are supposed to make investments on the CML, a rule-of-thumb investment advice is to allocate 40% to risk-free investments (bonds) and 60% to risky assets (stocks), and maintain this allocation by periodically rebalancing. A variation is to subtract one's age from 100 (recently upgraded to 110 due to increased longevity) and use that as the allocation to stocks, so in early years one invests in riskier assets and enjoys their expected long-term high returns. As one ages, the recommended allocation shifts toward safer investments.

Maintaining a prescribed allocation through rebalancing has the fortunate effect of buy-low, sell-high. For example, in the standard 60-40 portfolio, if stocks go up, then to maintain the 60-40 allocation, one needs to sell some of the stock holdings and buy bonds (sell high). Similarly, if stocks go down, one needs to buy more (buy low). A similar situation holds for the bond allocation.

3.6.2   Performance Measures

Recognizing that CAPM and APT are equilibrium results on returns, how does one evaluate actual returns? Starting with the regression model in Formula 3.14, we can calculate *Jensen's alpha*,

$$\hat{\alpha} = (\hat{\mu}_X - \hat{R}_0) - \hat{\beta}_X(\hat{\mu}_M - \hat{R}_0)$$

where $\hat{x}$ means the empirically estimated value of the x. According to CAPM, the equilibrium value of $\hat{\alpha}$ should be zero. Therefore, if a portfolio shows a persistent positive $\hat{\alpha}$, this can be construed as the portfolio's superior beta-adjusted return. Investment and portfolio managers tout their ability to beat the market and to generate "alpha," thereby attracting more investments and increasing assets under management (AUM) and enjoying the associated AUM fee income.

A similar measure inspired by CAPM is *Treynor's ratio*

$$\hat{T} = \frac{\hat{\mu}_X - \hat{R}_0}{\hat{\beta}_X}$$

which is the beta-adjusted excess return of a portfolio. According to CAPM, the above should equal the market portfolio's excess return, $\mu_M - R_0$. A portfolio showing persistent beta-adjusted excess return higher than the market's is an attractive investment.

The Sharpe ratio is the risk-adjusted empirical return of a portfolio and the empirical proxy for the slope of the line from the risk-free asset to the portfolio in the risk-reward (σ, μ) plane.

$$\hat{m} = \frac{\hat{\mu}_X - \hat{R}_0}{\hat{\sigma}_X}$$

According to the mean-variance theory, the CML has the highest slope, so any portfolio exhibiting persistent higher empirical slope than CML's slope, $(\mu_M - R_0)/\sigma_M$, is indicative of a superior risk-adjusted return.

3.6.3 Z-Scores, Mean-Reversion, Rich-Cheap

Regression analysis is the workhorse for extracting estimates of model parameters. Once estimated, the residuals are centered around their means and divided by their standard deviation to arrive at a standardized measure called the *Z-score*: the number of standard deviations a dependent variable is away from its mean where the mean and standard deviation are either known or calculated/estimated from the data.

It is often assumed that Z-scores revert to 0, resulting in *mean-reversion*: undervalued assets with high Z-scores for their returns are cheap and bought by astute investors bringing their values back to their equilibrium values. Similarly rich assets with negative Z-scores for their returns are shorted bringing their value back to equilibrium.

This is a version of *efficient market hypothesis (EMH)*, which posits that deviations from market equilibrium are short-term and will be arbitraged away, thereby restoring markets to equilibrium state and conditions.

3.6.4 Pairs Trading

Pairs trading is a common trading strategy where one buys a cheap asset while shorting a related rich asset based on the price difference. Specifically, for two stocks in the same sector, say technology, it is assumed that their prices are mainly driven by the same common factors and any large price discrepancy is temporary and will fade away. With this assumption, trading entry and exit signals are constructed based on the discrepancy.

The following shows the typical steps for constructing a simple pairs trade:

1. Obtain the historical prices of the two stocks, adjusted for any splits, dividends: let $X_1, \ldots, X_N$ be the adjusted price of the first asset, while $Y_1, \ldots, Y_N$ the adjusted price of the second asset.
2. Graph the adjusted price series (X_i, Y_i) and create a scatter plot.
3. Perform a regression analysis to obtain the slope and examine the statistics to ensure that the series are related: $Y = b_0 + b_1 X + \text{Noise}$.
4. Create trading signal $S_i = Y_i - b_1 X_i$.
5. Standardize the S_i series by subtracting its empirical mean and dividing the result by the empirical standard deviation to come up with the Z-score series.
6. If the Z-score is high, that means Y_i is too high: short Asset 2 while buying b_1 units of Asset 1 for each 1 unit of Asset 2. Similarly, if the Z-score is too low, buy Asset 2 and short b_1 units of Asset 1.
7. Create profit-taking (exit winning trades) and stop-loss (exit losing trades) signals based on the number of favorable or unfavorable changes in the Z-score.

Example 4

Figures 3.13 through 3.15 show the result of a pairs trade based on a 5-year monthly history of Amazon (AMZN) and Walmart (WMT). Table 3.3 shows the statistics of regression analysis, indicating a high R squared of 90.3% and confidence of at least $99.9539\% = 1 - 0.000461$ that the slope b_1 is significant.

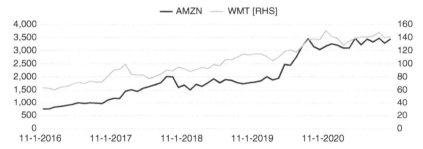

FIGURE 3.13   5-year monthly price history of Amazon (AMZN), Walmart (WMT).

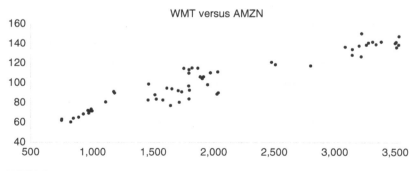

FIGURE 3.14   Walmart (WMT) versus Amazon (AMZN).

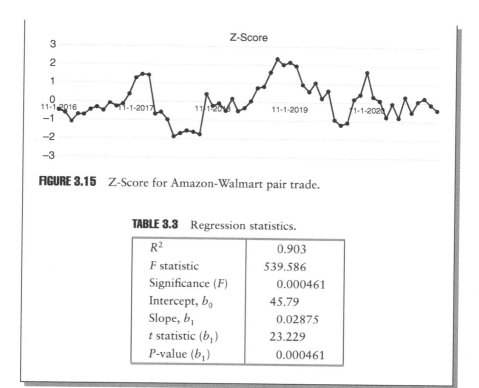

FIGURE 3.15 Z-Score for Amazon-Walmart pair trade.

TABLE 3.3 Regression statistics.

R^2	0.903
F statistic	539.586
Significance (F)	0.000461
Intercept, b_0	45.79
Slope, b_1	0.02875
t statistic (b_1)	23.229
P-value (b_1)	0.000461

3.6.5 Risk Management

It is often said that investment is all about risk management. Successful investors, traders, and gamblers know how to play the odds and how to size their bets. Optimal bet sizes, strategies, stopping times, and game durations in games of chance have been extensively studied under the rubric of gambling or betting systems [Dubins and Savage, 1965].

3.6.5.1 Gambler's Ruin Consider a game where you will win/lose $1 with probability $p, 1 - p$, for example, a *loaded* coin toss with $Prob[Heads] = p$, and you win/lose if the coin lands Heads/Tails. Assume that you begin with an initial amount $a \geq 0$ and will play this game until you reach a target amount $b \geq a$ or you lose all your money a, that is you get *ruined*. What is the probability of success, that is, reaching your target b before losing a?

Let S_a be the probability of success when starting with initial state a. We can form the following linear homogeneous recurrence equation

$$(0 < a < b) \quad S_a = pS_{a+1} + (1-p)S_{a-1}$$

with $S_0 = 0, S_b = 1$. Using the fundamental solution for recurrence, $S_n = x^n$, we have

$$px^2 - x + (1-p) = 0$$

as the characteristic equation. Let $\rho = (1-p)/p$. If $\rho \neq 1$, the characteristic equation has two distinct roots, $1, \rho$, leading to

$$S_n = A \times 1^n + B \times \rho^n$$

for constants A, B. When $\rho = 1$, the characteristic equation has a repeated root equaling 1, and

$$S_n = A \times 1^n + B \times n \times 1^n$$

Invoking the boundary conditions lets us solve for A, B

$$\begin{cases} A = 0, B = 1/n & \text{when } \rho = 1 \\ A = -1/(\rho^N - 1), B = 1/(\rho^N - 1) & \text{when } \rho \neq 1 \end{cases}$$

to arrive at

$$P[Success] = S_a = \begin{cases} a/b, & \text{if } \rho = 1 \ (p = 1/2) \\ \dfrac{\rho^a - 1}{\rho^b - 1} & \text{if } \rho \neq 1 \end{cases} \tag{3.25}$$

For example, with initial capital $a = \$900$ and the modest goal of $b = \$1,000$, the probability of success in a fair game, $\rho = 1$, is pretty good, $a/b = 90\%$. If the odds are slightly against you, say $p = 18/38$, $\rho = 20/18$—typical odds for a red/black bet at a casino roulette game—then the probability of success drops to 0.00003! Formula 3.25 shows that even if odds are only slightly against you, you are mostly like ruined.

3.6.5.2 Kelly's Ratio   In the Gambler's Ruin case, one could only bet $1 at each turn. Is there a way of improving one's chances by judiciously sizing one's bets? Specifically, let us follow the strategy of betting a constant fraction α of one's wealth, so that our wealth V increases by $V\alpha$ to $V(1 + \alpha)$ with probability p, and decreases by $-V\alpha$ to $V(1 - \alpha)$ with probability $1 - p$ at each turn. Starting with unit wealth $V_0 = 1$, after N tosses, one has

$$V_N = (1 + \alpha)^n(1 - \alpha)^{N-n}$$

where n is the number of wins (getting Heads). Taking log of both sides and dividing by N we have

$$\frac{1}{N} \ln V_N = \frac{n}{N} \ln(1 + \alpha) + (1 - \frac{n}{N}) \ln(1 - \alpha)$$

By the law of large numbers, $p = \lim_N n/N$, and the long-term return is

$$R = \lim_N \frac{1}{N} \ln V_N = p \ln(1 + \alpha) + (1 - p) \ln(1 - \alpha)$$

To maximize this return, we set its derivative to 0

$$\frac{dR}{d\alpha} = \frac{p}{1 + \alpha} - \frac{1 - p}{1 - \alpha} = 0$$

resulting in $\alpha^* = 2p - 1$ as the optimal fraction to maximize R for $p > 1/2$. The optimal fraction $2p - 1$ is known as *Kelly's ratio* [Kelly, 1956]. In practice, one might employ a fraction of Kelly's ratio, for example a *half-Kelly*, $1/2(2p - 1)$, to smooth out the large swings in one's PnL.

If $p \leq 1/2$, one should either not play, or, if one insists, it is shown that *bold play* is optimal, that is, one should bet all one's money at each try until one hits their target [Billingsley, 1979].

REFERENCES

Billingsley, P. (1979). *Probability and Measure*. New York: Wiley.

Dubins, L.E. and Savage, L.J. (1965). *How to Game If You Must (Inequalities for Stochastic Processes)*. Mineola, NY: Dover Publications, Inc.

Fama, E.F. and French, K.R. (1993). Common risk factors in the returns on stocks and bonds. *Journal of Financial Economics* **33**(1): 3–56.

French, C. (2003). The Treynor capital asset pricing model. *Journal of Investment Management* **1**(2): 60–72.

Hanoch, G. and Levy, H. (1969). The efficiency analysis of choices involving risk. *Review of Economic Studies* **36**(3): 335–346.

Ingersoll, J.E. Jr. (1987). *Theory of Financial Decision Making*. Lanham, MD: Rowman and Littlefield Publishing Group.

Kelly, J.L. (1956). A new interpretation of information rate. *IRE Trans. Inf. Theory* **2**: 185–189.

Lintner, J. (1965). The valuation of risk assets and the selection of risky investments in stock portfolios and capital budgets. *The Review of Economics and Statistics* **47**(1): 13–37.

Markowitz, H. (1952). Portfolio selection. *Journal of Finance* **7**(1): 77–91.

Merton, R.C. (1972). An analytic derivation of the efficient portfolio frontier. *The Journal of Financial and Quantitative Analysis* **7**(4): 1851–1872.

Mossin, J. (1966). Equilibrium in a capital asset market. *Econometrica* **34**(4): 768–783.

Rohatgi, V.K. (1976). *An Introduction to Probability Theory and Mathematical Statistics*. New York: John Wiley & Sons.

Ross, S.A. (1976). The arbitrage theory of capital asset pricing. *Journal of Economic Theory* **13**(3): 341–360.

Sharpe, W.F. (1964). Capital asset prices: A theory of market equilibrium under conditions of risk. *The Journal of Finance* **19**(3): 425–442.

Thorp, E. (2008). The Kelly criterion in blackjack, sports betting, and the stock market. *Handbook of Asset and Liability Management* **1**, 12.

Tobin, J. (1958). Liquidity preference as behavior towards risk. *The Review of Economic Studies* **25**(2): 65–86.

Tsay, R.S. (2010). *Analysis of Financial Time Series*. Hoboken, NJ: Wiley.

Wise, B., Ricker, N., Veltkamp, D., and Kowalski, B. (1990). A theoretical basis for the use of principal component models for monitoring multivariate processes. *Process Control and Quality* **1**, 11.

EXERCISES

1. Using the formulas for ARA and RRA
   (a) Show that exponential utility: $U(x) = 1 - e^{-cx}$ for some $c > 0$, has constant ARA (CARA).
   (b) For power utility: $U(x) = (x^{1-\alpha} - 1)/(1 - \alpha)$ for $\alpha \neq 1$
      i. Show that power utility is concave (risk averse) when $\alpha > 0$ and convex (risk seeking) when $\alpha < 0$.
      ii. What type of behavior is modeled when $\alpha = 0$?
      iii. Show that power utility has constant RRA (CRRA).
      iv. Using L'Hôpital's rule, show that power utility reduces to log utility, $U(x) = \ln(x)$, when $\alpha = 1$.

2. An investor has a base 10 log utility function: $U(x) = \log_{10}(x)$. Investment 1 has payoff (1, 100) with probabilities (0.8, 0.2). Investment 2 has payoff (10, 1000) with probabilities (0.99, 0.01).
   (a) Which investment is mean-variance dominant?
   (b) Which investment has higher expected utility?

3. Assume you have $100,000 to invest for one year, and decide to allocate 60% to an all equity fund trading at $400 per share and 40% to a bond

fund trading at \$100 per share. After one year, the equity fund is trading at \$450 per share and the bond fund is trading at \$95 per share.

(a) What is the value of your portfolio after one year?
(b) What is the 1-year rate of return on your portfolio?
(c) What are the allocations of your portfolio after one year?
(d) How do you rebalance your portfolio to maintain allocations at 60/40?

4. Show the steps to get from Formula 3.4 to Formula 3.5.

5. Let $R_1 \sim (\mu_1 = 4\%, \sigma_1 = 10\%)$ and $R_2 \sim (\mu_2 = 6\%, \sigma_2 = 6\%)$, $\rho(R_1, R_2) = 25\%$, where R_1, R_2 are the returns of two assets.
(a) Graph the feasible set (σ_P, μ_P) of all portfolios formed from the two assets.
(b) Calculate the weights (w_1^*, w_2^*) of the minimum variance portfolio (MVP) formed from the two assets.
(c) What is the standard deviation and expected value of the MVPs return?
(d) Although Asset 1 is dominated by Asset 2, depending on the correlation, it can be part of an efficient portfolio with positive weight. Identify the set of correlations where this can be the case. *Hint*: The efficient frontier starts at the MVP, so find MVP's with $w_1^* = 0$.

6. The canonical form of a shifted hyperbola in the (σ, μ) plane is $\sigma^2/c_\sigma^2 - (\mu - \mu_0)^2/c_\mu^2 = 1$.
(a) Derive the expression for the two asymptotes of the shifted hyperbola (μ intercept, slopes).
(b) Formula 3.9 shows that the weights for any portfolio on the MVF are a linear function of μ, $w^*(\mu) = a\mu + b$. Using this, show that the variance can be expressed as $\sigma^2(\mu) = A\mu^2 + B\mu + C$ for all points on the MVF, and express the parameters A, B, C in terms of a, b, c. *Hint*: For any μ, the MVF's variance is

$$\sigma^2(\mu) = (a\mu + b)^T C(a\mu + b)$$
$$= A\mu^2 + B\mu + C$$

(c) Complete the square above to show that MVF can be written as $\sigma^2/c_\sigma^2 - (\mu - \mu_0)^2/c_\mu^2 = 1$ and, hence, is a hyperbola, and express c_σ, c_μ, μ_0 in terms of A, B, C.
(d) For the two risky assets case, $R_1 \sim (\mu_1, \sigma_1)$ and $R_2 \sim (\mu_2, \sigma_2)$ with correlation ρ, $\mu = w\mu_1 + (1-w)\mu_2$ and, hence, w is a linear function of μ

$$w = \frac{1}{\mu_1 - \mu_2}\mu - \frac{\mu_2}{\mu_1 - \mu_2}$$

and the variance can be expressed as $\sigma^2 = A\mu^2 + B\mu + C$. Express A, B, C and the asymptotes in terms of $\mu_1, \mu_2, \sigma_1, \sigma_2, \rho$.

7. Given three assets whose returns' means, variances, and correlations are

$$\mu = \begin{bmatrix} 5\% \\ 6\% \\ 3\% \end{bmatrix} \qquad \sigma = \begin{bmatrix} 6\% \\ 8\% \\ 10\% \end{bmatrix} \qquad \rho = \begin{bmatrix} 100\% & 95\% & 90\% \\ 95\% & 100\% & 80\% \\ 90\% & 80\% & 100\% \end{bmatrix}$$

   (a) Compute a,b in Formula 3.10.
   (b) What is the MVF evaluated at $\mu = 6\%$?
   (c) Graph the MVF for $0 \le \mu \le 12\%$ in the risk-reward (σ, μ) plane.
   (d) Given a risk-free asset with return $R_0 = 3\%$, use Formula 3.11 to calculate the weights of the market portfolio and its risk and reward (σ_M, μ_M), and the slope of the capital market line (CML).

8. Assume that the risky returns are jointly normal and use the method of Lagrange multipliers to find the optimal location on the MVF for an investor with exponential utility, that is, maximize $\mu - c\sigma^2/2$ (see Section 3.5.2) subject to

$$\frac{\sigma^2}{c_\sigma^2} - \frac{(\mu - \mu_0)^2}{c_\mu^2} = 1$$

9. To derive Formula 3.11, we observe that the slope of the Capital Market Line connecting R_0 to M is the maximum among all lines connecting R_0 to any feasible portfolio. The weights for MP are derived by solving the following: maximize the slope $(\mathbf{w}^T\mu - R_0)/\sqrt{\mathbf{w}^T\mathbf{Cw}}$ subject to $\mathbf{w}^T\mathbf{u} = 1$. Derive the formula by completing the following steps:

   (a) Form the Lagrangian and using $(\partial/\partial\mathbf{w})\mathbf{w}^T\mathbf{Cw} = 2\mathbf{Cw}$ and the chain rule, show

$$\frac{\partial\mathcal{L}}{\partial\mathbf{w}} = \frac{\mu - \dfrac{\mathbf{Cw}}{\mathbf{w}^T\mathbf{Cw}}(\mathbf{w}^T\mu - R_0)}{\sqrt{\mathbf{w}^T\mathbf{Cw}}} - \lambda\mathbf{u}$$

   and set the Lagrangian to zero to get

$$\mu - \frac{\mathbf{w}^T\mu - R_0}{\mathbf{w}^T\mathbf{Cw}}\mathbf{Cw} = (\lambda\sqrt{\mathbf{w}^T\mathbf{Cw}})\mathbf{u}$$

   (b) Find the vector $\mathbf{v}$ so that when you pre-multiply both sides by $\mathbf{v}^T$, you end up with

$$\lambda = R_0/\sqrt{\mathbf{w}^T\mathbf{Cw}}$$

$$\mu - \frac{\mathbf{w}^T\mu - R_0}{\mathbf{w}^T\mathbf{Cw}}\mathbf{Cw} = R_0\mathbf{u}$$

(c) Find the matrix $\mathbf{A}$ so that when you pre-multiply both sides of the above by $\mathbf{A}$, you end up with

$$\frac{\mathbf{w}^T \boldsymbol{\mu} - R_0}{\mathbf{w}^T \mathbf{C} \mathbf{w}} \mathbf{w} = \mathbf{C}^{-1}(\boldsymbol{\mu} - R_0 \mathbf{u}) \qquad (3.26)$$

(d) Find the vector $\mathbf{v}$ so that when you pre-multiply both sides of Formula 3.26 by $\mathbf{v}^T$, you get an expression for the term $\dfrac{\mathbf{w}^T \boldsymbol{\mu} - R_0}{\mathbf{w}^T \mathbf{C} \mathbf{w}}$ multiplying $\mathbf{w}$, and divide both sides of Formula 3.26 by this expression to establish the result

$$\mathbf{w} = \frac{\mathbf{C}^{-1}(\boldsymbol{\mu} - R_0 \mathbf{u})}{\mathbf{u}^T \mathbf{C}^{-1}(\boldsymbol{\mu} - R_0 \mathbf{u})}$$

10. Let the risk-free rate be 3% and the market return and risk be ($\mu_M = 8\%, \sigma_M = 10\%$). Given an asset with $\beta = 0.8$ and a return standard deviation of 12%, you expect its price to be $110 in one year.
    (a) According to CAPM, what is today's price of the asset?
    (b) What is the correlation between the asset and market returns?
    (c) What fraction of the variance of the asset's return is diversifiable?
11. According to CAPM, μ_X is a linear function of β_X. The graph of μ_X versus β_X in the (β, μ) plane is called the security market line (*SML*).
    (a) What is the coordinate of the risk-free asset in the (β, μ) plane?
    (b) What is the coordinate of the market portfolio in the (β, μ) plane?
    (c) For a portfolio X on the CML with $R_X = wR_0 + (1 - w)R_M$, what is its coordinate in the (β, μ) plane?
    (d) Can the beta of a portfolio be negative? Can it be larger than 1? Explain.
    (e) Show that the beta of a portfolio is the weighted average of the betas of the portfolio's assets, where the weights are the asset allocations of each asset in the portfolio.
    (f) Show that the diversifiable risk, $Var(\epsilon_X)$, of a portfolio X on the CML is zero.
12. For two assets, let their 1-year simple returns, R_1, R_2, be independent and identically distributed as follows

$$P[R_i = r] = p, \quad P[R_i = -r] = 1 - p$$

for some $r > 0$ and $0 < p < 1$. A risk-averse investor with strictly concave utility function, $U'' < 0$, is considering a 1-year investment in a portfolio P of these two assets with allocation w

$$R_P = wR_1 + (1 - w)R_2$$

Starting with unit initial wealth $W_0 = 1$, the wealth after 1 year is

$$W_1 = W_0 \times (1 + R_P) = 1 + wR_1 + (1 - w)R_2$$

Find the optimal allocation to maximize expected utility of future wealth, $E[U(W_1)]$, via the following steps:
(a) Write the explicit expression for $E[U(W_1)]$ in terms of p, r, w

$$E[U(W_1)] = p^2 U(1 + wr + (1 - w)r)$$
$$+ p(1 - p)U(\ldots) + (1 - p)pU(\ldots)$$
$$+ (1 - p)^2 U(1 - wr - (1 - w)r)$$

(b) Using the chain rule, calculate $dE[U(W_1)]/dw$ as a function of $w, r, p, U'(\cdot)$ and set it to zero.
(c) Since $U'' < 0$, $U'(\cdot)$ is a strictly decreasing function, it implies $U'(x_1) = U'(x_2)$ if and only if $x_1 = x_2$. Use this result to find w^* that makes $dE[U(W_1)]/dw$ equal zero.
(d) Since $U''(\cdot) < 0$, show that $E[U(W_1)]$ is *maximized* at w^* by showing $d^2 E[U(W_1)]/dw^2$ evaluated at w^* is ≤ 0.
(e) What are the optimal weights $(w^*, 1 - w^*)$?
13. It is argued that in the commonly used 60/40 portfolio (60% stocks, 40% bonds), since stocks are much riskier than bonds, the stocks' relative contribution to the portfolio risk is too high. A remedy is to construct portfolios with equal risk contribution.

For a portfolio P, the marginal contribution of risk due to ith asset with allocation w_i is defined as $\partial \sigma_P / \partial w_i$ and its *risk contribution* as $w_i \partial \sigma_P / \partial w_i$. A portfolio with equal risk contribution from each asset is called an *equal risk parity (ERP)* portfolio.
(a) Using $\partial \sigma_P^2 / \partial \mathbf{w} = 2\mathbf{Cw}$ and the chain rule, show

$$\frac{\partial \sigma_P}{\partial \mathbf{w}} = \frac{\mathbf{Cw}}{\sigma_P}$$
$$\Rightarrow \quad \sigma_P = \mathbf{w}^T \frac{\partial \sigma_P}{\partial \mathbf{w}}$$

which shows the decomposition of portfolio risk as the weighted average of the marginal risk contribution of each asset.

(b) For a two-asset portfolio P, $R_P = w_1 R_1 + w_2 R_2$, with $R_i \sim (\mu_i, \sigma_i)$ and correlation $\rho = \rho(R_1, R_2)$, solve for the *positive* weights w_1, w_2 of the ERP portfolio.

(c) Using $R_{Bonds} \sim (3\%, 4\%)$, $R_{Stocks} \sim (8\%, 20\%)$, and $\rho = 10\%$, compute the risk and return of the ERP and 60/40 portfolios.

14. Starting with N assets, construct two portfolios P_1, P_2 with corresponding allocations $\{w_{11}, \ldots, w_{1N}\}$, and $\{w_{21}, \ldots, w_{2N}\}$. Create a new portfolio P from P_1, P_2 with corresponding allocations of $w_1, 1 - w_1$ to P_1, P_2. What is the allocation of the ith asset in P?

15. Prove Jensen's inequality for discrete random variables via induction as follows. For a convex function f:

(a) Let a random variable X take on two values $x_1 < x_2$ with corresponding probabilities p_1, p_2. Show that $f(E[X]) \le E[f(X)]$.

(b) Assume that $E[f(X)] \ge f(E[X])$ for any discrete random variable X that takes on N values. Show that $E[f(X)] \ge f(E[X])$ for any discrete random variable Y that takes on $N + 1$ values.

16. Arithmetic versus geometric average.

(a) Let $a_1, a_2 > 0$ and show that

$$\frac{a_1 + a_2}{2} \ge \sqrt{a_1 a_2}$$

(b) Use Jensen's inequality applied to the log function to show that the arithmetic average dominates the geometric average

$$\frac{1}{N} \sum_{i=1}^{N} a_i \ge (a_1 \times \ldots \times a_N)^{1/N}, \quad a_i > 0$$

(c) Let r_n be the periodic return of an asset $r_n = A_n / A_{n-1} - 1$. If the asset value cannot go negative, then $1 + r_n \ge 0$. What can you say about the N period arithmetic average, r_A, defined via

$$1 + r_A = \frac{1}{N} \sum_{i=1}^{N} (1 + r_i)$$

versus the compounded average, r_G, defined via

$$(1 + r_G)^N = (1 + r_1) \times \ldots \times (1 + r_N)$$

of the periodic returns?

PYTHON PROJECTS

1. Install numpy and matplotlib packages.

```
pip install numpy
pip install matplotlib
import math
import numpy as np
import matplotlib.pyplot as plt
```

2. Create the graph of the feasible region of two risky assets and the asymptotes of the hyperbola.

```
def feasible_region2(mu1, mu2, sigma1, sigma2, rho):
    mu_vector = np.empty(0)
    sigma_vector = np.empty(0)
    for w1 in np.linspace(-5,5,500):
        w2 = 1.0- w1
        mu = w1 * mu1 + ....
        sigma = math.sqrt( w1**2 * sigma1**2 + ...)
        mu_vector = np.append(mu_vector, mu)
        sigma_vector = np.append(sigma_vector, sigma)

    # Asymptotes

    mu0 = (mu1 + sigma2**2 + mu2 * simga1**2 - ...) /
      (sigma1**2 + ...)
    slope = ....
    sigma_axis = np.linspace(0, 0.25, 200)
    asymp1 = mu0 + slope * sigma_axis
    asymp2 = mu0 - slope * ....

    # Plot

    plt.plot(sigma_vector, mu_vector, "k")
    plt.plot(sigma_axis, asmpy1, "k-", linewidth = 0.1)
    plt.plot(sigma_axis, asmpy2, "k-", linewidth = 0.1)
```

3. Multiple risky assets. Create the graph of the minimum variance frontier of risk-free and risky assets, the capital market line, and plot random risky portfolios.

```
def plot_MVF(mu, sigma, corr, num_rands):
    # mu and sigma are 1xN vectors of mean and standard dev.
    # vectors for N risky assets, corr is the NxN corr matrix
```

```
# Create the covariance matrix and its inverse
sd = np.diag(sigma)
C = np.matmult(np.matmul(sd,corr),sd)
C_inv = np.linalg.inv(C)

# Find weights and mean, stdev of MVP, u is the unit vector
w_MVP = np.matmul(C_inv,u)/...
mu_MVP = np.matmul(w_MVP, mu)
sigma_MVP = math.sqrt(np.matmul(...))

# Select a risk free rate that is less than mu_MVP
# Find weigths and mean, stdev of Market portfolio
# and slope of CML
R0 = 0.6 * mu_MVP
w_M = np.matmul(C_inv,mu-R0*u) / ...
mu_M = ...
sigma_M = ...
CML_slope = (mu_M - R0) / sigma_M

# Create the 2x2 D_inv and D matrices
D_inv = np.zeros((2,2))
D_inv[0,1] = np.matmul(np.matmul(mu, C_inv), mu)
...
D_inv[1,1] =np.matmul(np.matmul(u, C_inv), u)
D = np.linalg.inv(D_inv)

# Compute the a, b vectors
a=D[0,0] * ...
b=D[1,0] * ...

# Compute MVF
mu_MVF = np.empty(0)
sigma_MVF = np.empty(0)
for x in np.linspace(mu_MVP - 0.10, mu_MVP + 0.10, 100):
    mu_MVF = np.append(mu_MVF, x)
    w = a * x + b
    s_w = math.sqrt(np.matmul(np.matmul(w,C),w))
    sigma_MVF = np.append(sigma_MVF, s_w)

# Create  random risky portfolios
mu_rand = np.empty(0)
sigma_rand = np.empty(0)
for r in np.arange(1,num_rands):
    # pick N(0,1) random variables, make them add up to 1
    w_rand = np.random.randn(np.size(mu))
    w_rand[-1] = 1 - np.sum(w_rand[0:w_rand.size-1])
    mu_rand = np.append(mu_rand, np.matmul(w_rand, mu))
    sigma_rand = np.append(sigma_rand, math.sqrt(...))
```

```
# Plot everything
plt.figure(figsize=(12,9))
plt.xlim([0,5*sigma_MVP])
plt.ylim([mu_MVP-0.10,mu_MVP+0.10])

plt.plot(sigma_MVF,mu_MVF,"k")

s=np.linspace(0, 5* sigma_MVP, 100)
plt.plot(s,R0+CML_slope * s, "k", linewidth=2)

plt.scatter(sigma_rand, mu_rand, c='k', marker=".")
```

4. Sample data for three risky assets, and 10,000 random risky portfolios (see Figure 3.16).

```
# Sample data
mu=np.array([0.05, 0.06, 0.03])
sigma=np.array([0.06, 0.08, 0.10])
corr = np.array([[1,0.95,.90],[0.95,1,.80],[.90,.80,1]])
plot_MVF(mu, sigma, corr, 10000)
```

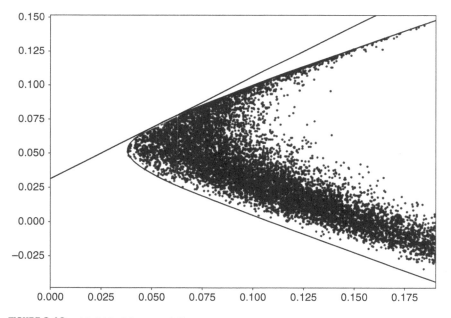

FIGURE 3.16   10,000 risky portfolios.

## CHAPTER 4

Forwards and Futures

Derivatives, or contingent claims, are contracts based on an *underlying* asset or transaction. The characteristics and design of these contracts can range from an agreement to buy or sell an asset in the future at a specific price to complex structured products with complicated payoffs.

4.1 FORWARDS

We shall start with the simplest contingent claim, a *forward contract*. On a given trading day (t), in a *spot* transaction between two counterparties—say exchange of money for an asset (buy/sell)—the transaction will happen at t. In a forward contract, the terms of the transaction are set and agreed to at t, but the transaction is shifted to some later *forward* date, $T > t$. For example, on trade date t, in a spot transaction one can buy 100 shares of a stock for its current (spot) market price, $A(t)$. Alternatively, on same trade date t, one can agree to buy the 100 shares in 3 months $T = t + 3$ months for some price K.

Forward contracts allow one to *lock in* the terms of a future transaction. Examples of the usage of forward contracts include

- An airline company might want to lock its future jet fuel purchase price a few months ahead of a peak travel season.
- An agricultural company might want to lock in the sales price of its products before the harvest and remove the future price uncertainty.
- The corporate treasurer of a company with large anticipated international sales might want to lock in the exchange rate at which future sales proceeds can be repatriated.
- A home buyer might ask their bank for a rate lock in a home mortgage loan in anticipation of successful completion of multiple steps (appraisal, title search, insurance, inspection, scheduling the closing, etc.), which could easily take a few months to complete before the actual purchase.

These are examples of forward contracts used for *hedging*. One could also use forward contracts for *speculation*: if one believes that the stock market is going up in three months, one could enter into a 3-month forward contract allowing the speculator to buy an index, say on the S&P 500, for a specific price.

As both counterparties are agreeing to a *future* transaction, how should they set the terms and how should they value the transaction in face of uncertainty? For example, if the contract is for sale of a stock for K by one counterparty to the other, the selling counterparty would be quite upset and the buyer quite happy if the actual future price turns out to be much higher than K. Similarly, the buyer will be quite upset and the seller happy if the future price turns out to be much lower than K. One's gain is the other's pain.

We now have the five salient moving parts of a forward contract:

1. Underlying transaction, usually a buy/sell of an asset, A.
2. Counterparties (e.g., buyer and seller, lender and borrower).
3. Agreement date t.
4. Forward transaction date $T > t$.
5. Terms of the agreement, usually price, K.

4.1.1 Forward Price

Depending on K, the *value of a forward contract*, $VF_A(t, T, K)$, can be positive or negative. In the previous S&P 500 example, from the buyer's point of view, if K is too large, then the forward contract is an agreement to buy an asset in the future at an inflated price, and, hence, has negative value, $VF_A(t, T, K) < 0$. Similarly, if K is too small, then one is buying an asset in the future on the cheap, and the value of the forward contract is positive, $VF_A(t, T, K)$. The price K, which would make the contract have zero value, is called the *forward price* of the asset, and is denoted by $F_A(t, T)$. We have

$$VF_A(t, T, F_A(t, T)) = 0$$

When the forward contract is done at the forward price, there is no exchange of money at t, just the commitment of the counterparties to honor the terms of the transaction at T. Note when $t = T$, a forward transaction is a spot transaction, and spot prices and forward prices are the same: $A(t) = F_A(t, t) = F_A(T, T) = A(T)$.

The difference between the forward price and the spot price is called the *basis*. Depending on the market, the basis is defined as either $A(t) - F_A(t, T)$ (bond markets) or $F_A(t, T) - A(t)$ (foreign exchange, equity index, crypto).

4.1.2 Cash and Carry

One might think that determining the fair forward price would involve fore-casting the future price of the asset. However, a simple *cash-and-carry* argu-ment shows that we can determine the forward price without resorting to forecasting. The seller in a forward contract has to deliver the asset at T for the contracted price K. The seller can replicate this liability as follows: buy the asset today t for $A(t)$ by taking a loan of size $A(t)$ with maturity T and hold on to the asset until T. At T, deliver the asset, receive K, and repay the loan plus the interest. As long as K equals the loan and the interest, the seller will have no risk, and should charge 0 at t to enter into the for-ward contract.

For notation convenience, we shall use continuous compounding inter-est rate r, and we shall further assume that interest rates are deterministic and constant. In this case, the above cash and carry argument implies that the forward price must equal

$$K = F_A(t, T) = A(t)e^{r(T-t)} \tag{4.1}$$

4.1.3 Interim Cash Flows

The cash-and-carry argument can be generalized for assets with known interim cash flows between the spot date t and the forward date T. Since the holder of the asset will benefit from these known cash flows, their value should be subtracted from the value in Formula 4.1. Specifically, if the underlying asset has known cash flows $CF_1, \ldots, CF_N$ with payments dates $t < T_1 < \ldots < T_N < T$, then the cash flows are future valued from their payment dates T_i to the forward date and their benefit subtracted from Formula 4.1

$$K = F_A(t, T) = A(t)e^{r(T-t)} - \sum_{i=1}^{N} CF_i e^{r(T-T_i)}$$

The forward price then is the t price *plus* the cost of carrying the asset *minus* any income that accrues to the holder of the asset, properly future valued to the forward date. For example, for a dividend-paying stock with known discrete dividends, the future value of the dividends must be subtracted from the carrying cost. Similarly, the future value of any coupon payments must be subtracted from the financing cost of a coupon bond.

4.1.4 Valuation of Forwards

What happens to the value of a forward contract as time goes by? Let us assume that the continuously compounded interest rate r for borrowing and lending is constant and known, and let us consider a forward contract where at inception $t = 0$ and the price K is set to the forward price $K = F_A(0, T)$, making the contract have 0 value at $t = 0$.

While K remains fixed for this contract, as time t goes by, the spot price $A(t)$, and, hence, the forward price $F_A(t, T) = A(t)e^{r(T-t)}$ change, and the value of a forward contract, $VF_A(t, T, K)$, will no longer remain at zero. To value the contract, we observe that at any time $t \leq T$, the original agreement with $K = F_A(0, T)$ can be offset by a zero-cost contract at $F_A(t, T)$. For example, the buyer in the original contract can enter into a new *zero-cost* forward contract as the seller with price set to $F_A(t, T)$. The net transaction at T is to buy the asset for K, and sell it at $F_A(t, T)$ with economic value $F_A(t, T) - K$ at T, which can be PV'ed to t, resulting in

$$VF_A(t, T, K) = e^{-r(T-t)}[F_A(t, T) - K]$$

The profit and loss (PnL) of a forward contract between two dates $t_1 < t_2$ is the change in the value of the contract

$$VF_A(t_2, T, K) - VF_A(t_1, T, K)$$

For a forward contract initiated at $t = 0$ at its initial forward value, $K = F_A(0, T)$, the total PnL from $t = 0$ to $t = T$ is

$$
\begin{aligned}
\text{Total PnL} &= VF_A(T, T, F_A(0, T)) - VF_A(0, T, F_A(0, T)) \\
&= VF_A(T, T, F_A(0, T)) - 0 \\
&= e^{-r(T-T)}[F_A(T, T) - F_A(0, T)] \\
&= A(T) - F_A(0, T)
\end{aligned}
$$

which is simply the economic value of paying the contracted price $K = F_A(0, T)$ instead of the actual price $A(T)$ for the underlying asset. In practice, many forward contracts stipulate *financial settlement*, i.e., payment of $A(T) - K$, rather than *physical settlement*, i.e., actual delivery of the underlying asset for the contracted price K.

4.1.5 Forward Curve

Forward prices are *not* future prices, $F_A(t, T) \neq A(T)$ when $t < T$, except by chance. It is common to graph the $F_A(t, T)$ as a function of the forward date T, see Figure 4.1, and think of this *forward curve* as the market forecast for the future prices of the asset. While the forward curve might be a guide for forecasting, its correct interpretation is the *indifference* curve for delivering an asset spot t versus later dates $T > t$.

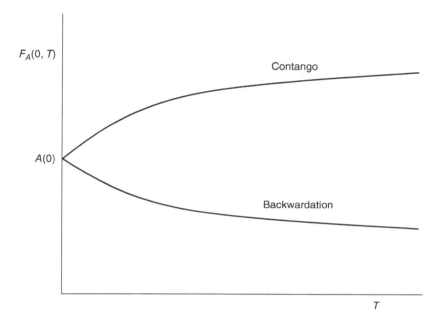

FIGURE 4.1 Contango versus backwardation.

If the slope of the forward curve is positive resulting in increasing forward prices relative to spot, the forwards are called being in *contango*, which is the usual case when one has to incur interest and other carrying costs such as storage for the underlying asset with not enough offsetting interim cash flows.

When the forward curve is inverted, the forwards are said to be in *backwardation*. This is usually the case for bonds where the earned yield is above the financing cost, or for stocks whose dividend yield exceeds their financing cost, resulting in a net benefit to the cash-and-carry holder.

EXAMPLE 1

The price of an asset on April 1st is \$100, and we are interested in a 3-month forward (July 1st) contract to buy the asset. Assume that the continuously compounded interest rate is deterministic and constant, $r = 3.9801\%$. We have $A(0) = 100, r = 3.9801\%, T = 0.25$ and

$$F_A(0, T) = 100e^{3.9801\%/4} = 101$$

(Continued)

Assume the spot price on July 1st ends up 2 points above the March 1st forward value, $A(T) = F_A(0, T) + 2 = 103$. Figure 4.2 and Table 4.1 show a possible evolution of the asset price and the associated forward price and the value of a forward contract initiated on March 1st to the buyer with $K = 101$.

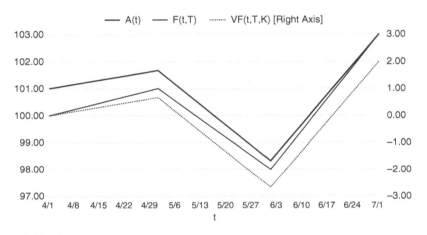

FIGURE 4.2   3-month evolution of an asset's spot and forward prices.

TABLE 4.1   3-month evolution of an asset and its forward price.

t	$A(t)$	T	$T - t$	$F_A(t, T)$	$VF_A(t, T, K)$
April 1st	$100	July 1st	0.25	$101	$0
May 1st	$101	July 1st	2/12	$101.67	$0.67
June 1st	$98	July 1st	1/12	$98.33	−$2.67
July 1st	$103	July 1st	0	$103	$2

4.2   FUTURES CONTRACTS

Exchange-traded *futures contracts* are forward contracts with standardized terms such as size and delivery date. For example, the popular E-mini S&P 500 futures contract traded on the Chicago Mercantile Exchange (CME) is a cash-settled contract based on $50 times the S&P 500 index with a quarterly delivery cycle on the 3rd Friday of each quarter (March, June, September, December).

As opposed to a forward contract, which is a fully customizable privately negotiated bilateral agreement between two counterparties, the futures contract provides liquidity and transparency (price, open interest, volume) with the exchange serving as the central counterparty (CCP): once a trade is done, the exchange becomes the seller to every buyer, and the buyer to every seller, reducing the credit risk to the customers.

4.2.1 Futures versus Forwards

Futures contracts are similar to forward contracts in that there is no exchange of funds when one buys or sells a futures contract: the futures price is the price making the contract have zero value at transaction time. However, as opposed to a forward contract whose delivery price remains fixed and its value can continue to change and its cumulative profit and loss, $A(T) - F_A(0, T)$, only paid at forward date T, the exchange requires daily *mark-to-market*: paying/receiving the day's gains or loss with no carry forward of the daily PnL to the forward date.

The daily mark-to-market changes the delivery price to each day's settlement price making the future contract have zero value again. Daily mark to market then is equivalent to liquidating one's position, and entering into a new zero-cost contract with a revised price. The PnL between two consecutive dates $t_1, t_2 = t_1 + 1$ day can be calculated as

$$\text{Daily PnL} = VF_A(t_2, T, F_A(t_1, T)) - VF_A(t_1, T, F_A(t_1, T))$$
$$= VF_A(t_2, T, F_A(t_1, T)) - 0$$
$$= e^{-r(T-t_2)}[F_A(t_2, T) - F_A(t_1, T)] \tag{4.2}$$

While Formula 4.2 is the *true* economic value of the daily PnL, futures contracts *by design* ignore the discounting and only require payment of

$$[F_A(t_2, T) - F_A(t_1, T)]$$

resulting in the futures price being different from the forward price, with the difference a function of the correlation of the ignored discounting and forward price. Note that the sum of daily cash flows of the futures contract equal the single cash flow of the forward contract

$$\sum_i [F_A(t_{i+1}, T) - F_A(t_i, T)] = F_A(T, T) - F_A(0, T)$$
$$= A(T) - F_A(0, T)$$

the difference being the *timing* of the cash flows.

For short-dated futures, the difference is usually small, and it can also be shown that if interest rates are deterministic, the futures price and forward price are the same: one can replicate one unit of a forward contract via a futures contract by daily adjusting the size of the futures contract to $e^{-r(T-t_2)}$ at t_1, thereby offsetting the ignored discounting [Cox et al., 1981]. In this case, the economic value of cash flows—daily cash flows for the futures contract versus one cash flow at the end for the forward contract—match, and the futures price must equal the forward price to avoid arbitrage. Note that since interest rates are assumed to be deterministic, the adjustment $e^{-r(T-t_2)}$ at t_1 is known for all t_1, t_2, and does not depend on the evolution of underlying $A(t)$ or the forwards, $F_A(t, T)$.

In the more realistic case that interest rates are non-deterministic, and especially for long-dated futures contracts based on forward interest rates, the difference can be significant and needs to be properly accounted for.

4.2.2 Zero-Cost, Leverage

While the initial value of a forward of futures contract with $K = F_A(0, T)$ is zero, its risk is not, and one cannot run an arbitrarily large position (infinite leverage). As spot prices move, the value of an existing contract changes and the gaining counterparty runs the risk of the losing counterparty unable or unwilling to pay, creating a credit risk.

For privately negotiated forward agreements between two counterparties, the counterparties can set a limit to the amount of this exposure and might require a periodic deposit of funds from the losing counterparty to the other.

For futures, the daily mark-to-market process does not allow the adverse PnL and credit risk to grow, however the credit risk *does* remain intraday, and the exchange requires posting of enough funds to withstand a potentially adverse movement during the day. For example, each E-mini S&P 500 contract requires a deposit of $12,000 per contract, protecting against $240 = 12000/50$ point daily movement in the S&P 500 index. The amount of the deposit per contract is known as the *performance bond* and is determined by the exchange and periodically updated in response to the changing volatility of the underlying asset.

4.2.3 Mark-to-Market Loss

While the forward price will converge to the spot price at contract expiry, and a properly constructed forward contract via a cash-and-carry calculation should not experience any ultimate PnL, the underlying asset and the contract can have large mark-to-market losses, requiring a large inflow of cash.

If the losing counterparty cannot provide the requisite cash, the position can be in default and get liquidated. When deciding to enter into a forward contract with an advantageous entry point from a cash-and-carry perspective, the mark-to-market risk and the price volatility need to be carefully analyzed and taken into consideration. For example, in the case shown in Table 4.1, although the position ends up with a positive value of $2 per contract, it might have already been force liquidated one month before when the asset price was $98 and the contract was valued at −$2.67.

4.3 STOCK DIVIDENDS

When calculating forward stock prices, if there are any known dividends between now and the forward date, the future value of these discrete dividends from the dividend dates to the forward date need to be subtracted from the cash-and-carry forward price. Specifically if there are known dividends $D_1, \ldots, D_n$ at $T_1, \ldots, T_n$ where $t < T_1 < \ldots < T_n < T$

$$F_A(t, T) = A(0)e^{r(T-t)} - \sum_i D_i e^{r(T-t_i)}$$

Instead of using the above formula, it is common practice to assume a continuously compounded *dividend yield* of q and that the dividends are reinvested in the asset, so that each unit of stock grows in quantity to e^{qt} over a time period of length t. In this case, the cash-and-carry argument implies that to deliver 1 unit of the stock at the agreed upon price and to avoid arbitrage, the seller must borrow enough to buy $e^{-q(T-t)}$ units of the stock trading at $A(0)$ to get

$$[e^{-q(T-t)}A(0)]e^{r(T-t)} = A(0)e^{(r-q)(T-t)} = F_A(t, T)$$

where the left-hand side is the amount owed at T and the right-hand side is the amount the seller receives.

4.4 FORWARD FOREIGN CURRENCY EXCHANGE RATE

Given two currencies, domestic and foreign, we can compute the forward exchange rate by considering the carrying cost of each currency. For example, let the 3-month simple interest rates be r_d, r_f, and let today's foreign currency exchange (FX) rate be $X(0)$: 1 unit of domestic currency buys $X(0)$ units of foreign currency.

The forward FX rate, $F_X(0,3m)$, that can be locked in today is calculated based on the following no-arbitrage argument known as *covered interest parity*: a unit domestic currency can be invested at r_d for three months to be worth $1 + r_d/4$ and converted at the agreed upon forward exchange rate, $F_X(0,3m)$. Alternatively, it can be converted today to $X(0)$ units of foreign currency and invested at r_f for three months to end up with $X(0)(1 + r_f/4)$ units of foreign currency. Lack of arbitrage requires these future amounts to be the same.

$$1 \times (1 + r_d/4) \times F_X(0,3m) = X(0) \times (1 + r_f/4)$$

$$\Rightarrow \quad F_X(0,3m) = X(0)\frac{1 + r_f/4}{1 + r_d/4} \tag{4.3}$$

In general, the forward exchange rate can be calculated with the formula

$$\frac{1}{D_d(t,T)} \times F_X(t,T) = X(t) \times \frac{1}{DF_f(t,T)}$$

where $DF_{d,f}(t,T)$ is domestic/foreign discount factors at time t for future date T.

EXAMPLE 2

Let the Canada versus U.S. exchange rate be 1.25, that is 1 USD buys 1.25 CAD, and let the 3-month USD and CAD simple interest rates be 3% and 2%, respectively. The 3-month forward CAD/USD exchange rate is

$$1.25 \times \frac{1 + 2\%/4}{1 + 3\%/4} = 1.2469$$

which is 31 pips (units of 0.0001) lower than spot. Note that the forward FX rate is *not* the future spot FX rate: $F_X(0,3m) \neq X(3m)$.

A persistent interest rate differential between two currencies together with a stable FX rate can lead to a profitable *FX carry* trade where one borrows in the currency with the low rate and invests in the currency with the high rate. As long as the FX rates remain steady, one can close out the trade, convert the profits into the low rate currency, and initiate a new trade.

This is akin to selling the high yielding currency forward and betting against the forward, i.e., betting that the future FX rates will be lower than the forward and that the forward will not be realized. The FX carry trade can last for a while, especially if the currencies are *pegged* by the government, but usually ends in tears for traders and the pegging countries when the peg is no longer sustainable leading to drastic devaluation and weakening (drop) of the high-yielding currency.

4.5 FORWARD INTEREST RATES

The cash-and-carry argument allows one to calculate the rate for a forward starting loan. For example, assume that a corporate treasurer expects to receive funds in six months and wants to lock in the 3-month interest rate that can be earned on those funds. Let the 6-month and 9-month simple interest rates be given as r_{6m}, r_{9m}. To calculate the implied simple (add-on) *forward rate, $F = f([6m, 9m])$,* referred to as *3-month rate, 6-months forward,* lack of arbitrage requires

$$(1 + r_{6m}/2) \times (1 + F/4) = (1 + r_{9m} \times 9/12)$$

Therefore

$$F = \left(\frac{(1 + r_{9m} \times 9/12)}{(1 + r_{6m}/2)} - 1 \right) /(1/4)$$

Note that today's locked-in interest rate for a forward deposit is *not* the future 3-month interest rate.

In general, if we have a discount factor curve, $D(T)$, we can calculate simple (add-on) forward rates as

$$f([T_1, T_2]) = \left(\frac{FV(T_2)}{FV(T_1)} - 1 \right) /(T_2 - T_1)$$

$$= \left(\frac{D(T_1)}{D(T_2)} - 1 \right) /(T_2 - T_1)$$

Similarly, the continuously compounded forward interest rates can be calculated as

$$FV(T_2) = FV(T_1)e^{f_c([T_1, T_2])(T_2 - T_1)}$$

$$\Rightarrow \quad f_c([T_1, T_2]) = -\frac{1}{T_2 - T_1} \ln \left(\frac{D(T_2)}{D(T_1)} \right) \tag{4.4}$$

which in the limit as $T_2 \to T_1$ leads to the instantaneous forward interest rates

$$f(T) = -\frac{\partial}{\partial T} \ln D(T) \qquad (4.5)$$

$$D(T) = e^{-\int_0^T f(u)du}$$

EXAMPLE 3

Let the 3-month and 6-month simple interest rates be quoted as 2% p.a. and 2.50% p.a., respectively. The 3-month rate, 3-months forward is the simple forward interest rate over $[3m, 6m]$

$$f([3m, 6m]) = (\frac{1 + 2.5\%/2}{1 + 2\%/4} - 1)/(0.5 - 0.25) = 2.9851\%$$

Note that forward interest rates can be thought of as the rate of growth of money during the forward deposit/loan period. In the example, money grows at the rate of 2% for three months, and at the rate of 2.5% for six months. The growth rate of money between three and six months to make these two rates consistent should be about 3%.

REFERENCES

Black, F. (1976). The pricing of commodity contracts. *Journal of Financial Economics* **31**: 167–179.
Cox, J.C., Ingersoll, J.E., and Ross, S.A. (1981). The relation between forward prices and futures prices. *Journal of Financial Economics* **9**(4): 321–346.

EXERCISES

1. Let $T_0 = 0, T_1, T_2, \ldots$ denote dates where T_n is n days from today (T_0). An asset's price is $1,000 today, $A(T_0) = 1000$, and the continuously compounded interest rate is constant, $r = 4\%$ with fractions of time calculated Act/365: $T_{i+1} - T_i = 1/365$.
(a) What is the 10-day forward price of the asset, $F_A(0, T_{10})$?
(b) You agree today $(T_0 = 0)$ to buy the asset in 10 days for $K = F_A(0, T_{10})$. How much do you need to pay/receive today to enter into this contract?

(c) Assume the asset's price increases by $10 each day for the next 10 days, $A(T_n) = A(0) + 10n$, and compute the missing entries in the following table where CF_{Fut} is the cash flow for one futures contract, CF_{Fwd} is the cash flow for one forward contract, Q_{Fut} is the number of futures contracts needed to replicate one forward contract, and $FV_{Fut} = FV(Q \times CF)$ is the corresponding cash flow of the modified futures contract, future valued to T_{10}.

n	$A(T_n)$	$F_A(T_n, T_{10})$	$VF_A(T_n, T_{10}, K)$	CF_{Fwd}	CF_{Fut}	Q_{Fut}	FV_{Fut}
0	1,000			0	0	0.999014	0
1	1,010		9.8904	0	9.900165	0.999124	9.900165
...							
10	1,100	1,100		98.9035			

(d) Compare the total cash flows of one (unmodified) futures contract versus the forward contract.

(e) Would Q_{Fut} be different if the underlying had instead dropped by $10 each day to settle at $900 at T_{10}?

2. Given a discount curve, $D(T)$, one can extract continuously compounded zero-coupon rates for any date via

$$D(T) = e^{-T \times Z(T)} \Leftrightarrow Z(T) = -\frac{1}{T} \ln D(T)$$

when interest rates are constant, $Z(T) = r$ for a constant r. The graph of $Z(T)$ versus T is known as the *zero-coupon curve*.

(a) Given two dates $0 < T_1 < T_2$, let $f_c([T_1, T_2])$ be the continuously compounded forward interest rate that can be locked in today $(t = 0)$ for the forward deposit period $[T_1, T_2]$. Provide an expression for $f_c([T_1, T_2])$ in terms of $Z(T_1), Z(T_2)$.

(b) Calculate the "1-year forward rate, 2 years forward," $f_c([2,3])$, for three cases:

   i. $Z(2) = 4\%, Z(3) = 5\%$
   ii. $Z(2) = 4\%, Z(3) = 4\%$
   iii. $Z(2) = 4\%, Z(3) = 3\%$

   Explain the resulting forward rates in each case.

3. Using the same no-arbitrage argument to derive Formula 4.3

(a) Provide an expression for the forward exchange rate, $F_X(0, T)$, for any T using simple (add-on) domestic and foreign interest rates, r_d, r_f.

(b) Using the Taylor Series approximation $(1 + x)^\alpha \approx 1 + \alpha x$ and ignoring terms of T^2 and higher, which is justified for small T, say $T < 0.5$, provide an approximate formula for the forward exchange rate in terms of spot exchange rate, $X(0)$, and simple (add-on) interest rate differential $r_f - r_d$.

(c) Derive an expression for $F_X(0, T)$ using continuously compounded r_d, r_f, and use the Taylor Series approximation $e^x \approx 1 + x$ and ignoring terms of T^2 and higher, provide an approximate formula for $F_X(0, T)$ in terms of $X(0)$ and $r_f - r_d$.

4. A 2-year bond with a semiannual coupon rate of 4% per annum is trading at par (100%).

(a) What is its spot semiannual yield?

(b) Assume one can borrow at 3% p.a. simple interest rate for three months (0.25 years) to purchase this bond on a leveraged basis. What is the forward price for a 3-month forward delivery?

(c) Use the 3-month forward price to calculate its *forward yield*, i.e., its semiannual yield on the forward date based on the above forward price. Note that in three months, the bond will be in the middle of the coupon period with 21 months left to maturity. Use Formula 2.5 with $w = 0.5$.

(d) A *positive carry* trade is one where the yield is higher than the financing cost. For bonds, a positive carry trade leads to a positive *yield carry* defined as the difference between the forward yield and the spot yield. Is purchase of this bond a positive carry trade?

(e) Recalculate the forward yield if the 3-month borrowing rate is 5%. Is the yield carry positive?

5. The n-year inflation rate, I_n, is the growth rate in the price of a basket of goods. In the United States, the Consumer Price Index (CPI) serves as the price index and is related to the inflation rate as

$$CPI(n \text{ year}) = CPI(0) \times (1 + I_n)^n$$

An often-used metric for inflation expectation is the 5-year, 5-year forward inflation rate, $I_{5,5}$ backed out of market levels for I_5, I_{10}.

(a) By relating them to the annually compounding growth rate of CPI, provide a formula for $I_{5,5}$ in terms of I_5, I_{10}.

(b) Compute the 5 year-5 year forward inflation rate when $I_5 = 2\%$, $I_{10} = 3\%$.

6. A stock trading at $100 per share can be financed at the continuously compounded interest rate of 5% per annum.

(a) What is the 1-year forward price of the stock if it pays quarterly dividend of $1 per quarter?

(b) What is the 1-year forward price if its dividend yield is 4% per annum?

(c) If the dividend yield is 4% per annum, is the forward curve in back-wardation or contango?

7. Assume that the spot JPY/USD exchange rate is 120 Yen per 1 USD, and that the continuously compounded interest rate in the United States and Japan are 1% and 2%, respectively.
   (a) What is the 3-month forward JPY/USD exchange rate?
   (b) What is the 3-month forward USD/JPY exchange rate?

8. Let the noncompounding (simple) 3-month and 6-month interest rates be 2% and 3%, respectively.
   (a) What is the $[3m, 6m]$ noncompounding forward rate?
   (b) What is the $[3m, 6m]$ continuously compounding forward rate?

9. If the continuously compounded interest rate is a constant r, what is the instantaneous forward interest rate (see Formula 4.5)?

## CHAPTER 5

Risk-Neutral Valuation

While forward contracts separate the agreement date and the forward transaction date, they require both counterparties to abide by the terms of the forward contract, regardless of any profit or loss consideration. For example, the buyer in a forward contract *has* to buy the asset for the previously agreed upon price, even if the market price of the asset is below the contract price. An option contract, on the other hand, provides the right, but not the obligation, to transact an asset at some future date for predetermined terms. While the cash-and-carry argument allowed us to price a variety of forward contracts, the pricing of options requires more advanced techniques, and their pricing falls under the modern pricing paradigm of *risk-neutral valuation*.

5.1 CONTINGENT CLAIMS

Option contracts are examples of contingent claims that allow the owner to transact at the option owner's sole discretion. We will focus on the economic value of the contract at transaction time and assume that an option owner will transact if and only if the economic value of the underlying transaction is positive.

The prime example of an option is a *European-style* exercise option, which has a specified payoff at a specific exercise/expiration date T in the future. For example, a European-style *call* option, $C(T)$, with *strike K* on an asset $A(T)$ gives the owner the right—but not the obligation as opposed to a forward contract—to buy the asset for K at expiry T. At expiration, if the asset price is below the strike K, the option owner can buy the asset in the market for a lower price than K, and, hence, will not exercise the option and let it expire worthless. If the asset price is above K, then the option owner can buy the asset for K and sell it immediately in the market for $A(T)$ for a profit of $A(T) - K$. The economic value of the option payoff is then

$$C(T) = \max(0, A(T) - K)$$

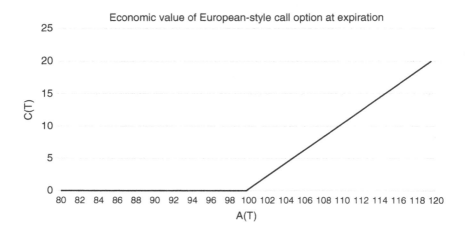

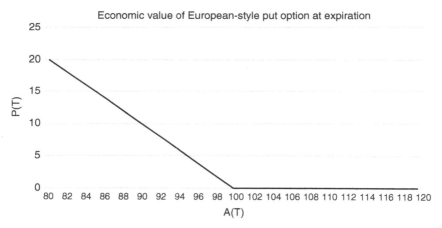

FIGURE 5.1   Economic value of European-style call and put options at expiration with strike $K = 100$.

Similarly, a *put* option with strike K allows the owner to sell the asset at K at expiry and its economic value at expiration is $P(T) = max(0, K - A(T))$ (see Figure 5.1).

While the value of the contingent claim is known at expiration, the goal of *contingent-claim pricing* is to determine its value prior to expiry. We will call the economic value of the option at expiry the option payoff, and focus on evaluating today's value of this future option payoff.

In 1973, the celebrated Black-Scholes-Merton (BSM) formula was derived to price European-style call and put options [Black and Scholes, 1973]. While BSM methodology used advanced mathematical techniques to derive the formula, it was shown later by Cox-Ross-Rubinstein (CRR) [Cox et al., 1979] that the same formula can be obtained and understood using much simpler techniques. This new methodology goes under the name of *risk-neutral valuation* and is the modern framework for contingent claim valuation. Its basic result is that *any contingent claim's value is its expected discounted value of its cash flows in a risk-neutral world* [Harrison and Kreps, 1979; Harrison and Pliska, 1981].

5.2 BINOMIAL MODEL

Given today's $t = 0$ price of an underlying asset $A_0 = A(0)$, consider a European-style contingent claim $C(t)$ with expiration $T > 0$. Assume that the underlying asset has no cash flows over the period $[0, T]$, and let us consider the simplest case where the underlying asset at expiration can only take on two values A_u, A_d, as shown in Figure 5.2. Let C_u and C_d denote the corresponding then-*known* values of the contingent claim in each state at expiration.

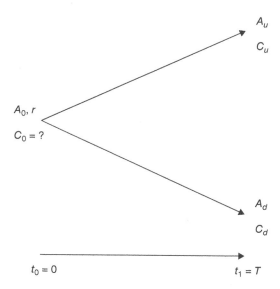

FIGURE 5.2 One-step binomial model.

Our goal is to construct a *replicating* portfolio today so that the portfolio value at expiration (T) replicates the value of the contingent claim. The fair price of the option today, C_0, would be today's value of this replicating portfolio.

Our portfolio consists of taking a position in the asset, Q_0 units of it, with positive Q_0 meaning buy and negative Q_0 meaning short, and entering into a loan or deposit at the prevalent continuously compounded risk-free rate r until T. If $L_0 < 0$, we are borrowing money and if $L_0 > 0$ we are lending. In either case, the value of the loan or deposit at expiration would be $L_0 e^{rT}$ regardless of the state of the world.

At T, if we are in A_u state of the world, we want this portfolio to be worth C_u

$$Q_0 \times A_u + L_0 e^{rT} = C_u$$

Similarly, if we are in A_d state of the world, we want the portfolio to be worth C_d

$$Q_0 \times A_d + L_0 e^{rT} = C_d$$

We have two equations and two unknowns, Q_0, L_0. Solving for these, we get

$$Q_0 = \frac{C_u - C_d}{A_u - A_d}, \tag{5.1}$$

$$L_0 = e^{-rT} \left(C_u - \frac{C_u - C_d}{A_u - A_d} A_u \right) \tag{5.2}$$

Today's value of the contingent claim is

$$
\begin{aligned}
C_0 &= Q_0 \times A_0 + L_0 \\
&= \frac{C_u - C_d}{A_u - A_d} A_0 + e^{-rT} \left(C_u - \frac{C_u - C_d}{A_u - A_d} A_u \right) \\
&= e^{-rT} \left[\frac{A_0 e^{rT} - A_d}{A_u - A_d} C_u + \left(1 - \frac{A_0 e^{rT} - A_d}{A_u - A_d} \right) C_d \right]
\end{aligned}
\tag{5.3}
$$

The seller of the option can charge C_0, borrow or lend L_0 at interest rate of r, and use the proceeds to have Q_0 units of the asset priced at A_0. At expiration, in either state of the world, A_u or A_d, the value of her holdings (Q_0 units of the asset) exactly offsets her liabilities: loan or deposit amount plus interest, $L_0 e^{rT}$, and payment of the economic value of the option (C_u or C_d) to the option owner.

EXAMPLE 1

Let today's price of a stock be $A_0 = \$100$, the 6-month continuously compounded interest rate $r = 4\%$, and assume that 6 months from today, the stock price can go up to $A_u = \$105$ or go down to $A_d = \$95$. For a 6-month expiration ($T = 0.5$) call option with strike $K = \$100$, we have

$$C_u = \max(0, A_u - 100) = 5$$
$$C_d = \max(0, A_d - 100) = 0$$

The replicating portfolio is computed as

$$Q_0 = \frac{5 - 0}{105 - 95} = 50\%$$
$$L_0 = e^{-0.04/2}(5 - (50\%)(105)) = -46.56$$

and today's price of the call option is

$$C_0 = (50\%)(100) + (-46.56) = 3.44$$

The economic value of the call at expiration can replicated as follows: starting with \$3.44 as the option premium, one can borrow \$46.56 for 6 months at 4% to end up with \$50 today, and use this to buy 50% of the stock trading at \$100 per share. At expiration, the loan principal and interest are $\$46.56e^{0.04/2} = \$47.50$. In the A_u state, one owns 50% of a stock trading at \$105 per share, and owes \$47.50 for the loan, resulting in net value of \$5, which is exactly the economic value of the option $C_u = 5$.

$$(50\%)(105) - 47.50 = 5$$

Similarly, in the A_d state, one owns 50% of a stock trading at \$95 and owes \$47.50 for the loan, resulting in the net value of 0, exactly the economic value of the option $C_d = 0$

$$(50\%)(95) - 47.50 = 0$$

In Example 1, we are assuming fractional (50%) shares for exposition. For a more realistic example, assume that the call option allows one to buy 100 shares of the stock at the price $K = \$100$ per share. To replicate this option, one needs to buy 50 shares of the asset today at the price of \$100 per share.

The replication argument allows the buyer and the seller of the option to agree on the arbitrage-free price of the option. The option buyer knows that by spending \$3.44 per option, she can replicate the economic value of the option at expiration, and paying any amount less than \$3.44 will result in a sure profit. In a competitive market with participants in search of sure profits, they will bid up the price of the option to the theoretical value until there are no sure profits left. Similarly, the option seller knows that by receiving \$3.44 per option, she can own and, hence, deliver the economic value of the option at expiration, so any amount higher than that is a sure profit. In a competitive market, other participants will offer the option lower and lower until there are no sure profits left.

5.2.1 Probability-Free Pricing

Note that in the above setup, we did not have to consider the probability of either state happening: as long as A_u, A_d can happen and are the only two possibilities, we are golden!

However, there are restrictions on the assumed future states. A bit of algebra allows us to rewrite the formula for C_0 as an expected value

$$C_0 = e^{-rT}[p_u C_u + (1 - p_u)C_d] \tag{5.4}$$

where

$$p_u = \frac{A_0 e^{rT} - A_d}{A_u - A_d} \tag{5.5}$$

and we recognize the $A_0 e^{rT}$ term as the forward price $F_A(0, T)$ (see Figure 5.3).

5.2.2 No Arbitrage

Lack of arbitrage is equivalent to p_u being a *probability*

$$0 \le p_u \le 1.$$

which is equivalent to the following restriction on assumed states

$$A_d \le F_A(0, T) \le A_u$$

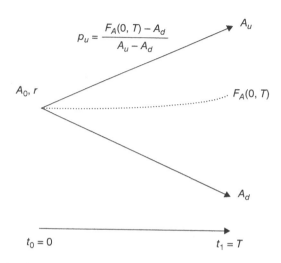

FIGURE 5.3 Lack of arbitrage.

To see this, consider the case $p_u > 1$, which means that the forward is higher than either state in the future: $F_A(0, T) > A_u > A_d$. In this case, we can sell the asset forward for $F_A(0, T)$, and deliver it at T by buying it at either A_u or A_d. Regardless, we have made money with no risk.

Similarly, if $p_u < 0$, then $F_A(0, T) < A_d < A_u$, and we can ensure a risk-less profit by buying the asset forward for $F_A(0, T)$, and selling it higher at expiration for A_u or A_d.

Therefore, if there is no arbitrage in the above simple economy, p_u can be considered as a probability, and today's value of the option is simply the expected discounted value of the option payoff under this probability per Formula 5.4.

5.2.3 Risk-Neutrality

We obtained C_0 by constructing a portfolio that replicates the option payoff regardless of the probability of each state. We then showed that we can get the same value by taking the expected value under a probability p_u. Other than a mathematical identity—p_u is the probability that gets you the correct option value, as long as you know the option value—is there another way of interpreting p_u? The answer is in the affirmative: p_u is the probability that a *risk-neutral* investor would apply to the above setting. Consider two alternatives:

1. Invest A_0 at the risk-free rate r, and receive $A_0 e^{rT}$ at T.
2. Buy an asset at A_0 and either get A_u or A_d at T.

For a risk-neutral investor, these two investments would be equivalent if

$$E[A(T)] = p_u A_u + (1 - p_u)A_d = A_0 e^{rT} \tag{5.6}$$

$$p_u = \frac{A_0 e^{rT} - A_d}{A_u - A_d} \tag{5.7}$$

which is identical to the expression in Formula 5.5. Therefore, rather than setting up a replicating portfolio and computing its value today, we can simply take the expected discounted value of the option payoff using *risk-neutral probabilities*. Notice that Formula 5.6 can be rewritten as

$$A(0) = e^{-rT}[p_u A_u + (1 - p_u)A_d]$$
$$= E[e^{-rT}A(T)] \tag{5.8}$$

relating the risk-neutral probabilities directly to the assumed evolution of the asset. We can also rewrite Formula 5.4 as

$$C(0) = E[e^{-rT}C(T)] \tag{5.9}$$

with both of the above expectations using risk-neutral probabilities.

5.3 FROM ONE TIME-STEP TO TWO

The two-state setup is obviously too simplistic. Assets can take a variety of values at expiration. However, using the above setup as a building block, we can arrive at more complex cases. The idea is to subdivide the time from now until expiration into multiple intervals, and for each state in each interval, generate two new arbitrage-free (bracketing the forward) future states. With enough sub-divisions, we can arrive at a richer and more real-life terminal distribution for the asset.

Consider a two time-step extension of the 1-step binomial model shown in Figure 5.4. For each intermediate node A_u, A_d at t_1, we can use the 1-step binomial model's Formulas, 5.8, and 5.9, to arrive at the risk-neutral probabilities that would provide the same values for C_u, C_d as the replicating portfolios $(Q_u, L_u), (Q_d, L_d)$. Having computed C_u, C_d, we can then use the 1-step binomial model again to compute the risk-neutral probabilities that would provide the same value as the replicating portfolio (Q_0, L_0) to compute C_0.

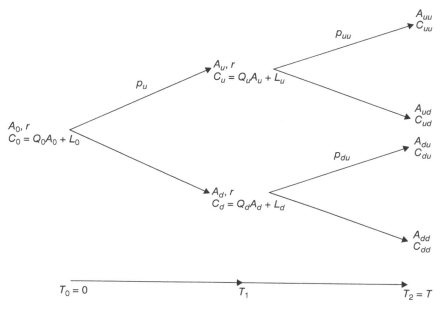

FIGURE 5.4 Two-step binomial model.

EXAMPLE 2

Continuing with Example 1, let us subdivide the time to expiration, $T = 6m$, into two 3-month intervals, and assume the stock's price evolves as shown in Figure 5.5. The replicating portfolio composition and the intermediate values of the option in A_u, A_d are shown. Note that the replicating portfolio initially consists of $Q_0 = 62.44\%$ of the stock funded in part by a 3-month loan of $L_0 = 59.35$. Depending on whether we end up in A_u or A_d in 3 months, the quantity and the loan size need to be dynamically adjusted. In the A_u state, the required replicating portfolio is $(Q_u, L_u) = (87.5\%, -85.76)$: one needs to borrow more to buy more of the stock. In the A_d state, the replicating portfolio is $(Q_d, L_d) = (12.5\%, -11.51)$: one needs to reduce the position in the stock by selling it and using the proceeds to reduce the loan size.

(Continued)

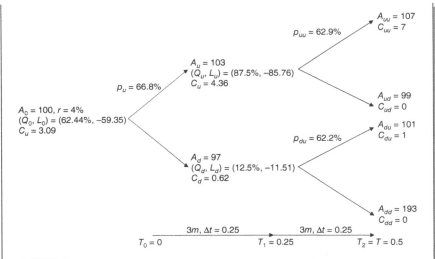

FIGURE 5.5 Two-period evolution of the replicating portfolio for a call option.

5.3.1 Self-Financing, Dynamic Hedging

As we subdivide the time to expiration into finer partitions, for the replication argument to hold, we have to ensure that the original portfolio is sufficient. We can change the composition of the portfolio, but cannot add new assets or unknown cash amounts. Therefore, at each interim state we can change the amount of the asset we hold by securing requisite funds at the prevailing financing rates. As we do this dynamic rebalancing (changing Qs), the value of the portfolio entering into each state must equal the value of the portfolio leaving the state, that is, the replicating portfolio should be *self-financing*.

Consider the *up* state A_u. As we enter it, we hold a portfolio that consists of Q_0 units of the asset now worth A_u, and a loan of size L_0 plus its interest worth $L_0 e^{rt_1}$. Therefore, the value of the portfolio value is

$$C_u = Q_0 A_u + L_0 e^{rt_1}$$

On the other hand, $C_u = Q_u A_u + L_u$, since (Q_u, L_u) is the required portfolio to replicate the option payoffs (C_{uu}, C_{ud}) at the next time step t_2. Therefore, we need to change our holding of the asset from Q_0 to Q_u only by changing the size of our loan from $L_0 e^{rt_1}$ to L_u, that is, the change in the underlying holding should only be financed by changing the loan size

$$(Q_u - Q_0)A_u = -(L_u - L_0 e^{rt_1})$$

ensuring that the portfolio is self-financing. Similarly, in the *down* state A_d, we have

$$(Q_d - Q_0)A_d = -(L_d - L_0 e^{rt_1})$$

EXAMPLE 2 (*Continued*)

Continuing with Example 2, note that the value of the portfolio coming into A_u state is

$$(62.44\%)(103) + (-59.35)e^{0.04/4} = 4.36$$

which is equal to the value of the portfolio after rebalancing

$$(87.5\%)(103) + (-85.76) = 4.36$$

Similarly, in the A_d state, the replicating portfolio is worth 0.62 before and after rebalancing:

$$(62.44\%)(97) + (-59.35)e^{0.04/4} = (12.5\%)(97) + (-11.51) = 0.62$$

5.3.2 Iterated Expectation

For the two time-step model, at node A_u, the risk-neutral probability p_{uu} must satisfy

$$A_u e^{r(T-t_1)} = [p_{uu}A_{uu} + (1 - p_{uu})A_{ud}]$$
$$\Rightarrow \quad A_u = E_{t_1}[e^{-r(T-t_1)}A(T)|A(t_1) = A_u]$$
$$\Rightarrow \quad p_{uu} = \frac{A_u e^{r(T-t_1)} - A_{ud}}{A_{uu} - A_{ud}}$$

Having found p_{uu}, we can compute C_u

$$C_u = e^{-r(T-t_1)}[p_{uu}C_{uu} + (1 - p_{uu})C_{ud}]$$
$$= E_{t_1}[e^{-r(T-t_1)}C(T)|A(t_1) = A_u]$$

Similarly, at node A_d, the risk-neutral probability p_{du} must satisfy

$$A_d = E_{t_1}[e^{-r(T-t_1)}A(T)|A(t_1) = A_d]$$
$$\Rightarrow \quad p_{du} = \frac{A_d e^{r(T-t_1)} - A_{dd}}{A_{du} - A_{dd}}$$

to compute C_d

$$C_d = E_{t_1}[e^{-r(T-t_1)}C(T)|A(t_1) = A_d]$$

The above formulas can be compactly written as conditional expectations conditioned on all information about an underlying asset up to t_1

$$A(t_1) = E_{t_1}[e^{-r(T-t_1)}A(T)|A(t_1)]$$
$$C(t_1) = E_{t_1}[e^{-r(T-t_1)}C(T)|A(t_1)] \tag{5.10}$$

where both $A(t_1), C(t_1)$ are random variables.

Having obtained C_u, C_d, we can compute the risk-neutral probability p_u via

$$A_0 e^{r(t_1-t_0)} = [p_u A_u + (1 - p_u)A_d]$$
$$\Rightarrow \quad p_u = \frac{A_0 e^{r(t_2-t_1)} - A_d}{A_u - A_d}$$

to get

$$A_0 = E_0[e^{-r(t_1-t_0)}A(t_1)]$$
$$= E_0[e^{-r(t_1-t_0)}E_{t_1}[e^{-r(T-t_1)}A(T)|A(t_1)]]$$
$$= E_0[e^{-rT}A(T)] \tag{5.11}$$

and to compute C_0

$$C_0 = E_0[e^{-r(t_1-t_0)}C(t_1)]$$
$$= E_0[e^{-r(t_1-t_0)}E_{t_1}[e^{-r(T-t_1)}C(T)|A(t_1)]]$$
$$= E_0[e^{-rT}C(T)] \tag{5.12}$$

where we have used the law of iterated expectation: For any pair of random variables X, Y

$$E[X] = E[E[X|Y]]$$

where the outer expectation is taken relative to all possible outcomes of Y, see Appendix A.2.3. Combining Formulas 5.11 and 5.12, we have

$$
\begin{aligned}
A_0 &= E_0[e^{-rT}A(T)] \\
C_0 &= E_0[e^{-rT}C(T)]
\end{aligned}
\tag{5.13}
$$

where the top equations in Formulas 5.10 and 5.13 characterize the risk-neutral probabilities solely based on the assumed evolution of the underlying asset, while the bottom equations provide the valuation for *any* contingent claim.

5.4 RELATIVE PRICES

Formulas 5.10 and 5.13 can be generalized to ($0 \leq t \leq T$)

$$
\begin{aligned}
A(t) &= E_t[e^{-r(T-t)}A(T)|A(t)] \\
C(t) &= E_t[e^{-r(T-t)}C(T)|A(t)]
\end{aligned}
\tag{5.14}
$$

which can be written as

$$
\begin{aligned}
\frac{A(t)}{e^{rt}} &= E_t\left[\frac{A(T)}{e^{rT}}\Big|A(t)\right] \\
\frac{C(t)}{e^{rt}} &= E_t\left[\frac{C(T)}{e^{rT}}\Big|A(t)\right]
\end{aligned}
\tag{5.15}
$$

Let $M(t)$ be the value of unit investment at a risk-free rate, that is $M(t)$ equals the value of a money market account started with unit currency and continuously reinvested at the risk-free rate. $M(0) = 1$ and $M(t) = e^{rt}$. We have

$$
\begin{aligned}
\frac{A(t)}{M(t)} &= E_t\left[\frac{A(T)}{M(T)}\Big|A(t)\right] \\
\frac{C(t)}{M(t)} &= E_t\left[\frac{C(T)}{M(T)}\Big|A(t)\right]
\end{aligned}
\tag{5.16}
$$

The first formula in 5.16 pins down the asset evolution in a risk-neutral setting, while the second is the valuation formula for contingent claims. Note that we can always form a contingent claim whose payoff equals the value of the underlying, $C(t) = A(t)$, therefore, the second formula already includes the first one and we can simply write

$$(0 \le t \le T) \quad \frac{C(t)}{M(t)} = E_t \left[\frac{C(T)}{M(T)} \bigg| A(t) \right] \tag{5.17}$$

Probing Formula 5.17 further, it states that under risk-neutral probabilities, *relative* prices for the asset and contingent claims on it relative to the money market account, $X(t) = C(t)/M(t)$, form a *martingale*: at any time $t \ge 0$, the conditional expected *future* (T) value is the t-value

$$(0 \le t \le T) \qquad E_t[X(T)] = X(t)$$

or said differently, the conditional expected change between any two times is zero

$$(0 \le t \le T) \qquad E_t[X(T) - X(t)] = 0$$

A prime example of a martingale is the symmetric random walk (see Figure 5.6). At each time-step, the expected value of the change is zero

$$E[X(t_{n+1}) - X(t_n)] = 1/2 \times (\Delta x) + 1/2 \times (\Delta x)$$

Furthermore, no matter where we are in the future, say point A or B after four time-steps, the expected value of the change from then on is still zero. This is a characterization of one's stake with payoff of ± 1 based on the outcome of a fair $(p = 1/2)$ coin. The expected amount of win or loss at each toss is 0 and the expected value of one's stake after any n tosses is the initial stake. The same holds for the future: if after m tosses we are at some level A, the expected value of the stake after another n tosses is still the same level A.

5.4.1 Risk-Neutral Valuation

We now have all the components of risk-neutral valuation:

1. Posit a random process for the evolution of the underlying assets.
2. Adjust the process to ensure risk-neutrality, equivalent to relative prices being martingales.
3. The price of any contingent claim is the risk-neutral expected discounted price of its cash flows.

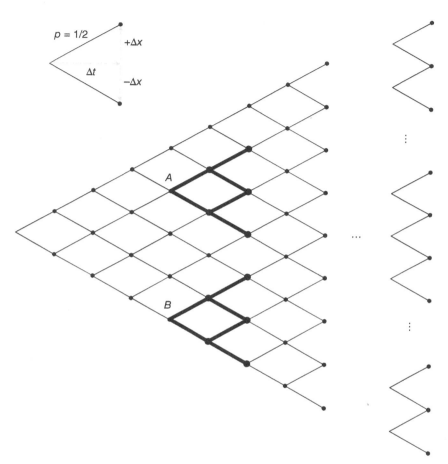

FIGURE 5.6 A symmetric random walk is a martingale.

Note that ensuring risk-neutrality is a condition on expectations that are composed of products of assumed states and their respective probabilities. This allows one to either fix the states and adjust the probabilities, or alternatively one can fix the probabilities and solve for the states. As long as expected relative prices satisfy Formula 5.17, we can use this probability-adjusted or state-adjusted evolution to price contingent claims.

The risk-neutral framework applies to non-constant and random interest rates. In this case, the money market account's value becomes

$$M(t, \omega) = e^{\int_0^t r(u, \omega)du}$$

where ω denotes the randomness of future interest rates. This allows the risk-neutral valuation framework to encompass interest rate derivatives (see Section 7.4.1).

5.4.2 Fundamental Theorems of Asset Pricing

The generalization of the above multi-step model to an arbitrary number of assets and contingent claims based on them gives rise to the following *Fundamental Theorems of Asset Pricing*:

1. For a given multi-asset economy, lack of arbitrage is equivalent to the existence of probability distributions, which would make relative prices martingales. Each such probability distribution is called a risk-neutral measure.
2. A *complete* market is where every contingent claim can be replicated via a self-financing trading strategy. A market is complete if and only if there exists a *unique* risk-neutral measure.

The first condition is a generalization of the result that to preclude arbitrage, forward prices should be bracketed by assumed future states.

The second condition is the generalization of our ability to solve the replication equations, i.e., two equations and two unknowns. Had we assumed that starting from two assets—a bank loan and an asset—the number of future states in the next time-step could be different than two, we would have had a different number of equations than unknowns, leading to generally either no solution or many solutions and, hence, a range of values for the contingent claim. In this case, the market would not be complete and contingent claims would not have a unique replicating portfolio or price.

REFERENCES

Black, F. and Scholes, M. (1973). The pricing of options and corporate liabilities. *Journal of Political Economy* 81: 637–659.

Cox, J.C., Ross, S.A., and Rubinstein, M. (1979). Option pricing: A simplified approach. *Journal of Financial Economics* 7: 229–263.

German, H., El Karoui, N., and Rochet, J.C. (1995). Changes of numeraire, changes of probability measure, and option pricing. *Journal of Applied Probability* 32: 443–458.

Harrison, J.M. and Kreps, D.M. (1979). Martingales and arbitrage in multi-period securities markets. *Journal of Economic Theory* 20: 381–408.

Harrison, J.M. and Pliska, S.R. (1981). Martingales and stochastic integrals in the theory of continuous trading. *Stochastic Processes and Their Applications* 11: 215–260.

EXERCISES

1. Assume the risk-free continuously compounded interest rate is 4% per annum. For an asset with today's price $A(0) = \$100$, you are told that its expected return is 10% per annum and that the asset in one year's time can be ($100, \$120$) with probabilities (50%, 50%). What is the expected value of the asset in one year in a risk-neutral setting?

2. For each step of the risk-neutral binomial model, what is the expected continuously compounded yield

$$\frac{1}{t_{i+1} - t_i} E_{t_i}\left[\ln\left(\frac{A(t_{i+1})}{A(t_i)}\right)\right]$$

3. Let r be the risk-free continuously compounded rate and $A(0)$ today's value of an asset. For a given horizon T, assume the asset can take on two values A_u, A_d with risk-neutral probabilities of $(1/2, 1/2)$. Provide an expression for A_u, A_d if $Var(A(T)) = \sigma^2 T$ for a given volatility parameter σ.

4. In a 1-step binomial model, compute the risk-neutral probabilities for some ΔA when
   (a) $A_{u,d} = A_0 \pm \Delta A$
   (b) $A_{u,d} = F_A(0, T) \pm \Delta A$

5. In the 1-step binomial model shown in Figure 5.2, consider the portfolio consisting of one long position in the contingent claim and short

$$Q_0 = (C_u - C_d)/(A_u - A_d)$$

of the asset, $P = C - Q_0 A$.
   (a) Show that the portfolio has the same value at $t_1 = T$ regardless of the terminal state A_u, A_d, that is $P(t_1) = P_1$ for a constant P_1 and the portfolio is risk-less.
   (b) Using an arbitrage argument, show that today's value of the portfolio should be its discounted future value

$$P_0 = C_0 - Q_0 A_0 = e^{-rT} P_1$$

   and compute C_0.
   (c) Show that the computed value of C_0 above is the same as Formula 5.3.

6. Using the same numerical values as in the 2-period binomial model in Example 2

  (a) Calculate today's price, P_0, of a 6-month European put option with strike $K = \$100$.
  (b) Calculate today's value of a 6-month forward contract with purchase price $K = \$100$.
  (c) Verify that $C_0 - P_0 = VF_A(0, T, K)$.
7. **Replication via Forward Contracts.** In the 1-step binomial model, replicate the option payoff at expiration via Q_0 amount of a forward contract with delivery price of K_0.
  (a) Solve for Q_0, K_0

$$Q_0(A_u - K_0) = C_u, \qquad Q_0(A_d - K_0) = C_d$$

  (b) Compute today's value of the above replicating forward contract: $Q_0 \times VF_A(0, T, K_0)$.
  (c) Is $C_0 = Q_0 \times VF_A(0, T, K_0)$ the same as Formula 5.3?
8. Given two independent random variables X_1, X_2
  (a) Provide an expression for $E[X_1 + X_2|X_1]$.
  (b) Evaluate the above when $E[X_1] = E[X_2] = 0$.
9. Let $X_1, X_2, \ldots$ be independent and identically distributed random variables with $E[X_i] = 0$, and let

$$S_n = \sum_{i=1}^{n} X_i$$

Show that $S_1, S_2, \ldots$ form a martingale

$$E[S_{n+1}|S_1, S_2, \ldots, S_n] = S_n$$

10. For the random walk shown in Figure 5.6
  (a) What is the expected movement during each period?
  (b) What is the standard deviation of the movement during each period?
  (c) What is the expected movement over n time periods

$$E[X(t_{i+n}) - X(t_i)]$$

  (d) What is the standard deviation of the movement over n time periods

$$\sqrt{Var(X(t_{i+n}) - X(t_i))}$$

## CHAPTER 6

Option Pricing

The risk-neutral valuation framework of Chapter 5 provides the mechanism for pricing any contingent claims. The celebrated Black-Scholes-Merton option pricing formula can be derived by following the steps of risk-neutral valuation: positing that an asset's returns follows the limiting form of a random walk, ensuring risk-neutrality by equating forward prices and expected prices, and computing the expected discounted value of the option payoff.

6.1 RANDOM WALK AND BROWNIAN MOTION

A symmetric *random walk* and its continuous time limit, a *Brownian Motion*, are typically used to model the evolution of the underlying asset or more typically the *return* of the underlying asset, leading to lognormal dynamics for the underlying asset.

6.1.1 Random Walk

A symmetric random walk is an example of a discrete time *random process*: a collection of random variables $X(t)$ indexed by time. Different realizations of the random variables as functions of time are called sample paths and denoted by the generic symbol ω, $X(t, \omega)$. We will generally suppress the second argument unless necessary.

The symmetric random walk starts at the origin, and at each time-step Δt increases or decreases by Δx with equal probability $p = 1/2$. At each time-step, the expected change is zero, and, hence, the expected movement during any time period is zero, i.e., a symmetric random walk is a martingale as shown in Figure 5.6. While the expected value of the change is zero, its variance increases over time.

Random walk is a *Markov process*: for any given future time t, the conditional probabilities of the process after t only depend on its position at time t and are impervious to the process history before t. Specifically, a discrete time process, $\{X(t_i)\}_{i\geq 0}$, is Markov if for any function f

$$(0 \leq n < m)\quad E[f(X(t_m))|X(t_0), X(t_1), \ldots, X(t_n)] = E[f(X(t_m))|X(t_n)]$$

6.1.2 Brownian Motion

A *diffusion* is a continuous time Markov random process with continuous sample paths (Karlin and Taylor, 1981). For the random walk, if we let the time interval and step size go to zero, while maintaining $\Delta x = \sigma\sqrt{\Delta t}$ for some diffusion coefficient $\sigma > 0$, we arrive at a diffusion process called *Brownian motion*, $B(t)$, where $B(t)$ has a normal distribution with mean 0 and variance $\sigma^2 t$, $B(t) \sim N(0, \sigma^2 t)$. When $\sigma = 1$, the Brownian motion is called a *standard* Brownian motion.

To see the convergence to a normal distribution, we subdivide any given interval $[0, t]$ into n segments, $\Delta t = t/n$, and let the movement $X_i(1 \leq i \leq n)$ for each segment be $\pm\Delta x$ with probability 1/2, with Δx set to $\Delta x = \sigma\sqrt{\Delta t}$.

We have $E[X_i] = 0, Var(X_i) = (\Delta x)^2 = \sigma^2 t/n$. By the central limit theorem

$$\lim_{n\to\infty} \frac{1}{\sqrt{n}} \sum_{i=1}^{n} \frac{X_i - 0}{\sqrt{\sigma^2 t/n}} \sim N(0, 1)$$

$$\frac{1}{\sigma\sqrt{t}} \sum_{i\geq 1} X_i \sim N(0, 1)$$

$$B(t) = \sum_{i\geq 1} X_i \sim N(0, \sigma^2 t)$$

Brownian motion is a deep mathematical subject and has many properties: (strong) Markov, martingale, independent increments, everywhere continuous, but nowhere differentiable. For our purposes, we will just use the fact that the increments of a Brownian motion $B(t)$ are independent and jointly normal: for any $t_1 < t_2 < t_3$, $B(t_3) - B(t_2)$ is independent of $B(t_2) - B(t_1)$ and

$$B(t_2) - B(t_1) \sim N(0, \sigma^2(t_2 - t_1))$$

The standard Brownian motion starts at 0, $B(0) = 0$, and has no drift, $E[B(t)] = 0$. If

$$B(t) \sim N(B(0) + \mu t, \sigma^2 t)$$

then $B(t)$ is called a Brownian motion started at $B(0)$ with *drift* μ and diffusion coefficient σ. It can be thought of as the limit of a scaled (by σ) standard random walk with a constant drift μ per unit time.

6.1.3 Lognormal Distribution, Geometric Brownian Motion

The process $e^{B(t)}$ is called a geometric Brownian motion (GBM), see Figure 6.2, and is typically used to model the evolution of asset prices. Figures 6.1 and 6.2 show a 20-sample realization of a standard and geometric Brownian motion, which can be thought of as the limiting behavior of a random walk with drift and exponentiated as shown in Figure 6.3.

Since $B(t)$ is normal, the geometric Brownian motion $e^{B(t)}$ is lognormal. A random variable Y is said to have a lognormal distribution, $Y \sim LN(\mu, \sigma^2)$, if its *natural* log is a $N(\mu, \sigma^2)$ random variable, or in other words, $Y \sim e^{N(\mu,\sigma^2)}$. While a normal random variable can take on any value, a $LN(\mu, \sigma^2)$ random variable can only take positive values. Table 6.1 shows some of the properties of normal and lognormal distributions, and Figure 6.4 shows the pdfs of the normal and lognormal random variables with the same mean and variance.

6.2 BLACK-SCHOLES-MERTON CALL FORMULA

The Black-Scholes-Merton (BSM) formula is based on modeling the return of the underlying asset as a Brownian motion. Specifically, we model

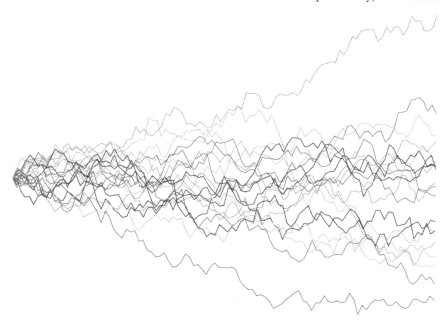

FIGURE 6.1 Standard Brownian motion.

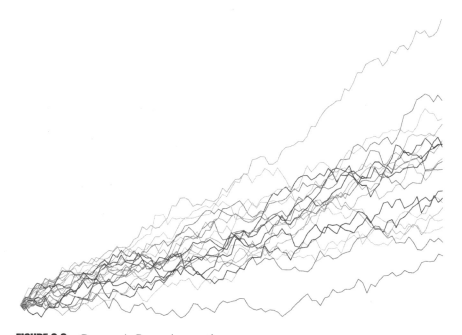

FIGURE 6.2   Geometric Brownian motion.

the underlying asset's evolution by focusing on its relative changes over time via

$$A(t) = A(0)e^{R(t)\times t}$$

where $R(t)$ is the continuously compounded *random* rate of return over $[0, t]$

$$R(t) = \frac{1}{t} \ln \frac{A(t)}{A(0)}$$

Assuming that $R(t) \times t$ follows a Brownian motion with drift μ, its distribution at any time is normal

$$R(t) \times t \sim N(\mu \times t, \sigma^2 \times t)$$

which implies the asset value will be lognormal

$$A(t)/A(0) \sim LN(\mu \times t, \sigma^2 \times t) \tag{6.1}$$

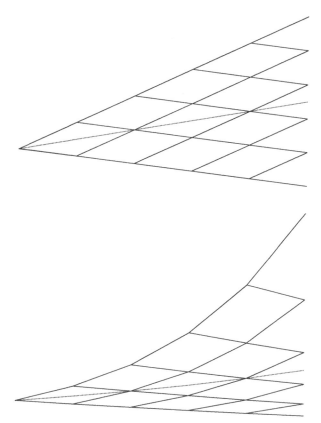

FIGURE 6.3 Random walk with drift (top); exponentiated random walk with drift leading to geometric Brownian motion (bottom).

The parameter σ is known as the percentage, proportional, or log volatility, or just *volatility*. The lognormal distribution is somewhat close to the empirical distributions observed for equities—although the empirical/realized distributions tend to have fatter tails than lognormal—and is commonly used for equity, FX, and commodity options.

Recall that in an arbitrage-free risk-neutral world with constant continuously compounded interest rates, Formula 5.13 must hold

$$A(0) = E[e^{-rt}A(t)]$$

$$\Rightarrow \quad E[A(t)] = A(0)e^{rt} = F_A(0, t) \qquad (6.2)$$

TABLE 6.1 Properties of normal and lognormal random variables.

	Normal $N(\mu, \sigma^2)$	Lognormal $LN(\mu, \sigma^2)$
pdf	$\dfrac{1}{\sqrt{2\pi\sigma^2}}e^{-\frac{(x-\mu)^2}{2\sigma^2}}$	$\dfrac{1}{x\sqrt{2\pi\sigma^2}}e^{-\frac{(\ln(x)-\mu)^2}{2\sigma^2}}$
Mean	μ	$e^{\mu+\sigma^2/2}$
Variance	σ^2	$e^{2\mu+\sigma^2}(e^{\sigma^2}-1)$
Mode	μ	$e^{\mu-\sigma^2}$

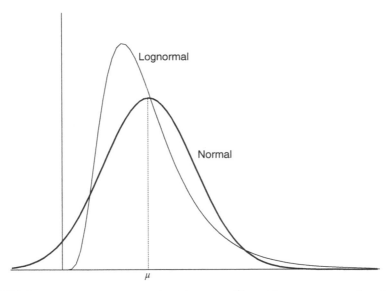

FIGURE 6.4 Normal and lognormal random variables with same mean and variance. Lognormal random variables have fatter tails than normal random variables.

Using the fact that the mean of a $LN(\mu, \sigma)$ random variable is $e^{\mu+\sigma^2/2}$, combining Formulas 6.1 and 6.2, we have

$$E[A(t)] = A(0)e^{rt} = A(0)e^{(\mu+\sigma^2/2)t}$$

which implies

$$\mu = r - \frac{1}{2}\sigma^2$$

in a risk-neutral setting. The distribution of $A(t)$ is then fully specified by the risk-free rate and volatility

$$A(t)/A(0) \sim LN\left(\left(r - \frac{1}{2}\sigma^2\right)t, \sigma^2 t\right)$$

or equivalently

$$A(t) = A(0)e^{N\left(\left(r - \frac{1}{2}\sigma^2\right)t, \sigma^2 t\right)} \tag{6.3}$$

Having adjusted the evolution process for the underlying to ensure risk-neutrality, we can compute the price of any contingent claim as the expected discounted value of its payoff. Specifically, for a call option with expiry T and strike K, we need to compute

$$C(0) = e^{-rT}E[\max(0, C(T) - K)]$$

To compute this, it will be helpful to define $X = A(t)/F_A(0, t)$. From Formula 6.3, we have

$$X = A(t)/F_A(0, t) \sim LN\left(-\frac{1}{2}\sigma^2 t, \sigma^2 t\right)$$

with density function

$$f_X(x) = \frac{1}{x\sqrt{2\pi\sigma^2 t}} e^{-\frac{(\ln(x) + \sigma^2 t/2)^2}{2\sigma^2 t}} \tag{6.4}$$

Using Formula 6.4, we can evaluate today's value of a call option as follows

$$C(0) = e^{-rT}E[\max(0, A(T) - K)]$$
$$= e^{-rT}F_A(0, T)E[\max(0, A(T)/F_A(0, T) - K/F_A(0, T))]$$
$$= e^{-rT}F_A(0, T)\int \max(0, x - K/F_A(0, T))f_X(x)dx$$
$$= e^{-rT}\left[F_A(0, T)\int_{K/F_A} xf_X(x)dx - K\int_{K/F_A} f_X(x)dx\right]$$

The first integral

$$I_1 = \int_{K/F_A} xf_X(x)dx$$

can be evaluated by completing a square (see Exercises) and equals $N(d_1)$ where $N(x)$ is the CDF of a standard normal random variable

$$N(x) = P[N(0,1) \leq x] = \int_{-\infty}^{x} \frac{1}{\sqrt{2\pi}} e^{-u^2/2} du$$

and

$$d_1 = \frac{\ln(F_A(0,T)/K)}{\sigma\sqrt{T}} + \frac{1}{2}\sigma\sqrt{T}$$

The second integral

$$I_2 = \int_{K/F_A} f_X(x)dx$$
$$= P[X > K/F_A]$$
$$= P[A(T) > K] = N(d_2) \qquad (6.5)$$

where $d_2 = d_1 - \sigma\sqrt{T}$. Putting the two pieces together, we have the celebrated BSM formula for a European exercise call option

$$C(0) = e^{-rT}[F_A(0,T)N(d_1) - KN(d_2)]$$
$$d_{1,2} = \frac{\ln(F_A(0,T)/K)}{\sigma\sqrt{T}} \pm \frac{1}{2}\sigma\sqrt{T} \qquad (6.6)$$

EXAMPLE 1

Let today's price of an asset be $A(0) = 100$, with volatility $\sigma = 10\%$, and continuously compounded risk-free interest rate $r = 3.9605\%$. The 6-month forward price is

$$F = F_A(0, 0.5) = 100e^{(3.9605\%)(0.5)} = 102$$

The prices of 6-month expiry ($T = 0.5$) call options with strike set to be *at-the-money* spot (ATM, $K = A(0)$), *at-the-money forward* (ATMF, $K = F$), one point *in-the-money* forward (ITM, $K < F$), and one point *out-of-the-money* forward (OTM, $K > F$) are shown in Table 6.2. For example, for the at-the-money spot $K = A(0)$ case

$$d_{1,2} = \frac{\ln(102/100)}{0.10\sqrt{0.5}} \pm \frac{1}{2}(0.10)\sqrt{0.5}$$

and for the at-the-money forward (ATMF) case

$$d_{1,2} = \frac{\ln(102/102)}{0.10\sqrt{0.5}} \pm \frac{1}{2}(0.10)\sqrt{0.5} = \pm\frac{1}{2}(0.10)\sqrt{0.5}$$

TABLE 6.2 Six-month call option prices with different strikes.

Type	$A(0)$	F	K	d_1	d_2	$N(d_1)$	$N(d_2)$	Call
ATM	100	102	100	0.315405	0.244964	62.38%	59.67%	3.882
ATMF	100	102	102	0.035355	−0.03536	51.41%	48.59%	2.82
ITM	100	102	101	0.174688	0.103977	59.63%	54.14%	3.324
OTM	100	102	103	−0.10262	−0.17333	45.91%	43.12%	2.371

As will be seen later, the term $N(d_1)$ is the amount of the underlying asset needed in a self-financing replicating portfolio, while $N(d_2)$ is the risk-neutral probability that the option finishes in the money, $N(d_2) = P[A(T) > K]$.

6.2.1 Put-Call Parity

To derive the value of a European put for an asset with no interim cash flows until expiration, rather than repeating the above procedure and evaluating the integral based on the put payoff, we appeal to an arbitrage argument by considering the following two portfolios:

1. A T-expiry call option with strike K, and cash holding equal to the present value of K, that is, Ke^{-rT}. At expiration, if $A(T) > K$, the payoff is $A(T) - K + K$, and if $A(T) \leq K$, the payoff is K. The payoff at expiration is, therefore, $\max(A(T), K)$.
2. A T-expiry put option with strike K, and the underlying asset, $A(0)$. At expiration, if $A(T) < K$, the payoff is $(K - A(T)) + A(T) = K$ and if $A(T) \geq K$, the payoff is $A(T)$. The payoff at expiration is, therefore, $\max(A(T), K)$.

Since the two portfolios will have the same value, $\max(A(T), K)$, at expiration T, they must have the same value today, and we must have

$$P(0) + A(0) = C(0) + Ke^{-rT} \qquad (6.7)$$

This identity is called a *put-call parity*, and holds for European-style options on underlying assets with no interim cash flows and is the financial restatement of the identity $x = \max(0, x) - \max(0, -x)$.

Using Formula 6.7, and setting $F = F_A(0, T) = A(0)e^{rT}$, we compute today's value of a European put option

$$P(0) = C(0) - e^{-rT}[K - A(0)e^{rT}]$$

$$= e^{-rT}[FN(d_1) - KN(d_2) + K - F]$$

$$= e^{-rT}[K(1 - N(d_2)) - F(1 - N(d_1))]$$

$$= e^{-rT}[KN(-d_2) - FN(-d_1)]$$

In Formula 6.7, when the strike equals the forward value $K = F_A(0, T) = A(0)e^{rT}$, we have an at-the-money forward (ATMF) option, and ATMF call and put option prices coincide: $P(0) = C(0)$.

Table 6.3 shows analogous put prices as Table 6.2. Note that the definition of the in-the-money and out-of-the-money options for puts are the reverse of those for calls.

6.2.2 Black's Formula: Options on Forwards

The BSM formula was extended in 1976 by Black (Black, 1976) to price options on forwards and the Black76 model and formulas are widely used for exchange-traded futures and options on them. A T_e-expiry call option on a T-delivery forward has payoff

$$\max(0, F_A(T_e, T) - K) = \max(0, A(T_e)e^{r(T-T_e)})$$

TABLE 6.3 Six-month put option prices with different strikes.

Type	$A(0)$	F	K	d_1	d_2	$N(-d_1)$	$N(-d_2)$	Put
ATM	100	102	100	0.315405	0.244964	37.62%	40.33%	1.921
ATMF	100	102	102	0.035355	−0.03536	48.59%	51.41%	2.82
OTM	100	102	101	0.174688	0.103977	43.07%	45.86%	2.344
ITM	100	102	103	−0.10262	−0.17333	54.09%	56.88%	3.351

at expiration, and its today's value can be computed via the BSM formula to provide

$$C(0) = e^{-rT_e} E[\max(0, F_A(T_e, T) - K)]$$

$$d_{1,2} = \frac{\ln(F_A(0, T)/K)}{\sigma\sqrt{T_e}} \pm \frac{1}{2}\sigma\sqrt{T_e} \qquad (6.8)$$

Note that when the option expiration equals the futures expiration, $T_e = T$, Black's formula reduces to the BSM formula.

6.2.3 Call Is All You Need

One can continue along the above lines to derive analytical formulas for European-Style options with more complicated payoffs. In practice, however, the call formula is all one really needs to evaluate European-style options. Indeed, any real-world option payoff is economically equal to—or can be approximated arbitrarily closely—via a portfolio of calls and puts, and since by put-call parity a put can be priced via a forward and a call, calls serve as the salient building blocks of European-style options.

The following is a list of some common European-style payoffs encountered in practice:

1. Straddle: A put and call with same strike K.
2. Strangle: A K_1-put and K_2-call where $K_1 < K_2$.
3. Collar, Risk-Reversal: Being long a collar is being long a K_2-call, and short a K_1-put with $K_1 < K_2$. The strikes K_1, K_2 are usually chosen around the forward rates, so that the package is worth 0, that is, a cost-less collar.
4. Call/Put Spread: Being long a call-spread is being long a K_1-call, and short a K_2-call, with $K_1 < K_2$.
5. Ratio: Most common is a 1 x 2 (1 by 2) ratio. Being long a 1 x 2 call ratio means being long one K_1-call, and short two K_2-calls.
6. Fly: Being long a call-fly is being long one K_1-call, short two K_2-calls, and long one K_3-calls, with $K_1 < K_2 < K_3$, and $K_2 - K_1 = K_3 - K_2$. This is usually used to pin down and express strong views on the underlying asset's value at expiration, leading to *pin risk* for the option-seller.
7. Digitals: Digi-calls, Digi-puts. These can be considered as limits of call or put spreads as the two strikes converge.
8. Knock-in Call: A K_1-strike call with K_2-knock-in ($K_1 < K_2$) has the same payoff of a K_1-call, but only if the underlying is above K_2 at expiration. The payoff is zero if the underlying is below K_2 at expiration. This can easily be priced as a K_2-call plus a K_2-Digi-call with payoff $K_2 - K_1$.

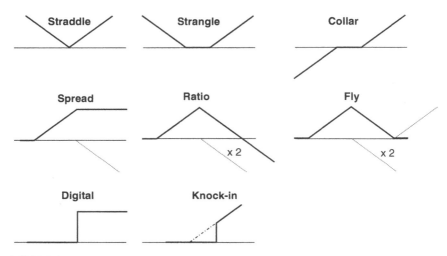

FIGURE 6.5 European-style option payoffs.

These are shown in Figure 6.5. All of the products can be priced via the BSM formula, as the payoffs are simple portfolios of different-strike calls/puts and digi-calls/puts.

6.3 IMPLIED VOLATILITY

Given a volatility parameter σ, the BSM formula provides today's value of a call option. Equivalently, given the market price of a call option, one can use the BSM formula to back out the *implied volatility* and use it to determine whether the call is rich, cheap, or fair.

EXAMPLE 2

With $A(0) = 100, r = 3.9605\%, F_A(0, 0.5) = 102$, let the market price of a $K = 103$ call option be $C(0) = 3$. The implied volatility of this price computed from the BSM call formula using a solver turns out to be $\sigma_{Implied} = 14\%$, which one might find to be too high relative to the standard deviation of the return history of the asset, say 12%. Alternatively, one might take a view that for the next six months, the price volatility will be higher than usual (12%) and, hence, the 14% is a fair value for volatility over this time period.

6.3.1 Skews, Smiles

The implied volatility parameter derived from market prices of options with different strikes and expirations are not constant and are both expiration and strike dependent, $\sigma(T, K)$. Moreover, even these $\sigma(T, K)$'s are not constant and change as underlying's price changes, $\sigma(T, K, A(T))$.

It is usually observed that implied volatility of options for low strikes is higher than the implied volatilities of ATM options, leading to volatility *skew*. Additionally, implied volatilities increase for out of the money options for both low *and* high strikes, leading to volatility *smile*. The skew is mainly due to the observation that market sell-offs are typically large and disruptive. The smile is primarily due to the reluctance of options sellers to sell deep out-of-the-money options (lottery tickets), see Figure 6.6.

Since a call option's payoff is $\max(0, A(T) - K)$, the first derivative with respect to K is a step function and the second derivative is a delta function, resulting in the following convolution integral

$$
\begin{aligned}
\frac{\partial^2 C}{\partial K^2} &= e^{-rT} \int \frac{\partial^2 \max(0, x - K)}{\partial K^2} f_A(x) dx \\
&= e^{-rT} \int \delta(x - K) f_A(x) dx \\
&= e^{-rT} f_A(K)
\end{aligned}
\tag{6.9}
$$

where $f_A(x)$ is the risk-neutral density function of the asset. Given the market prices for options of all strikes, Formula 6.9 can be used to extract the *market-implied* risk-neutral distribution.

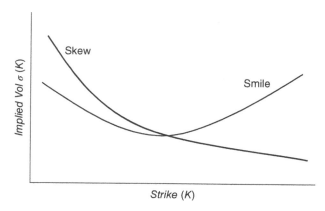

FIGURE 6.6 Skew and smile effect for out-of-the-money options.

6.4   GREEKS

Recall that BSM formulas were obtained as special instances of risk-neutral valuation under normal distributions for proportional returns. We should not forget that risk-neutral valuation gives the same value as a self-financing replicating portfolio. The question arises as to what happened to the replicating portfolio, and how do we replicate an option's payoff? The answer lies in the *Greeks*.

Recall that in our binomial setting, the replicating portfolio was Q_n units of the underlying asset financed via a risk-free loan. The Q_ns had to be (dynamically) changed in response to market movements. In the simple one-step binomial model, we computed

$$Q_0 = \frac{C_u - C_d}{A_u - A_d},$$

which can be interpreted as the sensitivity of the option price with respect to the underlying asset. In the continuous time limit

$$Q \to \frac{\partial C}{\partial A}$$

and the replicating portfolio consists of $\frac{\partial C}{\partial A}$ units of the asset. This is called the *delta* of the option. The delta of a call/put is a number with absolute value between 0 and 1, and expresses how much of the underlying asset is needed to replicate the option payoff.

As we saw in the two-step binomial model, the Delta changes. The rate of change of delta with respect to the underlying is called *gamma* and is defined as $\frac{\partial^2 C}{\partial A^2}$. Gamma measures the curvature of the option payoff, and is also called the *convexity*.

The *intrinsic value* of an option is its value if it could be exercised immediately—for example the difference between spot value and strike if positive and 0 otherwise for a call option—and the *time value* of an option is the difference between the option value and its intrinsic value. Time value converges to 0 as one gets closer to expiration. *Theta*, or time-decay, is defined as the rate of change of option value due to shrinking time to expiration, $\frac{\partial C(t,T)}{\partial t}$. An option holder typically loses time value as one gets closer to expiry.

Finally, the sensitivity of an option with respect to volatility $\frac{\partial C}{\partial \sigma}$ is called *vega*.

TABLE 6.4 BSM formulas and Greeks.

	Call $C(t,T)$	Put $P(t,T)$
Payoff at T	$\max(0, A(T) - K)$	$\max(0, K - A(T))$
Premium	$e^{-r(T-t)}[FN(d_1) - KN(d_2)]$	$e^{-r(T-t)}[KN(-d_2) - FN(-d_1)]$
Delta $\left(\frac{\partial}{\partial A}\right)$	$N(d_1)$	$N(d_1) - 1$
Gamma $\left(\frac{\partial^2}{\partial A^2}\right)$	$\dfrac{N'(d_1)}{A(t)\sigma\sqrt{T-t}}$	$\dfrac{N'(d_1)}{A(t)\sigma\sqrt{T-t}}$
Theta $\left(\frac{\partial}{\partial t}\right)$	$-\dfrac{\sigma A(t)N'(d_1)}{2\sqrt{T-t}} - re^{-r(T-t)}KN(d_2)$	$-\dfrac{\sigma A(t)N'(d_1)}{2\sqrt{T-t}} + re^{-r(T-t)}KN(-d_2)$
Vega $\left(\frac{\partial}{\partial \sigma}\right)$	$A(t)\sqrt{T-t}N'(d_1)$	$A(t)\sqrt{T-t}N'(d_1)$

6.4.1 Greeks Formulas

Table 6.4 summarizes various BSM formulas and their Greeks for $0 \leq t \leq T$

$$F = F_A(t, T) = A(t)e^{r(T-t)}, \qquad d_{1,2} = \frac{\ln(F/K)}{\sigma\sqrt{T-t}} \pm \frac{1}{2}\sigma\sqrt{T-t},$$

$$N(d) = \int_{-\infty}^{d} \frac{1}{\sqrt{2\pi}}e^{-x^2/2}dx, \qquad N'(x) = \frac{1}{\sqrt{2\pi}}e^{-x^2/2}.$$

6.4.2 Gamma versus Theta

As seen in Figures 6.7 and 6.8, the BSM call/put formulas are convex functions of the underlying asset, and their delta changes when the underlying asset moves.

Note than for *any* convex function, we have $f(y) - f(x) \geq f'(x)(y - x)$. This can be proven from the definition of a convex function

$$(0 \leq t \leq 1) \quad f(x + t(y - x)) = f((1 - t)x + ty) \leq (1 - t)f(x) + tf(y)$$

therefore

$$(y - x)\frac{f(x + t(y - x)) - f(x)}{t(y - x)} \leq f(y) - f(x)$$

Taking the limit as $t \to 0$ shows the result.

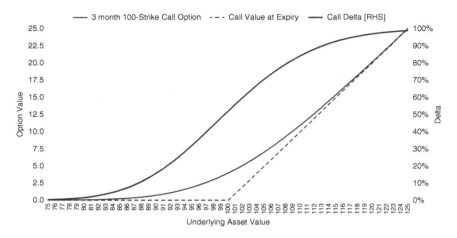

FIGURE 6.7   Call option value and its delta.

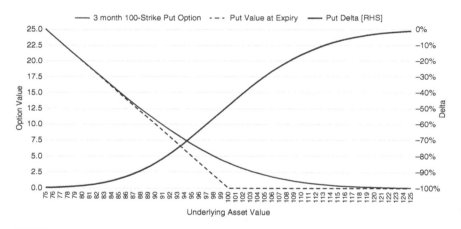

FIGURE 6.8   Put option value and its delta.

Since call/put is convex, the owner of a call/put can delta-hedge—take an offsetting position of size $\partial C/\partial A$ in the underlying—and always incur a positive PnL as the underlying asset moves

$$[C(A_2) - C(A_1)] - \frac{\partial C}{\partial A}(A_1)[A_2 - A_1] \geq 0$$

For example, the owner of a call option who wants to delta-hedge needs to sell $\partial C/\partial A$ of the underlying asset. If the underlying asset goes up in

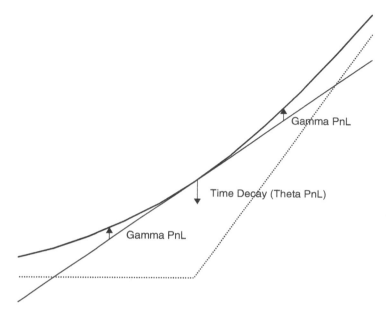

FIGURE 6.9 Convexity PnL versus time decay for a delta-hedged call option.

value, $\partial C/\partial A$ also increases due to convexity of the call formula, and the owner has to sell more at the higher price to remain delta-hedged. Similarly, if the underlying asset goes down in value, $\partial C/\partial A$ also decreases, and the owner needs to be short less, i.e., has to buy back the underlying asset at the lower price to remain delta-hedged. Each buying at a low price and selling at a high price to remain delta-hedged accrues a positive PnL (*gamma PnL*). However, as each day goes by, the option loses time value (*time decay*), see Figure 6.9.

The interplay of gamma and theta PnL is similar for a put. The delta of a put is negative, so the owner of a put option who wants to delta-hedge needs to buy $|\partial C/\partial A|$ of the underlying asset. If the underlying asset goes up in value, $|\partial C/\partial A|$ decreases, and the put owner needs to own less of the underlying asset, i.e., they have to sell at the higher price to remain delta-hedged. Similarly, if the underlying asset goes down in value, $|\partial C/\partial A|$ increases, and the put owner needs to buy more of the underlying asset at the lower price to remain delta-hedged.

For either the call or the put, the owner of the option who wants to remain delta-hedged needs to buy low, sell high, which is the benefit of being long gamma or convexity at the expense of time decay. The situation is the reverse for the seller: the seller of a call or a put who is delta-hedging is short convexity or gamma and has to buy high, sell low, but benefits from time decay.

If the *realized* volatility over the life of the option is higher/lower than the volatility used to price the option, then the option buyer who delta-hedges makes/loses money. Similarly an option seller who delta-hedges will make/lose money if realized volatility is less/more than the volatility used to price the option.

6.4.3 Delta, Gamma versus Time

As one gets closer to expiration, $T - t \to 0$, the delta approaches a step function (see Figure 6.10) and, hence, the gamma of an in-the-money or out-of-the-money call or put converges to 0. However, for at-the-money options, the gamma becomes the derivative of a step function evaluated at the step point. The derivative of a step function is characterized by Dirac's delta function, $\delta(x)$, with $\delta(0) = \infty$. For ATM options, gamma keeps rising as one gets closer to expiration, requiring constant balancing of the delta back and forth from 0% to 100% as the underlying moves around the strike and the option moves in and out of the money. This delta-hedging of high gamma ATM options is a major challenge to option traders who take options into expiration.

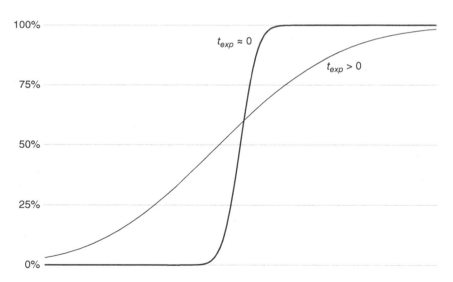

FIGURE 6.10 Delta as a function of time to expiration, $t_{exp} = T - t$.

6.5   DIFFUSIONS, ITO

The BSM call formula was originally derived by first setting up the relationship between the Greeks of a European-style contingent claim as a partial
differential equation (PDE) and then solving the PDE subject to the boundary condition of the claim's payoff at expiration. The BSM PDE requires
the following result, which can be considered as the chain rule applied to
diffusions.

Ito's Lemma. Let $A(t, \omega)$ be a diffusion following

$$dA(t, \omega) = \mu(t, \omega)dt + \sigma(t, \omega)dB(t, \omega) \qquad (6.10)$$

Then any function $f(t, A)$ satisfying some regularity conditions is also a diffusion following

$$df = \frac{\partial f}{\partial t}dt + \frac{\partial f}{\partial A}dA + \frac{1}{2}\frac{\partial^2 f}{\partial A2}(dA)^2$$

with the following multiplication rule for differentials (Oksendal, 1992)

$\times$	dt	$dB(t, \omega)$
dt	0	0
$dB(t, \omega)$	0	dt

Therefore

$$df = \left(\frac{\partial f}{\partial t} + \mu(t, \omega)\frac{\partial f}{\partial A} + \frac{1}{2}\frac{\partial^2 f}{\partial A^2}\sigma^2(t, \omega) \right) dt + \frac{\partial f}{\partial A}\sigma(t, \omega)dB$$

Formula 6.10 is a shorthand for the following integral equations

$$A(t) - A(0) = \int_0^t \mu dt + \int_0^t \sigma dB$$

where

$$\int \mu dt = \lim_n \sum_{i=1}^n \mu(t_i, \omega) \times (t_{i+1} - t_i) \qquad (6.11)$$

and

$$\int \sigma dB = \lim_{n} \sum_{i=1}^{n} \sigma(t_i, \omega)) \times (B(t_{i+1}) - B(t_i)) \qquad (6.12)$$

for partitions $\{t_i\}_{i=1}^{n}$ of $[0, t]$. The limit in Formula 6.11 is the standard point-wise convergence limit, albeit with potentially random terms $\mu(t_i, \omega)$. The second limit in Formula 6.12 is the *Ito integral* and is an L^2 limit: a sequence of random variables X_n is said to converge to X in L^2 sense if the L^2 distance between them vanishes

$$\lim_{n} E[(X_n - X)^2] = 0$$

6.5.1 Black-Scholes-Merton PDE

Given an asset A following a diffusion as above and given a contingent claim with payoff $f(t, A)$ form a delta-hedged portfolio P as follows

$$P = f - \frac{\partial f}{\partial A} A$$

Then

$$
\begin{aligned}
dP &= df - \frac{\partial f}{\partial A} dA \\
&= \left(\frac{\partial f}{\partial t} + \mu(t, \omega) \frac{\partial f}{\partial A} + \frac{1}{2} \frac{\partial^2 f}{\partial A^2} \sigma^2(t, \omega) \right) dt + \frac{\partial f}{\partial A} \sigma(t, \omega) dB(t, \omega) \\
&\quad - \frac{\partial f}{\partial A} (\mu(t, \omega) dt + \sigma(t, \omega) dB(t, \omega)) \\
&= \left(\frac{\partial f}{\partial t} + \frac{1}{2} \frac{\partial^2 f}{\partial A^2} \sigma^2(t, \omega) \right) dt \qquad (6.13)
\end{aligned}
$$

showing the relationship between theta and gamma of a delta-hedged portfolio.

Since there are no random/stochastic terms in Formula 6.13, the portfolio is instantaneously risk-less and, hence, lack of arbitrage implies it must earn the instantaneous risk-free rate r

$$\frac{dP}{P} = rdt$$

or $dP = rPdt$. By equating 6.13 to $rPdt$, we get

$$\left(\frac{\partial f}{\partial t} + \frac{1}{2}\frac{\partial^2 f}{\partial A^2}\sigma^2(t,\omega)\right) dt = r\left(f - \frac{\partial f}{\partial A}A\right) dt$$

$$\Rightarrow \frac{\partial f}{\partial t} + \frac{1}{2}\frac{\partial^2 f}{\partial A^2}\sigma^2(t,\omega) = r\left(f - \frac{\partial f}{\partial A}A\right)$$

$$\Rightarrow \frac{\partial f}{\partial t} + rA\frac{\partial f}{\partial A} + \frac{1}{2}\frac{\partial^2 f}{\partial A^2}\sigma^2(t,\omega) = rf \qquad (6.14)$$

clearly indicating the relationship between theta, delta, and gamma of any contingent claim.

The BSM formula was derived by assuming that the asset follows the following diffusion

$$\frac{dA(t,\omega)}{A(t,\omega)} = \mu \times dt + \sigma \times dB(t,\omega)$$

for constant parameters μ, σ, resulting in lognormal dynamics for the asset (see Exercises). This implies $\sigma(t,\omega) = \sigma \times A(t,\omega)$ in Formula 6.14, leading to the following BSM PDE

$$\frac{\partial f}{\partial t} + rA\frac{\partial f}{\partial A} + \frac{1}{2}\frac{\partial^2 f}{\partial A^2}\sigma^2 A^2 = rf \qquad (6.15)$$

By invoking the boundary condition $f(T, A(T)) = \max(0, A(T) - K)$, and converting Formula 6.15 into the classical *heat equation, u(x, t)*

$$\frac{\partial u}{\partial t} = \frac{\partial^2 u}{\partial x^2}, \qquad x, t \geq 0 \qquad (6.16)$$

via appropriate substitutions, BSM arrived at Formula 6.6 for the price of a call option (Black and Scholes, 1973).

6.5.2 Call Formula and Heat Equation

Deriving the BSM formula for call options by solving the PDE relies on the solution to the classic heat equations. The steps are as follows:

1. The following formula

$$u(x,t) = \frac{1}{2\sqrt{\pi t}} \int_{-\infty}^{\infty} u(x,0)e^{-(s-x)^2/4t}ds \qquad (6.17)$$

is the solution to the initial value problem

$$(-\infty < x < \infty, t > 0) \quad \frac{\partial u}{\partial t} = \frac{\partial^2 u}{\partial x^2}$$

for well-defined functions with initial boundary $u(x, 0)$ (Brown and Churchill, 2012).

2. Let $f(A, t)$ be the t-price of a European call option on an asset $A(t)$ with strike K and expiring at T. The BSM PDE applied to the call option is

$$\frac{\partial f}{\partial t} + \frac{1}{2}\sigma^2 A^2 \frac{\partial^2 f}{\partial A^2} + rA\frac{\partial f}{\partial A} - rf = 0$$

with terminal boundary conditions

$$f(A(T), T) = \max(0, A(T) - K)$$
$$f(A(t), t) \to 0 \text{ as } A(t) \to 0$$
$$f(A(t), t) \to A(t) \text{ as } A(t) \to \infty$$

3. The following transformation turns the backward equation with terminal boundary condition to a forward equation

$$f(A, t) = e^{-r(T-t)}g(B, \tau) \tag{6.18}$$

where

$$c = r - \sigma^2/2$$

$$B = (2c/\sigma^2)\ln(A/K) + c \times (T - t)$$

$$\tau = \frac{2c^2}{\sigma^2} \times (T - t)$$

satisfying

$$\frac{\partial g}{\partial \tau} = \frac{\partial^2 g}{\partial B^2}, \quad \tau \geq 0$$

with *initial* boundary condition

$$g(B, 0) = \begin{cases} 0, & B < 0 \\ K(e^{B\sigma^2/(2c)} - 1) & B \geq 0. \end{cases} \tag{6.19}$$

4. Using the result in Step 1, the solution to Formula 6.19 is

$$g(B, \tau) = \frac{1}{\sqrt{2\pi}} \int_{-B/\sqrt{2\tau}}^{\infty} K(e^{B+z\sqrt{2\tau}\sigma^2/(2c)} - 1)e^{-z^2/2}dz$$

Using the substitutions in Formula 6.18 and some tedious algebra recovers the BSM call Formula 6.6.

The equivalence of the BSM call formula as a solution to the parabolic heat equation and also as an expected value of a functional of a Brownian motion is not a coincidence, and is in fact a consequence of the Feynman-Kac formula.

6.6   CRR BINOMIAL MODEL

The Cox-Ross-Rubinstein (CRR) binomial model as shown in Figure 6.11 is a discrete time version of the asset evolution under the lognormal dynamics posited by BSM and recovers BSM call/put option prices in the limit

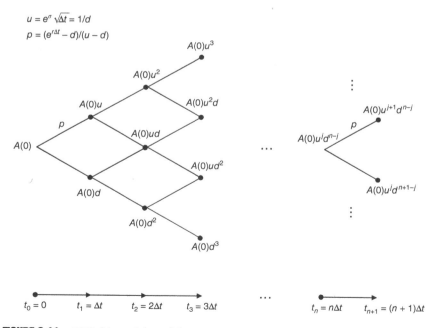

FIGURE 6.11   CRR binomial model.

as the length of time between steps converges to 0. Specifically, the time between now $t = 0$ and a horizon date—typically expiration T—is partitioned as $\{t_0 = 0, t_1, \ldots, t_N = T\}$ where

$$t_{i+1} - t_i = \Delta t = T/N$$

Given a volatility σ, let

$$u = e^{\sigma\sqrt{\Delta t}}, \quad d = 1/u = e^{-\sigma\sqrt{\Delta t}}$$

The process begins at $A(t_0) = A(0)$. At any time t_n, beginning from state $A(t_n, \cdot)$, the underlying moves up to $A(t_n, \cdot) \times u$ or down to $A(t_n, \cdot) \times d$ at t_{n+1} with up movement probability

$$p = \frac{e^{r\Delta t} - d}{u - d} = \frac{e^{r\Delta t} - e^{-\sigma\sqrt{\Delta t}}}{e^{\sigma\sqrt{\Delta t}} - e^{-\sigma\sqrt{\Delta t}}}$$

The above choice for p ensures risk-neutrality

$$E_{t_n}[A(t_{n+1})] = A(t_n)e^{r\Delta t}$$

and for sufficiently small Δt, we can ensure that the lattice is arbitrage-free, $0 \le p \le 1$

$$e^{-\sigma\sqrt{\Delta t}} \le e^{r\Delta t} \le e^{\sigma\sqrt{\Delta t}}$$

For each time t_n, we have

$$(0 \le n \le N)(0 \le j \le n) \quad P[A(t_n) = A(0)u^j d^{n-j}] = \binom{n}{j} p^j (1-p)^{n-j}$$

Today's value of a contingent claim with payoff $C(t_N, A(t_N))$ at expiration $t_N = T$ is

$$C(0) = e^{-rt_N} \sum_{j=0}^{N} P[A(t_N) = A(0)u^j d^{N-j}] C(t_N, A(0)u^j d^{N-j})$$

$$= e^{-rt_N} \sum_{j=0}^{N} \binom{n}{j} p^j (1-p)^{N-j} C(t_N, A(0)u^j d^{N-j})$$

For example, today's value of a call option with strike K is

$$C(0) = e^{-rt_N} \sum_{j=0}^{N} \binom{n}{j} p^j (1-p)^{N-j} \max(0, A(0)u^j d^{N-j} - K)$$

By using a variant of the central limit theorem, CRR (Cox et al., 1979), proved that this formula converges to the BSM call formula as $N \to \infty$ as expected.

6.6.1 CRR Greeks

It is possible to arrive at the interrelationship of the Greeks (delta, gamma, theta) in the CRR model. To this end, we can write

$$p_u C_u(t + \Delta t) + (1 - p_u)C_d(t + \Delta t) - C(t)e^{r\Delta t} = 0 \qquad (6.20)$$

where

$$C_{u,d}(t + \Delta t) = C(t + \Delta t, A(t)e^{\pm \sigma \sqrt{\Delta t}})$$

By expanding $C(t, A(t))$ and any exponential term via the Taylor series, and ignoring any terms with power of Δt higher than 1 ($o(\Delta t)$ terms), we have

$$C(t, A(t))e^{r\Delta t} \approx C(t, A(t)) + C(t, A(t))r\Delta t$$

$$p_{u,d} \approx \frac{1}{2} \pm \frac{r - \sigma^2 \Delta t/2}{2\sigma\sqrt{\Delta t}} \qquad (6.21)$$

$$C_{u,d}(t + \Delta t) \approx C(t, A(t)) + \left[\frac{\partial C}{\partial t} + \frac{1}{2}\frac{\partial^2 C}{\partial A^2}A^2\sigma^2 \right]\Delta t + \frac{\partial C}{\partial A}A\left[\frac{1}{2}\sigma^2 \Delta t \pm \sigma\sqrt{\Delta t} \right]$$

Substituting Formula 6.21 for Formula 6.20 and dividing by Δt recovers the BSM PDE, Formula 6.15

$$\frac{\partial C}{\partial t} + rA\frac{\partial C}{\partial A} + \frac{1}{2}\frac{\partial^2 C}{\partial A^2}\sigma^2 A^2 = rC$$

6.7 AMERICAN-STYLE OPTIONS

Options allowing the owner to exercise their right at *any* time until the option expiration date are called American-style exercise options. A common variant is *Bermudan* options where the option can be exercised at only a set of specific dates, for example, coupon dates for a bond with periodic coupon dates. In either case, the option owner has only one chance to exercise the option and once exercised the option expires.

The additional flexibility of early exercise versus holding on to the option until expiration makes an American option worth more than a European one. Let $C_E(t, T)$ and $C_A(t, T)$ be the t-price of a T-expiry European and American option, respectively, with the same underlying transaction, for example, purchase of an asset for a specific price K. Given that an American option can always be held and not exercised prior to T, $C_A(t, T) \geq C_E(t, T)$ for $t \leq T$.

6.7.1 American Call Options

For American-style *call* options on an underlying asset *with no interim cash flows*, there is no advantage in early exercise as one is just paying the strike K earlier than T and, hence, foregoing, potential positive interest on K from exercise date to T.

Specifically, assume $C_A(t, T, K) > C_E(t, T, K)$. In this case, one can sell the American call and buy a European call and either hold on to the positive difference or invest it at positive interest to T, ending up with $FV(C_A - C_E) \geq C_A - C_E > 0$ at T.

1. If the American call that was sold is not exercised prior to T, at expiry one is short and long call options with identical strikes having net economic value of 0.
2. If the American call that was sold is exercised earlier than T, then the seller can short the asset, deliver it to the American option holder, and receive K, which can be held or invested to earn positive interest until T. At T, one needs to cover the short position by buying the asset:
   (a) If $A(T) > K$, the European call can be exercised to buy the asset for K.
   (b) If $A(T) \leq K$, the European call option expires worthless, but one can purchase the asset and pay at most K.
   In either case, the cost of buying the asset to cover the short is at most K.

In all the above cases, one has generated at least the positive amount $(C_A - C_E) > 0$ with no future economic liability. In the absence of arbitrage, $C_A(t, T, K) = C_E(t, T, K)$ and the American call should not be exercised early.

American puts, however, can have a higher value than European ones. This is due to the fact that the asset price cannot go below zero and one is receiving the strike earlier. If the asset price is sufficiently low, the option is deep in the money, and receiving the strike price early offsets the low probability of the option getting deeper in the money, and, hence, early exercise might be optimal. Therefore, for American options, the put-call parity equality is replaced by an inequality

$$C_A(t, T, K) + PV(K) \leq P_A(t, T, K) + A(t)$$

6.7.2 Backward Induction

For American or Bermudan options where early exercise might be optimal, at each exercise date the owner needs to decide whether to exercise immediately or hold on to the option for a potentially larger payoff. The value of the American option is then the option payoff under the optimal exercise policy. Finding the optimal exercise policy to maximize the option payoff can be solved by *dynamic programming* techniques where the optimal solution to a larger problem includes the optimal solution to a smaller problem and can be obtained recursively. For example, if the shortest path from New York to Los Angeles goes through Chicago, then the Chicago to Los Angeles segment is the shortest path between those two cities. By starting at the destination Los Angeles and recursively calculating and updating the shortest paths between Los Angeles and intermediate cities closer and closer to New York, we can find the shortest path from New York to Los Angeles.

For Bermudan options, we divide the time until expiration into N time-steps, and apply the *backward induction* algorithm. Let $0 = t_0 < t_1 < \ldots < t_N = T$ denote the exercise dates in the time-discretized version of the process for the underlying asset, and express the option payoff as a function of the underlying asset, $C(t) = f(t, A(t))$, for example, $C(t) = \max(0, K - A(t))$ for a put option with strike K.

- At the last exercise date, t_N, set the option value as the immediate exercise (intrinsic) value $C(t_N, A(t_N)) = f(t_N, A(t_N))$.
- Having found the option value at exercise date t_{i+1}, move to the previous exercise date, t_i, and for each state, compute the option value as the higher of *immediate exercise value*, $f(t_i, A(t_i))$, versus *hold value*, $H(t_i)$

$$H(t_i) = E_{t_i}[\text{Discounted } C(t_{i+1})] = e^{-r(t_{i+1} - t_i)} E_{t_i}[C(t_{i+1}, A(t_{i+1}))]$$

resulting in

$$C(t_i, A(t_i)) = \max(f(t_i, A(t_i)), H(t_i))$$

at each state.

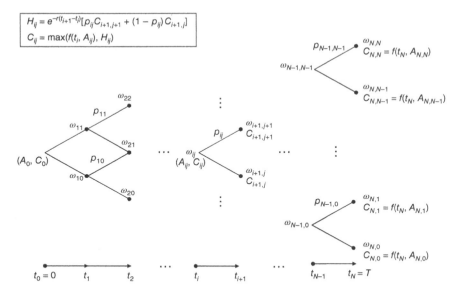

FIGURE 6.12 Backward induction algorithm.

Working backwards, we arrive at today's value of the option, $C(0)$. American options can be priced by computing Bermudan options with N exercise dates and letting $N \to \infty$.

An example of the algorithm in a binomial lattice setting like the CRR model is shown in Figure 6.12, where ω_{ij} denotes jth random state at time t_i, $0 \le i \le N, 0 \le j \le i$, and A_{ij}, C_{ij}, H_{ij} are the corresponding underlying asset, option, and hold value at state ω_{ij}. At expiration date $t_N = T$, for each state $0 \le j \le N$, $C_{N,j} = f(t_N, A_{N,j})$, and at each prior time t_i

$$H_{ij} = e^{-r(t_{i+1}-t_i)}[p_{ij}C_{i+1,j+1} + (1 - p_{ij})C_{i+1,j}]$$
$$C_{ij} = \max(f(t_i, A_{ij}), H_{ij})$$

By going one time-step back at each iteration, we arrive at $C(0)$.

6.8 PATH-DEPENDENT OPTIONS

We have so far considered options whose payoff only depends on the value of the underlying asset at exercise date. Path-dependent options have payoffs that depend on the value of the underlying asset on exercise date *and* previous dates. Examples of path-dependent options are:

1. Lookback options: The option payoff is a function of the maximum or minimum value of the underlying asset up to T.
2. Barrier/Knock-in/Knock-out options: The option payoff is some function of the underlying asset but only if the underlying asset *has* (knock-in) or *has not* (knock-out) crossed some barrier prior to exercise.
3. Asian options: The option payoff depends on the average price of the underlying up to the exercise date.

Note that path-dependent options can be European-style or American-/Bermudan-style exercise type.

Risk-neutral valuation remains the framework for the pricing of path-dependent options; however, the usual discretization of the underlying asset process into a lattice such as CRR breaks down: at each point, we not only need to know where the underlying asset is, but also the path it took to be there. For example, in a binomial model, after n time-steps, there are 2^n distinct paths that need to be considered. This *curse of dimensionality* forces one to resort to other methods to evaluate the risk-neutral pricing integral.

The usual technique to evaluate path-dependent options is the *Monte Carlo simulation* where the multidimensional risk-neutral integral is approximated as the arithmetic average of the option value for a randomly selected number of paths. For example, in an N-path simulation, we generate N random paths for the evolution of the underlying asset and calculate the option payoff under each path, and set the discounted value of the arithmetic average of the option payoff as the simulation price.

The simulation price is a random estimator of the value of the risk-neutral expectation. By the law of large numbers, it can be shown that as N gets larger, the simulation price converges to the value of the risk-neutral expectation at the rate of $1/\sqrt{N}$, but any N-path simulation produces a different estimate and, hence, simulation pricing suffers from run-to-run variability, referred to as *simulation noise*.

To reduce simulation noise, a few *variance reduction* techniques are employed, with *antithetic sampling* an easily implementable one for symmetric random variables driving the process equation for the underlying asset. For example, in simulating the Brownian motion driving the return of an asset in the BSM framework, we discretize the process as a random walk. For an N-path simulation of the random walk, we first generate $N/2$ paths, and add the $N/2$ *mirror images* of each of the first $N/2$ paths: if the random walk has gone up/down at a time-step, its mirror image path has gone down/up. This ensures that arithmetic average of the N sample paths have 0 mean. An example is shown in Figure 6.13.

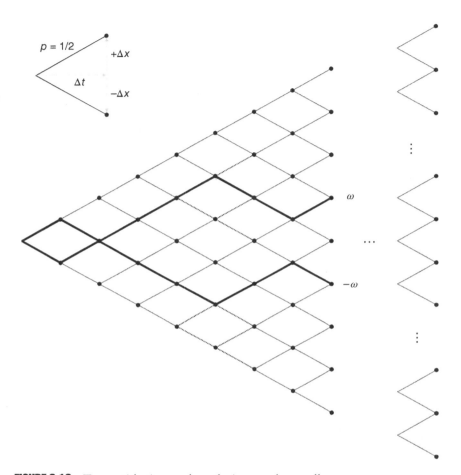

FIGURE 6.13   Two antithetic sample paths in a random walk.

Another variance reduction method is the *control variate* technique. In this method, the simulation price of an option with a known analytical solution is calculated and the difference between the simulation price and the correct price is used as a correction factor for a related option. For example, let P_{BSM} and P_{Sim} be the BSM and simulation prices of a call option, and let C_{Sim} be the simulation price of a contingent claim with similar features as a call option, say a call option with some path-dependent feature. The control-variate adjusted value of the related contingent claim is

$$C_{Sim} - (P_{Sim} - P_{BSM})$$

6.9 EUROPEAN OPTIONS IN PRACTICE

The BSM formula highlights the central role of volatility in option pricing, and prescribes the replicating strategy for a given option. While the BSM formula is commonly used, it has the following shortcomings:

- One of the main assumptions of the formula is the ability to continually delta-hedge as the underlying asset follows a diffusion with continuous sample paths. In practice, asset prices generally grind up in value, but experience sudden drops during periods of market turmoil.

    For example, a seller of a put option who needs to replicate the option needs to sell more and more as an asset price is falling, exacerbating the price drop. One of the culprits of the stock market crash of 1987 where the S&P 500 index dropped from 283 to 225 (a 20.5% drop) on Black Monday, October 19, 1987, was the delta-hedging activity of put sellers who had sold *portfolio insurance* products to institutional investors.

- The empirical distribution of stock price returns exhibit fatter tails than prescribed by a lognormal distribution.

- Skews, Smiles: The implied volatility parameter derived from market prices of options with different strikes and expirations are not constant and are both expiration and strike dependent, $\sigma(T, K)$. Moreover, even these $\sigma(T, K)$'s are not constant and change as underlying asset's price changes, $\sigma(T, K, A(t))$.

    For example, after the stock market crash of 1987, chastened option sellers increased the premiums for puts, leading to higher implied volatilities for low strike options (volatility skew). Moreover, the premiums for out-of-the-money call *and* put options were increased, leading to higher implied volatilities for high *and* low strikes (volatility smile).

While more sophisticated models such as jump-diffusion processes, stochastic volatility, and constant elasticity of variance (CEV) models have been offered to address the shortcomings, these remedies in turn have their own shortcomings and challenges, and the BSM model and formula remains the baseline model and quoting mechanism for options.

REFERENCES

Bertsekas, D.P. (1995). *Dynamic Programming and Optimal Control*. Belmont, MA: Athena Scientific.

Black, F. (1989). How we came up with the option formula. *The Journal of Portfolio Management* **15**(2): 4–8.

Black, F. (1976). The pricing of commodity contracts. *Journal of Financial Economics* **31**: 167–179.

Black, F. and Scholes, M. (1973). The pricing of options and corporate liabilities. *Journal of Political Economy* **81**: 637–659.

Brown, J.W. and Churchill, R.V. (2012). *Fourier Series and Boundary Value Problems*, Eighth Edition. New York: McGraw Hill.

Cox, J.C., Ross, S.A., and Rubinstein, M. (1979). Option pricing: a simplified approach. *Journal of Financial Economics* **7**: 229–263.

Cox, J.C. and Rubinstein, M. (1987). *Options Markets*. Upper Saddle River, NJ: Prentice Hall.

Karlin, S. and Taylor, H.M. (1981). *A Second Course in Stochastic Processes*. Cambridge, MA: Acadmic Press.

Oksendal, B. (1992). *Stochastic Differential Equations*, Third Edition. Berlin: Springer-Verlag.

EXERCISES

1. Let $r = 4\%, A(0) = 100$, and let the price of a 3-month ($T = 0.25$) ATMF ($K = 100e^{0.04/4}$) call option be 2.50.
    (a) Using your favorite solver, calculate the implied volatility of the call option.
    (b) Calculate the delta, gamma, and vega of the call option.
    (c) What is the price of an ATMF straddle (ATMF call + ATMF put)?
    (d) Holding volatility constant, how much does the price of the above straddle with $K = 100e^{0.04/4}$ change if the asset price $A(0)$ changes to 101?
    (e) Holding $A(0) = 100$ constant, how much does the price of the above straddle with $K = 100e^{0.04/4}$ change if volatility increases by 1%, $\sigma_{new} = \sigma_{old} + 0.01$?
    (f) Starting with the equation for the price of an ATMF straddle, use the Taylor series expansion of $N(x)$ at 0 to approximate the price of the ATMF straddle as a linear function of σ.
2. In the CRR model, let $A_0 = 100, r = 4\%, \sigma = 12\%, T = 1$, and $N = 12$.
    (a) Calculate the price of a 1-year call option with $K = 100$.
    (b) Calculate the price of the same option using the BSM call formula.
    (c) Calculate the price of a 1-year European-style option with the following exotic payoff at expiration: $C(T) = \max(0, A^2(T) - 10{,}000)$.
3. Normal and lognormal random variables.
    (a) Let $X \sim N(\mu, \sigma^2)$. Express CDF of X in terms of $N(\cdot)$, the CDF of a standard normal random variable, $N(0, 1)$.
    (b) Let $X \sim N(\mu, \sigma^2)$. Show that $P[|X - \mu| \le k\sigma] = 1 - 2N(-k)$, and evaluate this expression for $k = 1, 2, 3, 4$.

(c) Let $Y \sim LN(\mu, \sigma^2)$. Express CDF of Y in terms of $N(\cdot)$.

(d) Derive the probability density function of a $LN(\mu, \sigma^2)$ random variable

$$d/dy P[LN(\mu, \sigma^2) \le y]$$

(e) For a LN random variable $Y \sim LN(\mu, \sigma^2)$, we have

$$E[Y] = e^{\mu + \frac{1}{2}\sigma^2}, \quad Var(Y) = e^{2\mu + \sigma^2}(e^{\sigma^2} - 1)$$

For given constants α, β^2, solve for the parameters μ, σ^2 so that $E[Y] = \alpha$ and $Var(Y) = \beta^2$.

4. Derive the BSM call formula by completing the following steps. Let $F = F_A(0, T)$ for notation ease. We have

$$C(0)e^{rT} = E[\max(0, A(T) - K)]$$

$$= F \times E\left[\max\left(0, \frac{A(T)}{F} - \frac{K}{F}\right)\right]$$

$$= F \times \int_{-\infty}^{\infty} \max\left(0, x - \frac{K}{F}\right) f_X(x) dx$$

$$= F \times \int_{K/F}^{\infty} \left(x - \frac{K}{F}\right) f_X(x) dx$$

$$= F \times \int_{K/F}^{\infty} x f_X(x) dx - K \times \int_{K/F}^{\infty} f_X(x) dx \qquad (6.22)$$

where $f_X(\cdot)$ is the pdf of $A(T)/F \sim LN\left(-\frac{1}{2}\sigma^2 T, \sigma^2 T\right)$

$$f_X(x) = \frac{1}{x\sqrt{2\pi\sigma^2 T}} e^{-\frac{(\ln x + \sigma^2 T/2)^2}{2\sigma^2 T}}.$$

(a) The integral in the second term of Formula 6.22 is the area under the pdf of a $LN(-\sigma^2 T/2, \sigma^2 T)$ random variable, which is just the probability of falling in that region

$$I_2 = \int_{K/F}^{\infty} f_X(x) dx = P\left[LN\left(-\frac{1}{2}\sigma^2 T, \sigma^2 T\right) \ge K/F\right]$$

Compute I_2 in the above expression.

(b) To compute the first term in Formula 6.22, do a change of variable:

$$z = \frac{\ln x + \sigma^2 T/2}{\sigma\sqrt{T}}$$

hence

$$dx = \sigma\sqrt{T}e^{\sigma\sqrt{T}z - \sigma^2 T/2}dz$$

and complete the following steps

$$I_1 = \int_{K/F}^{\infty} x f_X(x)dx = \int_{K/F}^{\infty} \frac{1}{\sqrt{2\pi\sigma^2 T}}e^{-\frac{(\ln x + \sigma^2 T/2)^2}{2\sigma^2 T}}dx$$

$$= \int_{\frac{\ln K/F}{\sigma\sqrt{T}}+\sigma\sqrt{T}/2}^{\infty} \frac{1}{\sqrt{2\pi}}e^{-\frac{(z - \sigma\sqrt{T})^2}{2}}dz$$

$$= P\left[N(\sigma\sqrt{T}, 1) > \frac{\ln K/F}{\sigma\sqrt{T}} + \frac{1}{2}\sigma\sqrt{T}\right]$$

Compute I_1 in the above expression to arrive at the BSM formula: $C(0) = e^{-rT}(F \times I_1 - K \times I_2)$.
5. As seen in the proof of the BSM call formula, for a call

$$N(d_2) = P[A(T)/F \geq K/F] = P[A(T) > K]$$

that is, $N(d_2)$ is the probability that the call option finishes in the money.
(a) With $A(0) = 100, \sigma = 10\%, T = 1/2, r = 5\%$, compute the value of the following 6-month expiry digital payoff: \$1,000,000 if $A(T) > 100$ and 0 otherwise.
(b) Using same values as above, compute the value of a 6-month expiry *knock-in call* with payoff max$(0, A(T) - 100)$, but only if $A(T) > 110$ (see last payoff in Figure 6.5).
6. The BSM formula for a call is

$$C(0) = e^{-rT}[F_A(0, T)N(d_1) - KN(d_2)]$$
$$= A(0)N(d_1) - Ke^{-rT}N(d_2)$$

One might be tempted to calculate $N(d_1)$ as the delta, i.e.

$$\frac{\partial C}{\partial A} = N(d_1)$$

However, this overlooks the fact that $d_{1,2}$ are functions of $F_A(0, T) = A(0)e^{rT}$. Calculate delta using the chain rule as follows. Let $F = F_A(0, T)$ for notation convenience. Since $C(0)e^{rT} = FN(d_1) - KN(d_2)$ and $F = A(0)e^{rT}$

$$\frac{\partial C}{\partial A} = \frac{\partial [FN(d_1) - KN(d_2)]}{\partial F}$$

$$= N(d_1) + FN'(d_1)\frac{\partial d_1}{\partial F} - KN'(d_2)\frac{\partial d_2}{\partial F}$$

(a) Compute the terms

$$\frac{\partial d_1}{\partial F}, \quad \frac{\partial d_2}{\partial F}$$

(b) Complete the following steps and solve for Z

$$N'(d_{1,2}) = \frac{1}{\sqrt{2\pi}} e^{-\frac{1}{2}d_{1,2}^2}$$

$$\dots$$

$$= \frac{1}{\sqrt{2\pi}} \left(\frac{K}{F}\right)^{\pm 1/2} Z$$

(c) Using the above results, provide an expression for $\partial C/\partial A$.

7. In addition to futures, options on futures contracts are actively traded on exchanges. The expiration date T_e of the option need not coincide with the forward date T of the futures contract, and the payoff of a call option on a futures contract is

$$\max(0, F_A(T_e, T) - K)$$

(a) Derive the commonly used Black's formula for calls on futures by completing the missing steps below

$$C(0) = e^{-rT_e} E[\max(0, F_A(T_e, T) - K)]$$

$$\dots$$

$$= e^{-rT_e} e^{r(T-T_e)} E[\max(0, A(T_e) - Ke^{-r(T-T_e)})]$$

$$\dots$$

$$= e^{-rT_e} [F_A(0, T)N(d1) - KN(d2)]$$

where

$$d_{1,2} = \frac{\ln(F_A(0,T)/K)}{\sigma\sqrt{T_e}} \pm \frac{1}{2}\sigma\sqrt{T_e}$$

Note that when $T = T_e$, Black's formula reduces to the BSM formula.

(b) On Friday, November 13, 2020, the S&P 500 December futures contract, ESZ0, with a final settlement date of December 18, 2020 (third Friday of quarter-end) settled at 3580, and the 3600-strike end-of-month (expiration date November 20, 2020) call option on ESZ0 settled at 43.40. Using $r = 0.75\%$ (75 bps), and Act/365 for fractions of time, find the implied volatility of the call option.

8. **Normal and Lognormal Diffusions.** Let $A(t,\omega)$ be a diffusion, and let μ, σ be two constants.

(a) Let

$$dA(t,\omega) = \mu dt + \sigma dB(t,\omega)$$

and show that

$$A(t,\omega) \sim N(A(0) + \mu t, \sigma^2 t)$$

(b) Let

$$\frac{dA(t,\omega)}{A(t,\omega)} = \mu dt + \sigma dB(t,\omega)$$

and apply Ito's lemma to $f(t, A(t,\omega)) = \ln(A(t,\omega))$ to show that

$$A(t,\omega)/A(0) \sim LN((\mu - \frac{1}{2}\sigma^2)t, \sigma^2 t)$$

[Hint: Think of $\int dB(u,\omega)$ as a limiting sum of successive increments of a Brownian motion resulting in $\int_0^t dB(u,\omega) = B(t,\omega) - B(0) = B(t,\omega) \sim N(0,t)$ since $B(0) = 0$]

9. **Bermudan Options.** Using the CRR model with $A_0 = 100, r = 4\%$, $\sigma = 10\%, T = 0.5, N = 6$.

(a) Using backward induction, calculate the price of a 6-month ($T = 0.5$) Bermudan put option with $K = 100$ and monthly exercise dates.

(b) Calculate the prices of 1m, 2m, ..., 6m European put options with $K = 100$ (six prices).

(c) Is the Bermudan put the sum of the above six European puts? Is it the maximum of the above six European puts?

(d) Using backward induction, calculate the price of a 6-month Bermudan call option with $K = 100$ and monthly exercise dates and compare it to the price of a 6-month European call option with $K = 100$.

10. Confirm that the call Formula 6.6 is a solution to the BSM PDE.

11. Show that the European call and put formulas are convex functions of the underlying asset price.

12. Let the volatility σ be nonconstant and a function of the underlying asset, $\sigma(A(t))$. Use the chain rule to compute the smile-adjusted delta of a call option.

13. A chooser option allows the owner to decide on T_1 whether to own a European-style K-strike call or put option with expiry $T_2 > T_1$.

(a) At T_1, the payoff of the chooser option is

$$\max(C(T_1, T_2, K), P(T_1, T_2, K))$$

Provide a formula for the chooser option by using the put-call parity at T_1.

(b) Show that the chooser option becomes a straddle when $T_1 = T_2$.

(c) Let $A(0) = 100, r = 4\%, \sigma = 12\%$, and price a 6-month final expiry $(T_2 = 0.5)$ ATMF $(K = F_A(0, 0.5))$ chooser option where the option holder chooses the option type in three months $(T_1 = 0.25)$.

PYTHON PROJECTS

1. Install numpy, scipy, and matplotlib packages.

```
pip install numpy
pip install scipy
pip install matplotlib
import math
import scipy.stats
import numpy as np
import matplotlib.pyplot as plt
```

2. BSM formulas.

```
def BSM(init_value, r, texp, sigma, K, call_put):
    df = math.exp(-r*texp)
    F = init_value * math.exp(r*texp)
    st = sigma * math.sqrt(texp)
    d1 = math.log(F/K) / st + .5 * st
    # calculate d2
    call = df * ( F * scipy.stats.norm.cdf(d1,0,1) - K * ...
```

```
if call_put == 'call':
res = call
elif call_put == 'put':
res = call + K * df - init_value
else
res = 0.0
return res
```

3. CRR model for calls, puts.

```
def CRR_model(init_value, r, texp, num_steps, sigma, K, call_put):
    dt = exp_time / num_steps
    u = math.exp(sigma * math.sqrt(dt))
    # caclulate d, p, df (discount factor)
    ...
    rng = np.arange(0,num_steps+1)
    final_value = init_value * (u**rng) * (d**np.flip(rng))
    bin_pmf = scipy.stats.binom.pmf(rng)
    if call_put == 'call':
    option_payoff = np.maximum(0,final_value - K)
    ...

    option_value = df * np.sum(option_payoff * pmf)
    return option_value
```

4. Investigate convergence of CRR model to the BSM formulas (see Figure 6.14).

```
def CRR_convergence(init_value, r, texp, sigma, K, call_put,
    max_steps):
    bsm = np.full(max_steps, BSM(...))
    crr = np.empty(0)
    for n in np.arange(1,max_steps):
    crr.append(crr, CRR_model(...))

    plt.plot(crr,'k')
    plt.plot(bsm,'k-',linewidth=0.5)

    # Test convergence
    CRR_convergence(100, 0.04, 1, 0.12, 100, 'call', 100)
```

5. Create a CRR binomial tree and implement the backward induction algorithm.

```
def CRR_tree(init_value, r, texp, num_steps, sigma):
    # calculate u, d
    tree = np.zeros(num_steps + 1, num_steps + 1)
    tree[0,0] = init_value
```

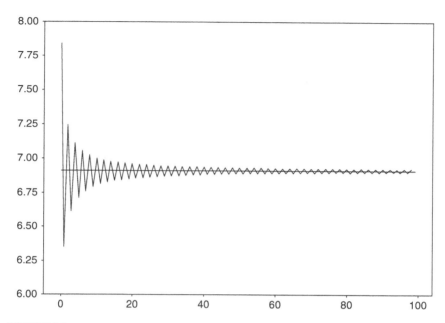

FIGURE 6.14 Convergence of CRR model to BSM Formula.

```
for t in np.arange(0, num_steps):
    for s in np.arange(0, t+1):
        tree[t+1,s] = tree[t,s] * u
        tree[t+1,s+1] = tree[t,s] * d

return tree
```

6. Implement backward induction algorithm.

```
def CRR_BI(init_value, r, texp, num_steps, sigma, K, call_put):
    # calculate dt, u, d, p
    df = math.exp(-r*dt)   # 1-period discount factor
    tree = CRR_tree(...)
    # Immediate exercise values
    exer_value = np.zeros(np.shape(tree))
    if call_put == 'call':
        exer_value = np.maximum(tree-K)
        ....

    option_value = exer_value
    for t in np.flip(np.arange(0,num_steps)):
```

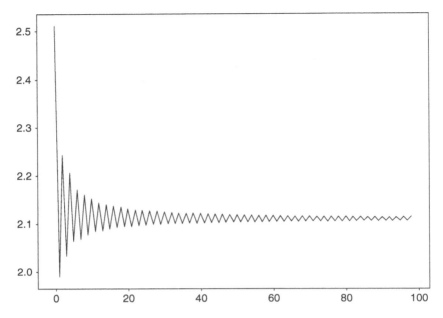

FIGURE 6.15   Convergence of backward induction model to the American option.

```
for s in np.arange(0,t+1):
    hold_value = df * (p * option_value[t+1,s] + ...)
    option_value[t,s] = max(exer_value[t,s], hold_value)

return option_value[0,0]
```

7. Show convergence of Bermudan options to American options (see Figure 6.15).

```
def CRR_American(init_value, r, texp, sigma, K, call_put,
    max_steps):
    american = np.empty(0)
    for n in np.arange(1,max_steps):
        american = np.append(american, CRR_BI(...))

    # plot it

# Test convergence
CRR_American(100, 0.04, 0.5, 0.12, 100, 'put', 100)
```

8. Monte Carlo simulation of Brownian motion: A common numerical method to generate sample paths of a Brownian motion with drift μ and diffusion coefficient σ is to use the *Euler approximation*, $B(0) = 0$

$$B(t + \Delta t) = B(t) + \mu \Delta t + \sigma \sqrt{\Delta t} N(0, 1)$$

where $N(0, 1)$ is a sample draw from a standard normal distribution. Generate num_paths paths of a Brownian motion for n time-steps

$$B = [B(0) = 0, B(dt), B(2dt), \ldots, B(ndt)]$$

```
def generate_normals(num_paths, num_steps):
    std_normals = np.random.normal(0,1,(num_paths,num_steps))
    return std_normals

def generate_increments(texp, num_steps, mu, sigma, num_paths):
    # Generate standard normals
    ...
    dt = texp / num_steps
    return mu * dt + sigma * math.sqrt(dt) * std_normals

def generate_BM(texp, num_steps, mu, sigma, num_paths):
    # X is the num_paths x num_steps increment matrix
    ...
    BM = np.zeros(numPaths, num_steps + 1)
    for t in range(0, num_steps):
        BM[:,t+1] = BM[:,t] + X[:,t]

    return BM
```

9. Generate prices for an asset starting with $A(0)$ following a geometric Brownian motion in a risk-neutral setting

```
def generate_asset(init_value, r, texp, num_steps, sigma,
        num_paths):
    mu = r - 1/2 * math.pow(sigma, 2)
    # Generate BM
    ...
    return init_value * np.exp(BM)
```

10. Graph 500 paths of a 1-year monthly simulation of an asset with $A(0) = 100$ that follows a geometric Brownian motion in a risk-neutral setting with $r = 4\%, \sigma = 10\%$

```
# Generate asset prices
...
for i in range(0, num_paths):
    plt.plot(asset_prices[i])

plt.show()
```

11. Using the same parameters as above, price a 1-year 105-strike European call option with 1000 simulated paths, and repeat the pricing for 10 simulation runs. Report the statistics of the simulation runs: average, standard deviation, minimum, maximum.

```
def price:call(init_value, r, texp, num_steps, sigma, K,
       num_paths):
    # Generate asset prices
    ...
    asset_final_value = asset.prices[:,num_steps]
    option_payoff = np.maximum(0, asset_final_value - K)
    df = math.exp(-r * texp)
    option_value = df * np.average(option_payoff)

    return option_value

def run_simulations(num_sims):
    sims = np.zeros(num_sims)
    for i in range(0, num_sims):
    sims[i] = price:call(100, 0.04, 1, 12, 0.10, 105, 1000)

    print(np.average(sims), np.std(sims), np.amin(sims), ...)
```

12. Repeat the above step using antithetic variance reduction: generate num_paths/2 standard normals and set the next num_paths/2 as their negative to generate the simulated BM. To see if there is a reduction in variance, fix the seed of the random number generator, say np.random.seed(2021), and compare the standard deviation of the 10 simulation runs with and without antithetic variables.

```
def generate_increments(texp, num_steps, mu, sigma, num_paths):
    # Generate num_paths/2 (num_paths is even) standard normals
    normals = generate_normals(num_paths//2, num_steps)
    # Generate the other half as the negative, and stack them
    std_normals = np.vstack((normals, -normals))
    # Continue as before
    return mu * dt + sigma * math.sqrt(dt) * std_normals
```

13. Add a 120 knock-out feature: the option expires worthless if at any month before expiration the underlying asset's value exceeds 120. Does this feature reduce the cost of the call option?

```
def KO_call(init_value, r, texp, num_steps, sigma, K, KO,
       num_paths):
    # Generate asset prices
```

TABLE 6.5 10 x 1000-path simulation runs, random.seed(2021).

	Average Price	StdDev	Antithetic Average	Antithetic StdDev
Call (BSM)	$3.579			
Call (Simulation)	$3.591	$0.241	$3.543	$0.115
KO Call (Simulation)	$1.952	$0.125	$1.933	$0.080
KO Call (Control Variate)	$1.941		$1.969	

```
# Keep track of whether the option is not knocked out
    (alive)
alive = np.ones(num_paths)
for t in range(1,num_steps+1):
alive = alive * (asset_prices:,t] <= KO)
final_value = asset.prices[:,num_steps]
option_payoff = alive * np.maximum(0, final_value - K)
# proceed as before
```

## CHAPTER 7

Interest Rate Derivatives

In the previous chapters, we made the simplifying assumption that interest rates are deterministic and can be represented by a single constant quantity, r. In reality, interest rates for different maturities (terms) are different, giving rise to the *term structure* of interest rates. For example, a 3-month deposit earns a different interest rate than a 6-month deposit, with the 6-month interest rate typically higher.

7.1   TERM STRUCTURE OF INTEREST RATES

There are a variety of equivalent ways to represent the term structure, among them the discount factor curve, the zero curve, and the forward rate curve (see Figure 7.1). Starting with the market prices of actively traded instruments, we can use the bootstrap method introduced in Section 2.7 to extract the discount factor curve.

7.1.1   Zero Curve

Once we have extracted the discount factor curve, $D(T), T \geq 0$, we can price any fixed income instrument and extract any spot or forward rates. For example, we can compute the zero-coupon curve, which is the yield of zero-coupon bonds versus their maturity. We can express the yields using any quote convention, for example, with semiannual compounding, we have

$$(0 \leq T) \quad \frac{1}{(1 + y(T)/2)^{2T}} = D(T)$$

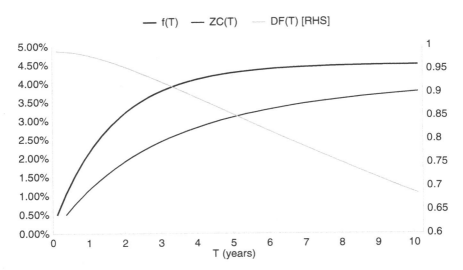

FIGURE 7.1   Forward-rate, zero-coupon, and discount-factor curves.

while continuous compounding gives

$$(0 \leq T) \quad e^{-Ty(T)} = D(T)$$

$$(0 < T) \quad y(T) = -\frac{1}{T} \ln D(T)$$

Note that the discount factor curve and the zero-coupon curve are interchangeable: if we know $D(T)$ for all T, we have $y(T)$ for all T, and vice versa.

7.1.2   Forward Rate Curve

A more common way to represent the discount curve is via simple (add-on) forward rates. Recall from Section 4.5 that the simple forward rate, $f([T_1, T_2])$, that can be locked today for a forward deposit period, $[T_1, T_2]$, and can be derived via the following arbitrage argument

$$FV(T_1) \times [1 + f([T_1, T_2]) \times (T_2 - T_1)] = FV(T_2)$$

leading to

$$(0 \le T_1 < T_2) \quad f([T_1, T_2]) = \frac{1}{T_2 - T_1} \left(\frac{D(T_1)}{D(T_2)} - 1 \right) \tag{7.1}$$

$$D(T_2) = \frac{D(T_1)}{1 + f([T_1, T_2]) \times (T_2 - T_1)} \tag{7.2}$$

Given a series of consecutive forward rates $f([T_i, T_{i+1}]), 0 = T_0 < T_1 < \ldots$, starting with $D(T_0 = 0) = 1$, one can use Formula 7.2 recursively to solve for any discount factor

$$D(T_n) = \frac{1}{1 + f([0, T_1]) \times T_1} \times \ldots \times \frac{1}{1 + f([T_{n-1}, T_n]) \times (T_n - T_{n-1})} \tag{7.3}$$

7.2   INTEREST RATE SWAPS

An interest rate swap is a contract between two counterparties to period-ically exchange interest rate payments based on a notional (hypothetical) principal for the term of the swap. In a standard *fixed-for-floating* inter-est rate swap, the interest payments of a fixed-rate loan versus those of a floating-rate loan are exchanged. The floating rate is periodically reset to a short-term interest rate benchmark, traditionally the 3-month rate in the United States. For USD swaps, the fixed-interest payments are semiannual, while the floating-interest payments are reset and paid quarterly. Specifically, for each quarterly calculation period, the 3-month rate is observed at the beginning, *accrued* for the length of the 3-month calculation period (cal-culated $Act/360 \approx 1/4$), and paid at the end of the calculation period (see Figure 7.2).

Interest rate swaps can be used to hedge interest rate risk and for asset-liability management. For example, a commercial bank typically takes in short-term deposits from individuals and businesses in the form of checking, savings, money-market, and Certificate of Deposit (CD) accounts and provides long-term home mortgage and commercial loans to them. This results in an asset-liability mismatch: the bank's revenue is fixed-interest income received from long-term loans, while its cost is due to variable interest paid on short-term deposits. An interest rate swap agreement allowing the bank to periodically pay a fixed interest versus receiving a floating interest can alleviate this mismatch.

Tables 7.1 and 7.2 show the cash flows of a 1-year swap with a semian-nual fixed rate of 4% p.a. if today's 3-month interest rate is 3.5% and future 3-month interest rates turn out to be 3.75%, 4%, and 4.25% in 3, 6, and 9 months, respectively.

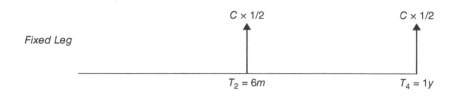

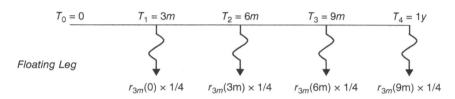

FIGURE 7.2   Cash flows of a 1-year USD fixed versus floating interest rate swap.

TABLE 7.1   Fixed leg's cash flows of a $100M 1-year 4% fixed versus floating swap.

Calc Period	Notional	Fixed Rate	Accrual (years)	Cash Flow	Pay Date
$[0m, 6m]$	100,000,000	4%	1/2	2,000,000	6m
$[6m, 1y]$	100,000,000	4%	1/2	2,000,000	1y

TABLE 7.2   Floating leg's cash flows of a $100M 1-year 4% fixed versus floating swap.

Calc Period	Notional	Floating Rate	Accrual (years)	Cash Flow	Pay Date
$[0m, 3m]$	100,000,000	3.5%	1/4	875,000	3m
$[3m, 6m]$	100,000,000	3.75%	1/4	937,500	6m
$[6m, 9m]$	100,000,000	4%	1/4	1,000,000	9m
$[9m, 1y]$	100,000,000	4.25%	1/4	1,062,500	1y

7.2.1   Swap Valuation

The stream of fixed and floating interest cash flows are respectively known as the fixed and floating legs. The fixed leg can be valued by computing the present value of its known interest payments. For the 1-year swap in Figure 7.2, it is $C/2[D(6m) + D(1y)]$ for unit notional.

For the floating leg, the cash flows depend on the future floating interest rates observed at the beginning of each calculation period. If the term of the floating interest rate matches the length of the calculation period, i.e., 3-month rate accrued for 3 months, then these unknown cash flows can be replicated by a portfolio of two zero-coupon bonds as follows.

For a given calculation period, $[T_i, T_{i+1}]$, a portfolio consisting of a long position in a T_i-maturity zero-coupon bond and a short position in a T_{i+1}-maturity zero-coupon bond will ensure that one *owns* unit currency at T_i and *owes* unit currency at T_{i+1}. At T_i, the unit currency from the maturing zero-coupon bond can be invested at the prevailing interest rate for the calculation period, $r(T_i)$, to end up with

$$1 + r(T_i) \times (T_{i+1} - T_i)$$

at T_{i+1}. At $T_i + 1$ the short position in the maturing T_{i+1} zero-coupon bond requires payment of unit currency, leaving $r(T_i) \times (T_{i+1} - T_i)$, which is exactly the cash flow of the floating leg for that calculation period. Today's value of the floating leg's cash flow is, therefore, today's value of being long a T_i zero-coupon bond and short a T_{i+1} zero-coupon bond

$$D(T_i) - D(T_{i+1}) \tag{7.4}$$

This replication argument applies to any of the floating leg's cash flows and today's value of the floating leg of a swap with n calculation periods and floating payments is

$$\text{Value of Floating Leg} = \sum_{i=0}^{n-1}(D(T_i) - D(T_{i+1})) = D(T_0) - D(T_n)$$

Combining the values of the fixed and floating legs, the value of a swap to the receiver of the periodic fixed-interest payments of C/m at $T_1, \ldots, T_n$ is

$$\text{Swap Value} = \frac{C}{m} \sum_{i=1}^{n} D(T_i) - [D(T_0) - D(T_n)] \tag{7.5}$$

Depending on the discount factor curve and the fixed rate C, the value in Formula 7.5 can be positive, negative, or zero. The fixed rate C that makes today's value of the swap zero is called the *par swap rate*

$$C = \frac{D(T_0) - D(T_n)}{1/m \sum_{i=1}^{n} D(T_i)}$$

TABLE 7.3 Discount factor curve, forward 6-month rate curve, and swap rates with semiannual fixed rate.

T (years)	$D(T)$	$f([T, T + 6m])$	$S(T)$
0	1	4.082%	
0.5	0.98	4.167%	4.082%
1	0.96	4.255%	4.124%
1.5	0.94	4.348%	4.167%
2	0.92	4.444%	4.211%
2.5	0.90	4.545%	4.255%
3	0.88		4.301%

and the graph of par swap rate as a function of the swap maturity is known as the par *swap curve*.

A swap can start today, $T_0 = 0$, or at a future date, $T_0 > 0$. For forward swaps starting at $T_0 > 0$, the fixed rate that would make today's value of the swap zero is called the *forward swap rate*.

EXAMPLE 1

Using the discount factors in Table 7.3, the 2-year par swap rate with semiannual ($m = 2$) payments on the fixed leg is

$$S_2 = \frac{1 - 0.92}{1/2(0.98 + 0.96 + 0.94 + 0.92)} = 4.211\%$$

while the 2-year par swap rate, 1-year forward is

$$F1y, 2y = \frac{0.96 - 0.88}{1/2(0.94 + 0.92 + 0.90 + 0.88)} = 4.396\%$$

The value to the receiver of the fixed rate in a \$1M 6-month forward 2-year swap with a semiannual fixed rate of 4% p.a. is

$$\$1,000,000 \times \left[\frac{0.04}{2}(0.96 + 0.94 + 0.92 + 0.90) - (0.98 - 0.90) \right]$$

$$= -\$5,600$$

The value to the payer of the fixed rate is +\$5,600.

7.2.2   Swap = Bone − 100%

By adding a hypothetical final principal payment to each leg, the cash flows of the fixed leg become identical to those of a fixed-rate bond paying a coupon rate of C, while the floating leg's cash flows match cash flows of a flating-rate note (FRN), a bond whose coupon is reset periodically to the prevailing short-term interest rate.

The value of the fixed leg augmented by the principal payment is the same as a regular bond, while the value of the augmented floating leg is $D(T_0)$. For a spot starting $(T_0 = 0)$ swap, the augmented floating leg is worth $D(0) = 1$. Receiving the fixed rate C in a swap is, therefore, economically equivalent to paying par (100%) for a bond with coupon rate C: Swap = Bond − 100%.

Since the second term is constant, the sensitivities of a swap to interest rates such as PV01, convexity is similar to those of a bond.

7.2.3   Discounting the Forwards

The replication argument for the floating payments holds as long as the tenor of the floating rate matches the calculation period and the floating rate is reflective of one's funding cost and can be used to discount the cash flows. The value of the replicating portfolio, Formula 7.4 can be related to the forward rate as follows

$$
\begin{aligned}
D(T_i) - D(T_{i+1}) &= \frac{D(T_i) - D(T_{i+1})}{D(T_{i+1})} \times D(T_{i+1}) \\
&= \left(\frac{D(T_i)}{D(T_{i+1})} - 1 \right) \Big/ (T_{i+1} - T_i) \times (T_{i+1} - T_i) \times D(T_{i+1}) \\
&= f([T_1, T_2]) \times (T_{i+1} - T_i) \times D(T_{i+1})
\end{aligned}
$$

showing that one can value each cash flow of the floating leg by setting the unknown future interest rate to the forward rate, accruing it for the length of the calculation period, $(T_{i+1} - T_i)$, and discounting this projected cash flow from the payment date T_{i+1}. Note that the actual cash flow will depend on the future setting of the floating rate, but for the purpose of valuation, one can use the forward rate and discount the resulting cash flow, leading to *discounting the forward*.

7.2.4   Swap Rate as Average Forward Rate

Since the floating leg value can be written as a sum of discounted forward rates, the par swap rate can be considered as a weighted average of forward rates if the fixed and floating leg have the same payment frequency. Specifically, for an N-year swap with m payments per year starting on T_0 with payment dates $\{T_1, \ldots, T_{Nm}\}$, we have

$$
\begin{aligned}
S &= \frac{D(T_0) - D(T_{Nm})}{1/m \sum_{i=1}^{Nm} D(T_i)} \\
&= \frac{1/m \sum_{i=1}^{Nm} f([T_{i-1}, T_i]) D(T_i)}{1/m \sum_{i=1}^{Nm} D(T_i)} \\
&= \sum_{i=1}^{Nm} w_i f([T_{i-1}, T_i])
\end{aligned}
$$

where

$$
w_i = \frac{D(T_i)}{\sum_{i=1}^{Nm} D(T_i)}
$$

7.3   INTEREST RATE DERIVATIVES

The earlier replication argument to value a swap breaks down when the floating interest rate's term does not match the length of the calculation period. For example, the floating rate could be the 6-month rate, or the 5-year par swap rate, reset and paid quarterly. For these swap variants and fixed income and interest rate contingent claims, such as bond options, callable bonds, and European-style options to enter into a swap (*swaptions*), one needs to model the evolution of the underlying assets in a risk-neutral arbitrage-free setting and apply the risk-neutral valuation framework. As these models can become quite elaborate, they are mainly used for complicated interest rate derivatives and simpler techniques and heuristics are used for simpler products.

7.3.1   Black's Normal Model

The log normal dynamics for asset prices is the result of modeling the asset's return as a Brownian motion with drift. As interest rates themselves are measures of return, interest rate products and their derivatives are modeled via a Brownian motion leading to *normal* dynamics. Specifically, the underlying asset's *absolute* change is modeled via a Brownian motion leading to

$$
A(t) - A(0) \sim N(\mu t, \sigma_N^2 t)
$$

where σ_N is known as the *Normalized, or Normal* volatility. In a risk-neutral world, we must have

$$E[A(t)] = F_A(0, t)$$

leading to the risk-neutral distribution

$$A(t) \sim N(F_A(0, t)), \sigma_N^2 t)$$

Today's value of a European call can be computed as

$$C(0) = D(T) \int_{-\infty}^{\infty} \max(0, x - K) f_{A(T)}(x) dx$$

where

$$f_{A(T)}(x) = \frac{1}{\sqrt{2\pi\sigma_N^2 T}} e^{-\frac{(x - F_A(0,T))^2}{2\sigma_N^2 T}}$$

To evaluate the integral, and using the shorthand $F = F_A(0, T)$, $f(x) = f_{A(T)}(x)$ and

$$d = \frac{F - K}{\sigma_N \sqrt{T}}$$

we observe

$$\int_{-\infty}^{\infty} \max(0, x - K) f(x) dx = \int_{K}^{\infty} (x - K) f(x) dx$$

$$= \int_{K}^{\infty} (x - F) f(x) dx + \int_{K}^{\infty} (F - K) f(x) dx$$

The first integral is evaluated as

$$\int_{K}^{\infty} (x - F) f(x) dx = \frac{-\sigma_N \sqrt{T}}{\sqrt{2\pi}} \int_{K}^{\infty} \frac{d}{dx} e^{-\frac{(x - F)^2}{2\sigma_N^2 T}} dx$$

$$= \sigma_N \sqrt{T} \frac{1}{\sqrt{2\pi}} e^{-d^2/2}$$

$$= \sigma_N \sqrt{T} N'(d)$$

The second integral is

$$(F - K) \int_K^\infty f(x)dx = (F - K)P[N(F, \sigma_N^2 T) \geq K]$$

$$= (F - K)N(d)$$

Putting the above two results together leads to Black's Normal call formula

$$C(0) = D(T)\sigma_N \sqrt{T}[N'(d) + dN(d)], \quad d = \frac{F_A(0, T) - K}{\sigma_N \sqrt{T}}$$

Using put-call parity, the formula for a put is

$$P(0) = D(T)\sigma_N \sqrt{T}[N'(d) - dN(-d)], \quad d = \frac{F_A(0, T) - K}{\sigma_N \sqrt{T}}$$

The above two formulas are widely used for European-style interest rate derivatives.

7.3.2 Caps and Floors

An interest rate cap is a series of periodic cash flows providing protection against rising rates. For example, a 1-year quarterly cap on a 3-month interest rate with strike K is a portfolio of four caplets based on four calculation periods, where the payoff of each caplet for the calculation period $[T_i, T_{i+1}]$ is

$$\text{Notional} \times \max(0, r_{3m}(T_i) - K) \times (T_{i+1} - T_i)$$

paid at the T_{i+1} (see Table 7.4). Today's value of each caplet is computed via Black's Normalized call formula

$$E[\max(0, r_{3m}(T_i) - K)] = \sigma_N \sqrt{T}[N'(d) + dN(d)], \quad d = \frac{f([T_i, T_{i+1}])}{\sigma_N \sqrt{T_i}}$$

where $f([T_i, T_{i+1}])$ is the simple (add-on) forward rate for $[T_i, T_{i+1}]$

$$f([T_i, T_{i+1}]) = \left(\frac{D(T_i)}{D(T_{i+1})} - 1 \right) \bigg/ (T_{i+1} - T_i)$$

Similarly, a floor is a collection of floorlets, where the payoff of each floorlet for the calculation period $[T_i, T_{i+1}]$ is

$$\text{Notional} \times \max(0, r_{3m}(T_i) - K) \times (T_{i+1} - T_i)$$

paid at the T_{i+1}. Each floorlet is computed via Black's Normal put formula

$$E[\max(0, K - r_{3m}(T_i))] = \sigma_N \sqrt{T}[N'(d) - dN(-d)], \quad d = \frac{f([T_i, T_{i+1}])}{\sigma_N \sqrt{T_i}}$$

EXAMPLE 2

Using linear interpolation in the discount factors in Table 7.3, the value of a \$1M 1-year forward start 1-year quarterly cap on 3-month rates using $\sigma_N = 0.80\%$ (80 bps/annum) as shown in Table 7.4 is \$4,930.97. A similar calculation based on Black's Normal put formulas shows the value of a 1-year forward 1-year quarterly 4% floor to be \$2,330.97.

TABLE 7.4   1-year forward start 1-year quarterly cap with strike $K = 4\%$, $\sigma_N = 0.80\%$.

Period $[T_i, T_{i+1}]$	Notional x $(T_{i+1} - T_i)$	$f([T_i, T_{i+1}])$	d	Caplet	$DF(T_{i+1})$	Today's Value
$[1y, 1y3m]$	\$250,000	4.211%	0.263158	0.004354	0.95	\$1,034.09
$[1y3m, 1y6m]$	\$250,000	4.255%	0.285455	0.004989	0.94	\$1,172.47
$[1y6m, 1y9m]$	\$250,000	4.301%	0.307284	0.005597	0.93	\$1,301.37
$[1y9m, 2y]$	\$250,000	4.348%	0.328665	0.006187	0.92	\$1,423.04
						\$4,930.97

7.3.3   European Swaptions

A T_e-expiry into N-year European swaption is the option to enter into an N-year swap at the expiration date T_e. A *receiver* swaption with strike K is the option to enter into a swap where one receives the fixed rate K. Similarly, a *payer* swaption with strike K is the option to enter into a swap where one pays the fixed rate K.

To value a payer swaption with strike K, we observe that at expiration, the owner will exercise the option only if the N-year par swap rate, $S(T_e)$, is above K. In this case, it is advantageous to pay a below-market fixed rate K for the next N years in exchange for receiving the floating rates. Since one can enter into an offsetting swap where one *receives* the par swap rate $S(T_e)$ for zero cost, the combination of the two swaps cancels out the floating legs resulting in a series of net periodic cash flows of size

$$\frac{1}{m}(S(T_e) - K)$$

for the next N years, where m is fixed leg's payment frequency ($m = 2$ for semiannual swaps). These net payments will only happen if the swaption is exercised, $S(T_e) > K$. The payoff of the payer swaption is then the series of periodic cash flows of size

$$\frac{1}{m}\max(0, S(T_e) - K)$$

at $T_1, T_2, \ldots, T_{Nm}$, where T_i is the payment date of the ith cash flow of the fixed leg (see Figure 7.3).

Today's value of the payer swaption is computed as

$$E[\max(0, S(T_e) - K)] \times \frac{1}{m}\sum_{i=1}^{Nm} D(T_i)$$

with the expectation calculated via Black's Normal *call* formula. Similarly, a receiver swaption is calculated as

$$E[\max(0, K - S(T_e))] \times \frac{1}{m}\sum_{i=1}^{Nm} D(T_i)$$

using Black's Normal *put* formula. Notice that the term

$$A = \frac{1}{m}\sum_{i=1}^{Nm} D(T_i)$$

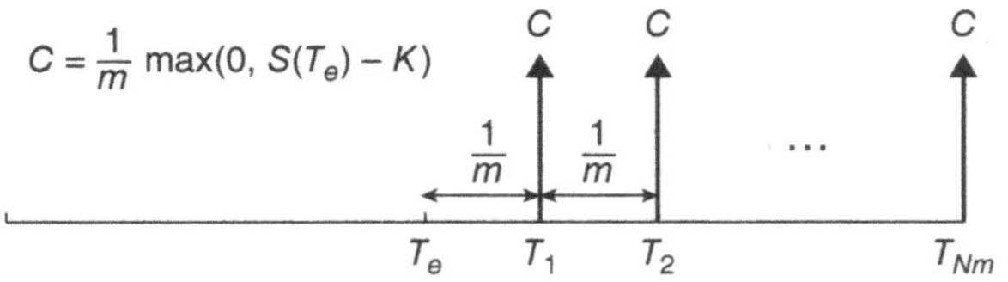

FIGURE 7.3   Payoff of a T_e into N-year payer swaption.

is the value of a N-year forward annuity starting at T_e paying unit cash flow per year, m times per year.

EXAMPLE 3

Let the Normalized volatility of a 1-year into 2-year forward swap rate be given as 1.20% per annum, $\sigma_N = 1.20\%$. Using the discount factors in Table 7.3, we compute the premium for a \$1M 1-year expiry into a 2-year semiannual ($m = 2$) payer swaption with strike $K = 4\%$ as follows. We first calculate the forward 1 year into a 2-year par swap rate and the annuity value

$$F = \frac{D(1y) - D(3y)}{1/2[D(1.5y) + D(2y) + D(2.5y) + D(3y)]} = 4.396\%$$

$$A = \frac{1}{m}\sum_{i=1}^{Nm} D(T_i) = \frac{1}{2}(0.94 + 0.92 + 0.90 + 0.88) = 1.82$$

Using Black's Normal call formula, we have

$$d = \frac{F - K}{\sigma_N \sqrt{T_e}} = \frac{0.04396 - 0.04}{0.012 \times \sqrt{1}} = 0.32967$$

$$E[\max(0, S(T_e) - K)] = (0.012)\sqrt{1}\left[\frac{1}{\sqrt{2\pi}}e^{-d^2/2} + dN(d)\right] = 0.007023$$

and the premium is calculated as

$$\$1,000,000 \times 0.007023 \times 1.82 = \$12,782.13$$

The value of a 1-year into 2-year receiver swaption with strike $K = 4\%$ is calculated using Black's Normal put formula

$$E[\max(0, K - S(T_e))] = (0.012)\sqrt{1}\left[\frac{1}{\sqrt{2\pi}}e^{-d^2/2} - dN(-d)\right] = 0.003067$$

with the premium given as

$$\$1,000,000 \times 0.003067 \times 1.82 = \$5,582.13$$

7.3.4 Constant Maturity Swaps

In a swap where the floating index is the N-year par swap rate, the swap is known as a constant maturity swap (CMS). For example, a 2-year fixed for floating swap of a 5-year CMS rate would require the periodic payments of a fixed rate in exchange for periodic, say quarterly, payments of the 5-year CMS rate for two years. While the replication argument for the floating payments is no longer applicable—the length of the calculation period's accrual period (1/4 for quarterly) is different than the tenor of the index (5 years)—one might still value the swap by discounting the forward CMS rate with an appropriate adjustment.

The adjustment is based on the following heuristic argument. By recalling that swap = bond − 100%, we start with the bond price-yield formula and Taylor-expand it around the forward CMS rate F

$$P(y) - P(F) = P'(F)(y - F) + 1/2P''(y - F)^2$$

Taking expected values of both sides in a risk-neutral setting where forward prices are expected prices, $E[P(y)] = P(F)$, we arrive at the approximation

$$0 = (E[y] - F)P'(F) + 1/2P''E[(y - F)]^2$$

Using the approximation

$$E[(y - F)^2] \approx \sigma_N^2 T$$

we arrive at the following CMS *convexity adjustment*

$$E[y] - F = -\frac{1}{2}\frac{P''(F)}{P'(F)}\sigma_N^2 T$$

$$\left[\frac{1}{F} - \frac{N/m}{(1 + F/m)^{N+1} - (1 + F/m)}\right]\sigma_N^2 T \qquad (7.6)$$

where we have used Formulas 2.8 and 2.12 for a par ($C = y = F$) bond.

CMS swaps are typically valued by discounting the forward CMS rate adjusted by Formula 7.6. Similarly, caps and floors on CMS rates are priced via Black's Normal formula with the forward rate adjusted by Formula 7.6.

7.4 INTEREST RATE MODELS

While Black's Normal model is widely used to price European-style options on interest rates, its use is not entirely justified as it conflates forward rates and forward prices. The risk-neutral valuation framework was established by replicating options on tradeable assets via self-financing replicating portfolios. In fixed income and for interest rates, the tradeable assets are loans and bonds, not interest rates or yields. The latter are simply measures of rate of return on traded assets and are not directly traded.

To price interest rate derivatives in a consistent manner in the risk-neutral valuation framework, we need to start with traded assets. The fundamental underlying assets in fixed income are unit cash flows at future dates T, that is, T-maturity zero-coupon bonds. The t-price of a unit cash flow at $T > t$ is the discount factor $D(t, T)$ with $D(t, t) = D(T, T) = 1$. Recall that in a risk-neutral world we must have

$$(0 \leq t \leq T) \qquad \frac{D(t, T, \omega)}{M(t, \omega)} = E_t \left[\frac{D(T, T, \omega)}{M(T, \omega)} \right] = E_t \left[\frac{1}{M(T, \omega)} \right] \qquad (7.7)$$

where $M(t, \omega)$ is the t-value of a money market account initiated with unit currency along the random sample path ω.

7.4.1 Money Market Account, Short Rate

Let $0 = T_0 < T_1 < \ldots$ be a discretization of time. Given a forward rate curve, $\{f([T_i, T_{i+1}])\}_{i \geq 0}$, the first rate $f([T_0, T_1])$ is the interest rate for a loan/deposit starting today $T_0 = 0$ for a short-term deposit $[0, T_1]$ and is known as the *short rate*.

The short rate is the interest rate in a money market account, $M(T)$, where the interest rate periodically (daily, weekly, or monthly) resets to the prevailing interest rate. Setting $\Delta T_i = T_{i+1} - T_i$, if we use simple (add-on) short rates, we have

$$M(T_n, \omega) = 1 \times (1 + r(0)\Delta T_1) \times \ldots \times (1 + r(T_{n-1}, \omega)\Delta T_N)$$

where we have introduced the term ω to emphasize that future short rates are random and unknown.

Focusing on today, since $M(0) = 1$, and $D(T_n, T_n) = 1$, we have

$$\frac{D(0, T_n)}{M(0)} = E_0 \left[\frac{D(T_n, T_n)}{M(T_n, \omega)} \right]$$

$$\Rightarrow D(0, T_n) = E_0 \left[\prod_{i=0}^{n-1} \frac{1}{1 + r(T_i, \omega)\Delta T_i} \right] \qquad (7.8)$$

which is the arbitrage-free martingale condition in a risk-neutral world. The term inside the bracket in Formula 7.8 is the stochastic version of the discount factor showing that for each random sample path, unit currency at T_n

gets discounted back to today along the series of consecutive random short rates along that path.

The notation simplifies if we use continuously compounded short rates

$$M(T_n, \omega) = e^{\sum_{i=0}^{n-1} r(T_i, \omega) \Delta T_i}$$

$$D(0, T_n) = E_0[e^{-\sum_{i=0}^{n-1} r(T_i, \omega) \Delta T_i}] \tag{7.9}$$

As $\Delta T_i \to 0$, we arrive at the continuous time versions of the above formulas

$$M(T) = e^{\int_0^T r(t, \omega) dt}, \quad D(t, T, \omega) = E_t[e^{-\int_t^T r(u, \omega) du}]$$

reducing to $M(T) = e^{rT}, D(t, T) = e^{-r(T-t)}$ for constant interest rates.

7.4.2 Short Rate Models

Applying the risk-neutral valuation framework, if we posit a process for the evolution of the short rates satisfying Formula 7.8 or 7.9, then today's price of any European-style interest rate derivative with payoff $C(T_N, \omega)$ for expiration date T_N is

$$C(0) = E_0\left[\frac{C(T_N, \omega)}{M(T_N, \omega)}\right] = E_0\left[\left(\prod_{i=0}^{N-1} \frac{1}{1 + r(T_i, \omega) \Delta T_i}\right) C(T_N, \omega)\right] \tag{7.10}$$

or

$$C(0) = E_0[e^{-\sum_{i=0}^{N-1} r(T_i, \omega) \Delta T_i} C(T_N, \omega)] \tag{7.11}$$

if we use continuous compounding. The term in the parentheses is the *path discounting* of the payoff along sample path ω, and the value of an interest rate derivative is the risk-neutral expected value of its path-discounted payoff.

7.4.3 Mean Reversion, Vasicek and Hull-White Models

Interest rates as opposed to stock prices are range-bound and exhibit mean reversion. A simple random process for $r(t, \omega)$ that incorporates mean reversion is an adaptation of the Ornstein-Uhlenbeck process proposed by Vasicek (Vasicek, 1977).

$$dr(t, \omega) = a \times [b - r(t, \omega)]dt + \sigma dB(t, \omega)$$

for positive $a > 0$, $b > 0$ known as the *mean reversion speed* and *level*, respectively.

When $r(t, \omega) > b$, the term in the bracket is negative and is multiplied by a positive mean reversion speed a, therefore, the drift term in the diffusion is negative and there is downward pressure on $r(t, \omega)$. The larger the difference between $r(t, \omega)$ and the mean reversion level b, the larger the downward pressure. Similarly, when $r(t, \omega) < b$, the drift term is positive and there is upward pressure on $r(t, \omega)$. The lower the $r(t, \omega)$, the larger the difference between $r(t)$ and b, and the upward pressure. When $r(t, \omega) = b$, then the drift term vanishes and $r(t, \omega)$ follows a Brownian motion, i.e., it has zero expected change and meanders around b.

The mean-reverting short rate model proposed by Vasicek was extended in a series of papers by Hull and White, (Hull and White, 1993) culminating in the Hull-White (HW) model with time-dependent mean reversion speeds, levels, and volatilities, replacing a, b, and σ from constants to deterministic functions of time, $a(t), b(t)$, and $\sigma(t)$. These models result in Gaussian short rates allowing for the short rate to go negative. If the short rate is a continuously compounding rate, then zero-coupon bond prices, which are equivalent to discount factors, are lognormal

$$D(t, T, \omega) = E_t\left[e^{-\int_t^T r(u, \omega)du}\right] \qquad (7.12)$$

since for a Gaussian process r, the integral $\int r(t, \omega)dt$ is conditionally Gaussian (Karlin and Taylor, 1975).

It is possible to derive analytic expressions for the short rate and discount factors. For the Vasicek model, we have

$$dr + ardt = abdt + \sigma dB$$

Multiplying both sides by the integrating factor $e^{\int a} = e^{at}$, we have

$$e^{\int a}dr + ae^{\int a}rdt = abe^{\int a}dt + \sigma e^{\int a}dB$$

$$\Rightarrow \quad d(e^{\int a}r) = abe^{\int a} + \sigma e^{\int a}dB$$

$$\Rightarrow \quad r(T) = e^{-aT}\left[r(0) + \int_0^T abe^{at}dt + \int_0^T \sigma e^{at}dB(t)\right]$$

For any deterministic function $f(t)$, the stochastic integral $\int f dB$ is Gaussian

$$\int_{t_1}^{t_2} f(t)dB(t) \sim N\left(0, \int_{t_1}^{t_2} f^2(t)dt\right)$$

This can be understood by thinking of the integral as the limit of

$$\sum f(t_i)[B(t_{i+1}) - B(t_i)]$$

and recalling that the increments of the Brownian motion are independent and a $[t_i, t_{i+1}]$ increment is an $N(0, t_{i+1} - t_i)$ random variable. We have

$$r(T) = r(0)e^{-aT} + b(1 - e^{-aT}) + N\left(0, \frac{\sigma^2}{2a}(1 - e^{-2aT})\right)$$

showing that r is a Gaussian process. The zero-coupon bond prices or the discount factors in Formula 7.12 can be evaluated (Mamon, 2004) to arrive at

$$D(t, T, r(t)) = e^{A(t, T)r(t) + B(t, T)}$$

$$A(t, T) = \frac{e^{-a\times(T-t)} - 1}{a}$$

$$B(t, T) = \left(\frac{\sigma^2}{2a^2} - b\right)[A(t, T) + (T - t)] - \frac{\sigma^2 A^2(t, T)}{4a} \qquad (7.13)$$

7.4.4 Short Rate Lattice Model

While Formula 7.13 provides insight into the behavior of zero-coupon bond prices and can be used to compute option prices on them, for more common interest rate derivatives, one resorts to a discrete time computer implementation of the model. Following the original papers by Hull-White, the HW model is usually implemented as a trinomial lattice, and both the probabilities and states have to be computed to jointly satisfy the arbitrage-free constraint of Formula 7.8. Below are the typical computer implementation steps.

1. *Discretization.* Discretize the HW process equation,

$$dr(t, \omega) = a(t)[b(t) - r(t, \omega)]dt + \sigma(t)dB(t, \omega)$$

    for lattice dates, $0 = t_0 < t_1 < \ldots < t_{N+1}$, to arrive at discretized mean-reversion speeds, levels, and local volatilities: $a_i = a(t_i), b_i = b(t_i), \sigma_i = \sigma(t_i), \Delta t_i = t_{i+1} - t_i, 0 \le i < N$. The mean reversion levels b_i's are used to make the lattice arbitrage-free, while the mean reversion speeds and local volatilities a_i, σ_i are used to fit the model to the market prices of actively traded interest rate derivative products such as cap/floors and European swaptions.

2. *Evolution.* Starting from $r_0 = r(t_0 = 0)$, let $r_{ij} = r(t_i, \omega_j)$ denote the jth state at the ith time t_i. At each time t_i, each node r_{ij} leads to three nodes

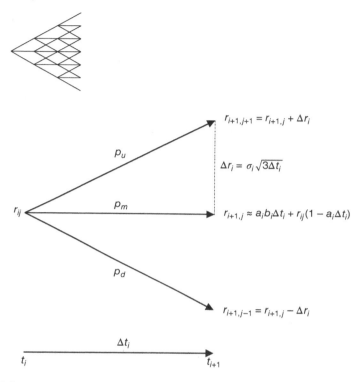

FIGURE 7.4 Typical implementation of the Hull-White model.

as shown in Figure 7.4, with the middle node $r_{i+1,j}$ chosen to ensure that the lattice recombines by letting k be the closest integer to $r_{ij}(1 - a_i \Delta t_i)/\sigma_i\sqrt{3\Delta t_i}$, and setting

$$r_{i+1,j} = a_i b_i \Delta t_i + k\sigma_i \sqrt{3\Delta t_i}.$$

The choice of spacing $\Delta r_i = \sigma_i \sqrt{3\Delta t_i}$ is motivated by lattice stability issues as $\Delta t_i \to 0$, coming from insights of finite-difference disciplines. With this choice, the transition probabilities defined as

$$p_m = \frac{2}{3} - \frac{(r_{ij}(1 - a_i \Delta t_i) - k\sigma_i \sqrt{3\Delta t_i})^2}{3\sigma_i^2 \Delta t_i}$$

$$p_{u,d} = \frac{1 - p_m}{2} \pm \frac{r_{ij}(1 - a_i \Delta t_i) - k\sigma_i \sqrt{3\Delta t_i}}{2\sigma_i \sqrt{3\Delta t_i}}$$

are all non-negative, and ensure that the process dynamics (local means and volatilities) are respected.

3. *Risk-neutral, Arbitrage-free.* Solve for b_i so that the arbitrage-free condition in Formula 7.8 is satisfied for $D(0, t_{i+1})$, i.e., recover today's discount factor curve, $D(0, \cdot)$. This step is sometimes called *inverting* the yield curve.

4. *Calibration.* Once an arbitrage-free lattice is constructed, tune the parameters a_i, σ_i and repeat the above steps to arrive at an arbitrage-free lattice that recovers today's discount factor curve *and* market prices of a chosen set of interest rate derivative products such as cap/floors or European swaptions.

5. *DF Curve Extraction.* Given a calibrated arbitrage-free lattice, starting at the last node, recursively extract the discount factor curve at each previous node via

$$\frac{D(t, T, \omega)}{M(t, \omega)} = E_t \left[\frac{D(T, T, \omega)}{M(T, \omega)} \right] \quad \Rightarrow \quad D(t, T, \omega) = E_t \left[\frac{M(t, \omega)}{M(T, \omega)} \right]$$

which for the discretized process can be written

$$(0 \leq i \leq n) \quad D(t_i, t_n, \omega) = E_{t_i} \left[\prod_{j=i}^{n-1} \frac{1}{1 + r(t_j, \omega)\Delta t_j} \right]$$

This means that at each node on the lattice, we can extract the discount factor curve at that node by focusing on the sublattice starting at that node and path-discounting future unit cash flows to that node along the series of short rates that originate from the node (see Figure 7.5).

6. *Pricing.* Equipped with the discount factor curve at each lattice node in a calibrated arbitrage-free risk-neutral setting, price any interest rate contingent claim by path-discounting its cash flows to today using Formula 7.11.

7.4.5 Pure Securities

A (t_i, j) *pure* security, also known as an Arrow-Debreu security, is a contingent claim that has a unit payoff at the jth state at t_i and 0 elsewhere. A t_i-maturity zero-coupon bond has a unit payoff at *any* state at t_i and can be considered as a portfolio of pure securities and its value today is simply

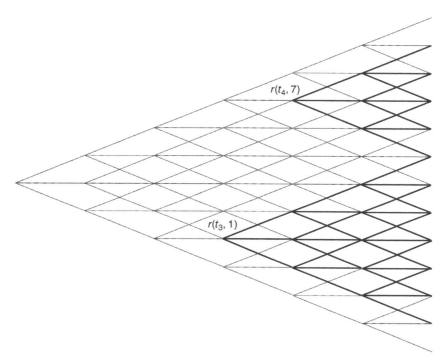

FIGURE 7.5 Navigating the sublattice originating from each node to extract the discount factor curve at the node.

the sum of the prices of these securities. Specifically let $AD(t_i, j)$ be today's $(t_0 = 0)$ price of a (t_i, j) pure security. Then

$$D(0, t_i) = \sum_j AD(t_i, j)$$

where j spans all the potential states at future time t_i. Similarly, today's price of any contingent claim with payoff $C(t_i, j)$ at (t_i, j) state is

$$C(0) = \sum_j C(t_i, j)AD(t_i, j) \qquad (7.14)$$

Today's price of a (t_i, j) pure security is the expected path-discounted of all paths leading to state j at t_i. The collection of AD prices satisfy the

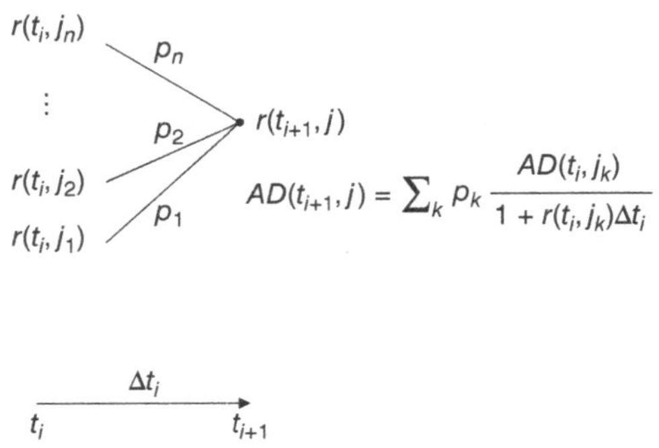

FIGURE 7.6 Forward induction and pure security prices.

Green's function and can be systematically calculated via the *forward induction* technique, (Jamshidian, 1991) as follows: $AD(0,0) = 1$

$$AD(t_{i+1}, j) = \sum_k AD(t_i, j_k)P[(t_i, j_k) \rightarrow (t_{i+1}, j)]D(t_i, t_{i+1}, j_k)$$

where $D(t_i, t_{i+1}, j_k)$ is the 1-period discount factor at state (t_i, j_k) for t_{i+1} and can be related to the simple (add-on) short rate $r(t_i, j_k)$

$$D(t_i, t_{i+1}, j_k) = \frac{1}{1 + r(t_i, j_k)\Delta t_i}$$

as shown in Figure 7.6.

The calculation and updating of $AD(t_i)$'s at each step greatly simplifies the yield curve inversion step during the construction of the lattice and simplifies the pricing of contingent claims to the calculation of the sum in Formula 7.14 instead of computing the expected path-discounted value of the payoff in Formula 7.11.

7.5 BERMUDAN SWAPTIONS

A Bermudan swaption is Bermudan option to enter into a swap with a fixed maturity date at one of a given set of exercise dates. For example, a 1-year into 2-year Bermudan payer with semiannual exercise dates and fixed payments allows one to enter as a fixed-rate payer into a 2-year swap in 1 year, or a 1.5-year swap in 1.5 years, or a 1-year swap in 2 years, or a 6-month swap

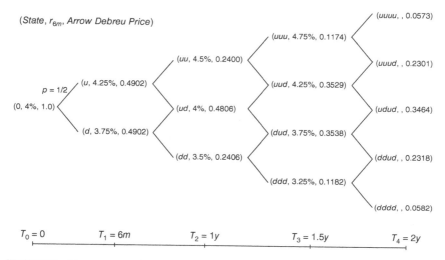

FIGURE 7.7 Two-year evolution of the 6-month rate.

TABLE 7.5 Discount factor curve at each node.

Tree Date	State	$DF(T_0)$	$DF(T_1)$	$DF(T_2)$	$DF(T_3)$	$DF(T_4)$
T_0	0	1	0.98039	0.96117	0.94233	0.92386
$T_1 = 6m$	u		1	0.97919	0.95882	0.93887
	d		1	0.9816	0.96353	0.9458
$T_2 = 1y$	uu			1	0.978	0.95648
	ud			1	0.98039	0.96117
	dd			1	0.9828	0.9659
$T_3 = 1y6m$	uuu				1	0.9768
	uud				1	0.97919
	dud				1	0.98160
	ddd				1	0.98401

in 2.5 years. The owner of the option can decide to exercise on any—but only one—of the above exercise dates. Bermudan swaptions are typically priced via backward induction in an interest rate lattice.

EXAMPLE 4

Consider an arbitrage-free short rate tree model shown in Figure 7.7 with all transition probabilities set to 1/2, and with its extracted discount factor curve at each node shown in Table 7.5. To price a $1M 6 month into 1.5-year Bermudan 4% p.a. fixed-rate payer swaption with semiannual exercise dates, we evaluate the underlying swap at each node as shown in Table 7.6. Starting with the last exercise date $T_3 = 1.5y$, we calculate the immediate exercise value, that is $\max(0, \text{Swap Value})$. We then step back and at each step and for each node, calculate the higher of the immediate exercise value and the discounted expected hold value until we arrive at today's value of $1,904.32.

A similar calculation shows the value of the 6 month into 1.5-year Bermudan 4% *receiver* swaption with semiannual exercise dates to be $1,918.61.

TABLE 7.6 Value of $1M 6 month into a 1.5-year Bermudan 4% p.a. semiannual swaption with semiannual exercise dates.

Tree Date	State	Payer swap	Bermudan payer swaption	Bermudan receiver swaption
$T_0 = 0$	0	−14.29	1,904.32	1,918.61
$T_1 = 6m$	u	3,590.33	3,590.33	294.48
	d	−3,619.49	294.48	3,619.49
$T_2 = 1y$	uu	4,834.72	4,834.72	0
	ud	−1.47	600	601.47
	dd	−4,873.23	0	4,873.23
$T_3 = 1y6m$	uuu	3,663	3,663	0
	uud	1,223.99	1,223.99	0
	dud	−1,226.99	0	1,226.99
	ddd	−3,690.04	0	3,690.04

7.6   TERM STRUCTURE MODELS

The state variable in short rate models is the short rate $r(t)$ and its evolution from any node determines the discount curve at that node. For example, in the HW model implementation the yield curve inversion step requires solving for the mean reversion level $b'_i s$ to recover today's yield curve. Similarly, to extract the DF curve at any future state, one needs to navigate the sublattice spawned from that state. Short rate models, therefore, are *implicitly* evolving the full term structure.

By selecting the full term structure in any of its equivalent representations—discount factor curve, zero-coupon curve, forward rate curve—as the state variables and evolving the full curve, one can obviate the yield curve inversion and extraction steps. Term structure models stating with the full yield curve, typically the forward rate curve, are called full term structure models (Heath et al., 1992). Their implementation is more technical and nuanced (Sadr, 2009), but they have the intuitive appeal of directly representing the yield curve at each state (see Figure 7.8).

Note that when evolving the forward rate curve, the initial point of the forward curve is the short rate, hence, a full term structure model is an implicit short rate model, and vice versa.

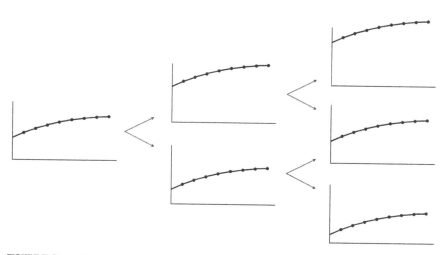

FIGURE 7.8   Full term structure model.

7.7 INTEREST RATE DERIVATIVES IN PRACTICE

In the United States, there is an active market for OTC forward rate agreements (FRA's) based on 3-month deposits. There are also actively traded futures contracts based on short-term interest rates (STIR) and options on futures contracts. The most common underlying rate has traditionally been the 3-month Libor rate currently being replaced by SOFR (secured overnight funding rate), serving as the index for popular and liquid Euro-dollar futures contract series. Various expiry options on Euro-dollar futures contracts are traded actively and used as benchmark instruments for calibration of interest rate models.

Par swap rates for various benchmark maturities (2 year, 3 year, 5 year, 7 year, 10 year, 12 year, 15 year, 20 year, 25 year, and 30 year) are actively quoted and traded. Given a series of par swap rates and cash and forward rate agreements and futures contracts based on the same floating rate, the swap market discount factor curve is extracted using the bootstrap method. Starting with this discount factor curve, a short rate or a full term structure model is constructed and calibrated to the liquid options such as futures options and Europen-style swaptions. Once the model is constructed, the price of more complicated interest rate derivative products such as Bermudan cancellable swaps and swaps with exotic payoffs can be computed.

7.7.1 Interest Rate Risk

For bonds, the single yield to maturity captures all the interest rate and discounting information in the price-yield formula, and the interest rate risk is captured by the PV01 dP/dy. Interest rate derivatives, on the other hand, depend on the full term structure and a variety of interest rates. A common method to compute the interest rate risk of an interest rate derivative product is the *bump and revalue* method: Starting with a set of liquid market instruments as inputs, bootstrap the discount factor curve, build and calibrate any models (short rate or full term structure), and compute the price. Next increase all the input rates used to bootstrap the discount factor curve by 1 bp, create a new bootstrapped discount factor curve, a new short rate or term structure model, and compute a new price. The difference between the new bumped price and the original price is called the *parallel PV01* of the instrument and measures the sensitivity to the overall level of interest rates. For a more detailed sensitivity analysis, one can do the same bump and revalue process, but increase each input instrument's rate one at a time while holding other rates unchanged to come up with a vector of sensitivities.

This vector is known as the *bucketed PV01*. Similar calculations can be done for second-order sensitivities.

Another method to measure risk is to revalue the instrument for a given interest rate shift scenario, for example, a 10 bp parallel shift, or a 100 bp steepening of the yield curve. These shift scenarios are applied to the input instruments, a new discount curve and interest rate model is created, and the instrument repriced. One can either value the instrument, or compute parallel or bucketed PV01 under the shift scenario, giving rise to scenario value or *scenario PV01*.

7.7.2   Value at Risk (VaR)

Valuing a portfolio of interest rate sensitive products under a variety of shift scenarios is the basis of *value at risk (VaR)*. For VaR calculations, one generates a set of N shift scenarios to compute N potential future values. Focusing on the statistics of the profit and loss of these scenarios, one can then compute an estimated maximum loss level for a given level of confidence, say 95%.

The shift scenarios can be based on historical movements, say daily movements over the last three years giving rise to about 750 scenarios (about 250 business days per year). Another method is to compute the mean and covariance matrix of the term structure movements from historical data and simulate N scenarios from a multivariate distribution—usually Gaussian—using the empirical covariance matrix.

REFERENCES

Heath, D., Jarrow, R., and Morton, A. (1992). Bond pricing and the term structure of interest rates: a new methodology. *Econometrica*, **60**: 77–105.

Hull, J. and White A. (1993). Bond option pricing based on a model for the evolution of bond prices. *Advances in Futures and Options Research* **6**: 1–13.

Jamshidian, F. (1991). Forward induction and construction of yield curve diffusion models. *The Journal of Fixed Income* **1**(1): 62–74.

Karlin, S. and Taylor, H.M. (1975). *A First Course in Stochastic Processes*. Cambridge, MA: Acadmic Press.

Mamon, R. (2004). Three ways to solve for bond prices in the vasicek model. *Journal of Applied Mathematics and Decision Sciences* **8**, 03.

Sadr, A. (2009). *Interest Rate Swaps and Their Derivatives: A Practitioner's Guide*. Hoboken, NJ: Wiley.

Vasicek, O. (1977). An equilibrium characterization of the term structure. *Journal of Financial Economics* **5**: 177–188.

EXERCISES

1. Using Table 7.3 and linear interpolation in discount factors
   (a) Calculate the spot and quarterly forward 3-month simple (add-on) rates, $f([T_i, T_{i+1}])$ for $T_0 = 0, T_1 = 3m, \ldots, T_{12} = 2y9m$.
   (b) Calculate the 2-year forward swap rate, 3-month forward with semi-annual payments on the fixed leg.
   (c) Calculate the value to the fixed-rate receiver of a \$1M 3-month into 2-year forward swap with semiannual fixed rate of 3% per annum.
   (d) What is the value of the above swap to the fixed-rate payer?
2. Using Table 7.3 and linear interpolation in discount factors, for a \$1M 1-year swap with semiannual fixed rate of 4% per annum and quarterly floating leg based on 3-month rates
   (a) Compute the value of the semiannual fixed leg.
   (b) Compute the value of the quarterly floating leg via discounting the forward 3-month rates.
   (c) Compute the value of the floating leg via replication.
   (d) What is the value of the swap to the fixed-rate receiver?
3. Using the same setup as Example 2
   (a) Compute today's value of each of the four floorlets for a \$1M 1-year forward start 1-year $K = 4\%$ quarterly floor on 3-month rates.
   (b) Compute today's value to the payer of the fixed rate for a \$1M 1-year forward start 1-year swap with quarterly payments at the fixed rate of 4% p.a.
   (c) Using the above results, show that put-call parity holds: Cap - Floor = Swap value to fixed rate payer.
4. Using the data in Table 7.3
   (a) Compute the semiannual forward swap rate for a 1-year swap, 2-year forward, $F_{2,1}$.
   (b) Using Black's normal formula with $\sigma_N = 0.80\%$, compute the value of a \$1M 2 year into a 1-year ATMF payer swaption with semiannual fixed rate $K = F_{2,1}$.
   (c) Using Black's normal formula with $\sigma_N = 0.80\%$, compute the value of a \$1M 2 year into 1-year ATMF receiver swaption with semiannual fixed rate $K = F_{2,1}$.
   (d) Solve for the implied volatility σ_N if the market value of a \$1M 2-year into 1-year semiannual payer swaption with $K = 5\%$ p.a. is \$5,000.
5. Let R, P be the value of a European receiver, payer swaption with the same expiry, swap term, and strike K.
   (a) Let S be the value to the receiver of the underlying swap with fixed rate K. Prove put-call parity for European-style swaptions: $R - P = S$.

(b) Using Table 7.3, calculate the value to the fixed-rate receiver of a $1M 1 year into 2-year forward swap with semiannual fixed rate of 4% per annum.

(c) Using the results of Example 3, show that put-call parity holds.

6. Using the Black's normal call formula
   (a) Show that the delta of a call option, $\partial C(0)/\partial A(0)$, equals $N(d)$.
   (b) Using put-call parity, compute the delta of a put option.
   (c) What is the delta of an ATMF call?
   (d) What is the delta of an ATMF call when using BSM's lognormal formula?

7. Consider an ATMF straddle's price under lognormal and normal dynamics, and use the first central difference approximation

$$N'(x) \times x \approx N(x/2) - N(-x/2)$$

to relate the normalized volatility to lognormal volatility

$$\sigma_N \approx \sigma \times F$$

8. Using the example in Figure 7.7 and the results in Table 7.5
   (a) Show the computations for the T_1 discount factor curves in each of the (u, d) states starting from the T_2 discount factor curves.
   (b) Show the computation for the Arrow-Debreu prices of the three T_2 states (uu, ud, dd) from the T_1 AD prices.
   (c) Calculate the semiannual 1-year CMS (par swap) rate in each of the (u, d) states at T_1.
   (d) Calculate today's value of a $1M European-style 6 month into 1-year payer swaption with semiannual fixed rate of 4% per annum.

9. A European cancelable swap allows the owner to cancel a swap at some point before the swap maturity. The cancellation option is economically equivalent to a European swaption into an offsetting remaining swap, and the value of the cancelable swap is a swap plus the cancellation option. Using DFs in Table 7.3, and 1 year into 2-year swaption volatility $\sigma_N = 1.20\%$, consider a 3-year swap with semiannual fixed rate of K per annum.
   (a) Solve for K so that today's value of the swap is 0, that is, the 3-year semiannual par swap rate.
   (b) The fixed rate payer in the above swap has the option to cancel the swap in 1 year. The cancellation option is economically equivalent to a 1 year into 2-year receiver swaption with strike K. Solve for K that would make today's value of the cancelable swap 0. Is K above or below the 3-year par swap rate?

(c) The fixed-rate receiver in the above swap has the option to cancel the swap in 1 year. The cancellation option is economically equivalent to a 1 year into 2-year payer swaption with strike K. Solve for K that would make today's value of the cancelable swap 0. Is K above or below the 3-year par swap rate?

10. A Bermudan cancelable swap allows the owner to cancel a swap at some point before the swap maturity. The cancellation option is economically equivalent to a Bermudan swaption into an offsetting swap. Using the same setup as Example 3, consider a 2-year swap with semiannual fixed rate of K per annum.

(a) Solve for K so that today's value of the swap is 0, that is, the 2-year par swap rate.

(b) The fixed-rate payer in the above swap has the Bermudan option to cancel the swap in 6 months, 1 year, or 1.5 years. The cancellation option is economically equivalent to a 6 month into 2-year Bermudan receiver swaption with strike K. Solve for K that would make today's value of the cancelable swap 0. Is K above or below the 2-year par swap rate?

(c) The fixed-rate receiver in the above swap has the option to cancel the swap in 6 months, 1 year, or 1.5 years. The cancellation option is economically equivalent to a 6 month into 2-year Bermudan payer swaption with strike K. Solve for K that would make today's value of the cancelable swap 0. Is K above or below the 2-year par swap rate?

Math and Probability Review

A.1 CALCULUS AND DIFFERENTIATION RULES

For a given function $f(x)$, its *derivative*, $f'(x) = df(x)/dx$, is defined as

$$\frac{d}{dx}f(x) = f'(x) = \lim_{h \to 0} \frac{f(x+h) - f(x)}{h}$$

For a constant c, if $f(x) = c$, $f'(x) = 0$ and $(c \times f)'(x) = c \times f'(x)$. For two given functions $f(x), g(x)$, the following relations hold:

1. *Product Rule*: $(f \times g)' = f' \times g + g' \times f$
2. *Quotient Rule*:

$$\left(\frac{f}{g}\right)' = \frac{f' \times g - g' \times f}{g^2}$$

3. *Chain Rule*: Let $h(x) = f(g(x)) = (f \circ g)(x)$. Then

$$h'(x) = f'(g(x)) \times g'(x)$$

4. *Power Rule, Exponential, Logarithm*

$$\frac{dx^n}{dx} = nx^{n-1} \quad (n \neq 0), \quad \frac{d}{dx}e^x = e^x, \quad \frac{d}{dx}\ln(x) = \frac{1}{x}$$

5. *L'Hôpital's Rule*: Subject to some regularity conditions, given two functions f, g, if their ratios in the limit results to an *indeterminate* form

$$\lim_{x \to a} \frac{f(x)}{g(x)} = \frac{0}{0} \text{ or } \lim_{x \to a} \frac{f(x)}{g(x)} = \frac{\pm\infty}{\pm\infty}$$

then

$$\lim_{x \to a} \frac{f(x)}{g(x)} = \lim_{x \to a} \frac{f'(x)}{g'(x)}$$

A.1.1   Taylor Series

The Taylor Series expansion of a function $f(x)$ around x is given by

$$f(x + \Delta x) = f(x) + f'(x)\Delta x + 1/2 f''(\Delta x)^2 + \ldots + \frac{1}{n!} f^{(n)}(x)(\Delta x)^n + \ldots$$

where $f^{(n)}(x)$ is the nth derivative of the function. Similarly, a function of n variables can be Taylor-expanded by considering all the single and mixed partial derivatives

$$\Delta f(x_1 + \Delta x_1, \ldots, x_n + \Delta x_n) = \sum_{i=1}^{n} \frac{\partial f}{\partial x_i} \Delta x_i$$

$$+ 1/2 \sum_{i,j=1}^{n} \frac{\partial f}{\partial x_i} \frac{\partial f}{\partial x_j} (\Delta x_i)(\Delta x_j)$$

$$+ \ldots$$

A.2   PROBABILITY REVIEW

A random variable is a real-valued function whose value is based on the outcome of random phenomena. For example, assigning numerical values to each potential outcome of a coin flip, say 1 for heads and 0 for tails, gives rise to a random variable X with two possible values (0,1) each with probability 1/2, written as

$$P[X = 0] = Prob(\text{Coin toss is Tails}) = Prob(\{T\}) = 1/2$$

$$P[X = 1] = Prob(\text{Coin toss is Heads}) = Prob(\{H\}) = 1/2$$

We can flip the coin a second time, and create a new random variable, Y

$$P[Y = 0] = Prob(\text{Second coin toss is Tails}) = 1/2$$

$$P[Y = 1] = Prob(\text{Second coin toss is Heads}) = 1/2$$

Depending on how the random phenomena are related, we can calculate probabilities such as

$$P[X = Y = 1] = Prob(\{H, H\})$$

If the two coin tosses are unrelated, then we have *independent* random variables X, Y and the joint probabilities are the *product* of each random variable's probability

$$P[X = i, Y = j] = P[X = i] \times P[Y = j] = 1/2 \times 1/2 = 1/4 \quad (i, j = 0, 1)$$

The probability of a collection of mutually exclusive outcomes is the *sum* of the probabilities, so

$$P[X + Y = 1] = Prob(\{(H, T)\} \text{ or } \{(T, H)\})$$
$$= Prob(\{(H, T)\}) + Prob(\{(T, H)\})$$
$$= (1/2)(1/2) + (1/2)(1/2) = 1/2$$

A.2.1 Density and Distribution Functions

In general, a random variable X can take on a multiple—even infinite—number of values. For random variables that take on *discrete* values, say $(x_1, x_2, \dots)$, their collection of respective probabilities $(p_1, p_2, \dots)$

$$P[X = x_i] = p_i > 0, \quad \sum_i p_i = 1$$

is known as the *probability mass function (pmf)*.

Random variables are generally categorized according to their type of pmf. The simplest pmf, the *Bernoulli* distribution, is a generalization of the coin toss random variable

$$(0 \le p \le 1) \quad P[X = 1] = p, P[X = 0] = 1 - p$$

which can be thought of as the result of tossing a weighted (loaded) coin. A random variable X having the Bernoulli distribution is written as $X \sim b(1, p)$.

A sequence of n Bernoulli random variables gives rise to a *binomial* random variable, written as $Y \sim b(n, p)$

$$(k = 0, 1, \dots, n) \quad P[Y = k] = \binom{n}{k} p^k (1 - p)^{n-k}, \quad \binom{n}{k} = \frac{n!}{k!(n-k)!}$$

This is the generalization of tossing n loaded coin tosses. Using combinatorics, one can show that if $X_1, X_2, \dots, X_n$ are independent and identically distributed (i.i.d.) where each $X_i \sim b(1, p)$, then their sum $Y = \sum_{i=1}^n X_i$ is a binomial random variable, $Y \sim b(n, p)$.

Random variables that can take on a continuum of values are known as *continuous* random variables, and are described via their *probability density function (pdf)*. A continuous random variable X with pdf f_X is written as $X \sim f_X$, where

$$P[x_1 \leq X \leq x_2] = \int_{x_1}^{x_2} f_X(x)dx$$

i.e., probability of X is computed as the area under the curve f_X. The total area under the pdf has to be 1

$$\int f_X(x)dx = 1$$

similar to the condition $\sum_i p_i = 1$ for discrete random variables.

For any random variable X, its *cumulative distribution function (CDF)*, $F_X(x)$ is defined as

$$F_X(x) = P[X \leq x]$$

For a continuous random variable X, its pdf $f_X(x)$ is the derivative of its CDF

$$\frac{d}{dx}F_X(x) = \frac{d}{dx}\int_{-\infty}^{x} f_X(u)du = f_X(x)$$

A.2.2   Expected Values, Moments

The *mean* or *expected value* of a continuous random variable X with density $f_X(\cdot)$ is defined as

$$E[X] = \int xf_X(x)dx$$

For a discrete random variable, the expected value is

$$E[X] = \sum_i x_i P[X = x_i] = \sum_i x_i p_i$$

In general, for any function $g(\cdot)$ of a random variable X, its mean is defined as

$$E[g(X)] = \int g(x)f_X(x)dx$$

or

$$E[g(X)] = \sum_i g(x_i)P[X = x_i] = \sum_i g(x_i)p_i$$

for discrete random variables.

The *variance* or the second *central moment* of a random variable is defined as

$$Var(X) = E[(X - E[X])^2] = E[X^2] - (E[X])^2.$$

The square root of variance is called the *standard deviation* and is usually denoted by $\sigma_X = \sqrt{Var(X)}$.

Two random variables X, Y are said to be *independent*, if

$$E[f(X) \times g(Y)] = E[f(X)] \times E[g(Y)],$$

for any arbitrary functions f, g. For independent random variables, their variances—*not* their standard deviations—add up

$$Var(X + Y) = Var(X) + Var(Y)$$

The *covariance* of two random variables X, Y is defined as

$$Cov(X, Y) = E[(X - EX)(Y - EY)]$$
$$= E[XY] - E[X]E[Y]$$

while the *correlation* is the covariance normalized by the standard deviations:

$$\rho = \rho_{X,Y} = Corr(X, Y) = \frac{E[(X - EX)(Y - EY)]}{\sqrt{Var(X)}\sqrt{Var(Y)}}$$
$$= \frac{E[XY] - E[X]E[Y]}{\sigma_X \sigma_Y}$$

If two random variables X,Y are independent, then they are uncorrelated $\rho_{X,Y} = 0$.

The variance of a linear combination of random variables, $Y = \sum_{i=1}^{N} a_i X_i$, is related to the covariances as follows

$$Var(Y) = \sum_{i,j=1}^{N} a_i a_j Cov(X_i, X_j) = \mathbf{a}^T \mathbf{C} \mathbf{a}$$

where $\mathbf{a}$ is a column vector consisting of a_i's, $\mathbf{a}^T$ its transpose, and $\mathbf{C}$ is the covariance matrix, $C_{ij} = Cov(X_i, X_j)$.

A.2.3   Conditional Probability and Expectation

The *conditional probability* of an event A given B, $P[A|B]$, is defined as

$$P[A|B] = P[A, B]/P[B]$$

Given two discrete random variables X, Y, the *law of total probability* states

$$P[X = x_i] = \sum_j P[X = x_i, Y = y_j]$$

$$= \sum_j P[X = x_i|Y = y_j]P[Y = y_j]$$

The *conditional expectation* of a random variable X given another random variable Y is a random variable defined as

$$E[X|Y] = \sum_i x_i P[X = x_i|Y = y_j]$$

for discrete random variables. One can recover $E[X]$ from conditional expectation $E[X|Y]$ via the *law of iterated expectation*

$$E[X] = E[E[X|Y]]$$

$$= \sum_j E[X|Y]P[Y = y_j]$$

$$= \sum_j \sum_i x_i P[X = x_i|Y = y_j]P[Y = y_j]$$

$$= \sum_i x_i \sum_j P[X = x_i, Y = y_j]$$

$$= \sum_i x_i P[X = x_i]$$

The analogous versions of the above for continuous random variables are based on the *conditional density function* defined as

$$f_{X|Y}(x|y) = \frac{f_{X,Y}(x, y)}{f_Y(y)}$$

leading to

$$f_X(x) = \int_y f_{X,Y}(x, y)dy = \int_y f_{X|Y}(x|y)f_Y(y)dy$$

and

$$E[X|Y] = \int_x x f_{X|Y}(x|y)dx$$

and

$$E[X] = E[E[X|Y]]$$

$$= \int_y \left(\int_x x f_{X|Y}(x|y)dx \right) f_Y(y)dy$$

$$= \int_x x \left(\int_y f_{X,Y}(x,y)dy \right) dx$$

$$= \int_x x f_X(x)dx$$

A.2.4 Jensen's Inequality

A function f is said to be *convex* if for any for $x < y$ and $0 \le w \le 1$ the following holds

$$f(wx + (1-w)y) \le wf(x) + (1-w)f(y)$$

Jensen's Inequality: if f is a convex function, then $E[f(X)] \ge f(E[X])$.

A.2.5 Normal Distribution

The most important and commonly encountered continuous random variable is a *normal, or Gaussian* characterized by two parameters μ, σ. Specifically, the pdf of a *normal* random variable $X \sim N(\mu, \sigma^2)$ is the bell-shaped curve

$$X \sim N(\mu, \sigma^2) \quad \Longleftrightarrow \quad f_X(x) = \frac{1}{\sqrt{2\pi\sigma^2}} e^{-\frac{(x-\mu)^2}{2\sigma^2}}$$

For an $N(\mu, \sigma^2)$ random variable, its mean is μ, its variance is σ^2, and its standard deviation is σ.

A *standard* normal random variable has parameters $(\mu = 0, \sigma^2 = 1)$, $X \sim N(0,1)$, and its CDF

$$N(x) = P[N(0,1) \le x] = \int_{-\infty}^x \frac{1}{\sqrt{2\pi}} e^{-\frac{u^2}{2}} du$$

is widely available in many scientific and engineering numerical packages.

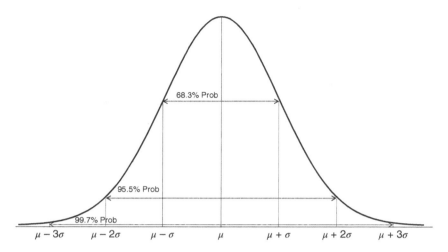

FIGURE A.1 Probability density function of a normal $N(\mu, \sigma^2)$ random variable.

The standard normal $N(0,1)$ is the building block for other normal random variables. Starting with a standard normal $X \sim N(0,1)$, for any given parameters (μ, σ^2), the random variable $Y = \mu + \sigma X \sim N(\mu, \sigma^2)$, i.e., any normal random variable can be obtained by scaling and shifting an $N(0,1)$ random variable.

For standard normal random variable, its pdf is $N'(x) = \frac{1}{\sqrt{2\pi}} e^{-x^2/2}$. Note that $N'(\cdot)$ is symmetric: $N'(x) = N'(-x)$, resulting in

$$P[N(0,1) \geq x] = 1 - P[N(0,1) \leq -x] = 1 - N(-x)$$

$$P[|N(0,1)| \leq x] = 1 - 2N(-x) \text{ for } x \geq 0$$

A.2.6 Central Limit Theorem

Let X_i be independent, identically distributed random variables with mean μ and variance σ^2. Then

$$\lim_{n \to \infty} \frac{1}{\sqrt{n}} \sum_{i=1}^{n} \frac{X_i - \mu}{\sigma} \sim N(0, 1)$$

This is one version of the *central limit theorem*, which essentially states the distribution of an average of any distribution converges to a normal distribution.

A.3 LINEAR REGRESSION ANALYSIS

It is often the case when looking at time series of financial data that they seem to be related and one set of variables seem to drive others. The standard method to extract this relationship is via regression analysis where one or more dependent variables are expressed as functions of independent or explanatory variables with some added noise. When the functional form is linear, we have *linear regression analysis*.

In the simplest and most common case, given two time series

$$\{(x_1, y_1), \ldots, (x_N, y_N)\}$$

we write

$$y_i = b_0 + b_1 x_i + e_i$$

for two constant parameters, *intercept* b_0 and *slope* b_1. In this setup, $\{x_1, \ldots, x_N\}$ is called the *independent* or explanatory variable, $\{y_1, \ldots, y_N\}$ the *dependent* variable, and the difference $e_i = y_i - (b_0 + b_1 x_i)$ the *residual*. The constant but unknown parameters b_0, b_1 are commonly estimated using the least squares method by minimizing

$$\min_{b_0, b_1} \sum_i e_i^2 = [y_i - (b_0 + b_1 x_i)]^2$$

resulting in

$$\hat{b}_1 = \frac{\sum_i (x_i - \bar{x})(y_i - \bar{y})}{\sum_i (x_i - \bar{x})^2}$$

$$\hat{b}_0 = \bar{y} - \hat{b}_1 \bar{x}$$

$$R^2 = \frac{(\overline{xy} - \bar{x}\bar{y})^2}{(\overline{x^2} - \bar{x}^2)(\overline{y^2} - \bar{y}^2)}$$

where $\hat{b}_0, \hat{b}_1$ are the random estimates of b_0, b_1, and the overbar notation denotes arithmetic average

$$\bar{z} = 1/N \sum_{i=1}^{N} z_i, \quad z_i = x_i, y_i, x_i^2, y_i^2, x_i y_i$$

The variable R^2 is called the coefficient of determination, and the higher it is, the smaller the residuals, i.e., the closer we are to a straight line.

It can be shown that the arithmetic mean of the residuals is zero and they are uncorrelated to x_i's

$$\bar{e} = 0, \quad \overline{xe} = 0$$

A.3.1 Regression Distributions

The following distributions arise if the residuals are assumed to be independent and jointly normal.

Chi-square distribution. Let $X_1, X_2, \ldots, X_n$ be i.i.d. random variables, $X_i \sim N(0,1)$, and let $S_n = \sum_{k=1}^{n} X_k^2$. Then S_n has a *chi-square* distribution with n degrees of freedom, $S_n \sim \chi^2(n)$ with pdf

$$(x \geq 0) \quad f_{S_n}(x) = \frac{x^{n/2-1}e^{-x/2}}{2^{n/2}\Gamma(n/2)}$$

where

$$\Gamma(z) = \int_0^\infty x^z e^{-x} dx$$

It can be shown that $\Gamma(z+1) = z\Gamma(z), \Gamma(1) = 1, \Gamma(1/2) = \sqrt{\pi}$, therefore $\Gamma(n) = (n-1)!$ and

$$\Gamma(n/2) = (n/2-1)(n/2-2)\ldots(1/2)\sqrt{\pi}$$

F distribution. Let X, Y be independent χ^2 random variables, $X \sim \chi^2(m), Y \sim \chi^2(n)$. The random variable $F = (X/m)/(Y/n)$ is said to have F distribution with (m, n) degrees of freedom, $F \sim F(m, n)$ with pdf

$$f(x) = \frac{\Gamma((m+n)/2)}{\Gamma(m/2)\Gamma(n/2)} \frac{m}{n} \left(\frac{m}{n}x\right)^{m/2-1} \left(1 + \frac{m}{n}x\right)^{-(m+n)/2}$$

F-statistic. Define the F-statistic as

$$F_0 = \frac{\sum_i(y_i - \bar{y})^2 - \sum_i e_i^2}{\sum_i e_i^2/(N-2)}$$

If e_i's are jointly normal i.i.d. random variables, $e_i \sim N(0, \sigma^2)$, then $F \sim \chi^2(1, N-2)$, and the F-statistic can be used in Analysis of Variance (ANOVA) to test the null hypothesis that a constant (intercept-only) model would have sufficed, i.e., x_i's do not aid in explaining the variance of y_i's:

$$H_0 : \{b_1 = 0\} \sim P[F(1, N-2) > F_0]$$

A high enough value of the *F*-statistic would allow us to reject the null hypothesis at a given level of significance and conclude that x_i's *do* have explanatory power and reduce the variance.

Student's *t* distribution. Let X, Y be independent random variables with $X \sim N(0,1)$, $Y \sim \chi^2(n)$. Then $T = X/\sqrt{Y/n}$ is said to have a Student's *t* distribution with n degrees of freedom, $T \sim t(n)$ with pdf

$$f_T(t) = \frac{\Gamma((n+1)/2)}{\Gamma(n/2)\sqrt{n\pi}}\left(1 + \frac{t^2}{n}\right)^{-(n+1)/2}$$

T-Statistics. Define

$$SE^2(Intercept) = \frac{\sum_i e_i^2}{N-2}\left(\frac{1}{N} + \frac{\overline{x}^2}{\sum_i (x_i - \overline{x})^2}\right), \quad T_{Intercept} = \frac{\hat{b}_0}{SE(Intercept)}$$

$$SE^2(Slope) = \frac{1}{N-2}\frac{\sum_i e_i^2}{\sum_i (x_i - \overline{x})^2}, \quad T_{Slope} = \frac{\hat{b}_1}{SE(Slope)}$$

If e_i's are jointly normal i.i.d. random variables, $e_i \sim N(0, \sigma^2)$, then both $T_{Intercept}, T_{Slope}$ statistics are $t(N-2)$ random variables and can be used to test the null hypothesis that slope or intercept are zero

$$H_0 : \{b_0 = 0\} \sim P[t(N-2) > T_{Intercept}]$$

$$H_0 : \{b_1 = 0\} \sim P[t(N-2) > T_{Slope}]$$

A high enough value of *T*-statistic would allow us to reject the null hypothesis that the particular coefficient is zero and we can conclude that the coefficient *does* have explanatory power at the desired level of significance.

Useful Excel Functions

1. TODAY - Today's date.
2. EDATE - The date of "n" months after a given date.
3. PRICE - Clean Price of a coupon bond. Use "1" as the last argument ([basis]) for Act/Act day count.
4. YIELD - Yield of a coupon bond given its Clean Price. Use "1" for Act/Act.
5. COUPPCD, COUPNCD - Dates of the previous, next coupon payment dates. Useful in calculating the accrued fraction w.
6. COUPNUM - Number of remaining coupons.
7. PMT - Periodic payments of a level pay loan.
8. GOAL SEEK tool (Alt-T-G), usually under 'Data' Tab (under What-If Analysis in some versions of Excel).
9. MMULT - Matrix multiplication.
10. MINVERSE - Matrix inverse.
11. RAND - Random number in [0,1].
12. NORMSDIST - Cumulative distribution function of a standard $N(0,1)$ random variable.
13. NORMSINV - Inverse of CDF of an $N(0,1)$ random variable. Combined with RAND, can be used to generate $N(0,1)$ random samples.
14. STDEV - Sample standard deviation: $\sqrt{1/(n-1)\sum(x_i - \overline{x})^2}$.
15. STDEVP - Population standard deviation: $\sqrt{1/n\sum(x_i - \overline{x})^2}$.
16. REGRESSION tool - From "Data Analysis" dialog box (in "Data" tab in new versions of Excel).
17. INTERCEPT, SLOPE - Least squares intercept and slope of two series.

About the Companion Website

This book is accompanied by a companion website for instructors:

www.wiley.com/go/sadr/mathtechniquesinfinance

The website includes:

- Solutions to all end-of-chapter problems.
- Jupyter notebooks with full Python code for all end-of-chapter projects.
- Multiple-choice questions for quizzes and exams.